Striving
TO BE HUMAN

EDITORIAL ADVISORY COMMITTEE

Rabbi Leah Cohen Tenenbaum, DMin, BCC-PCHAC, *co-chair*
Rabbi Douglas Kohn, *co-chair*
Rabbi Jordy Calman
Rabbi Lev R. Herrnson, MA, MAHL, EdM, BCC
Rabbi Rebecca Jaye
Rabbi Jill Maderer
Rabbi Geoffrey A. Mitelman
Rabbi Dean Shapiro
Rabbi Joseph Skloot, PhD
Rabbi Eleanor B. Steinman, EdD
Rabbi Ariel Tovlev

Rabbi Annie Villarreal-Belford, *Editor, CCAR Press*
Rafael Chaiken, *Director, CCAR Press*
Rabbi Hara E. Person, *Chief Executive,*
　Central Conference of American Rabbis

Striving TO BE HUMAN

Jewish Perspectives
on Twenty-First-Century Challenges

Edited by
Rabbi Leah Cohen Tenenbaum, DMin, BCC-PCHAC
and
Rabbi Douglas Kohn

Foreword by
Rabbanit Sara Tillinger Wolkenfeld

Reform Judaism Publishing, a division of CCAR Press
Central Conference of American Rabbis
5786 New York 2025

Copyright © 2025 by the Central Conference of American Rabbis. All rights reserved. No portion of this book may be copied in any form for any purpose without the written permission of the Central Conference of American Rabbis.

Published by Reform Judaism Publishing, a division of CCAR Press
Central Conference of American Rabbis
New York, NY
(212) 972-3636 | info@ccarpress.org | www.ccarpress.org

LIBRARY OF CONGRESS CATALOGING-IN-PUBLICATION DATA
Names: Tenenbaum, Leah Cohen, 1961– editor. | Kohn, Douglas, editor.
Title: Striving to be human: Jewish perspectives on twenty-first-century challenges / edited by Rabbi Leah Cohen Tenenbaum and Rabbi Douglas Kohn.
Description: First edition. | New York, NY: Reform Judaism Publishing, a division of CCAR Press, Central Conference of American Rabbis, [2025] | Summary: "A collection of Jewish perspectives on what it means to be human today, covering artificial intelligence, reproductive technologies, internet culture, animal rights, and much more." —Provided by publisher.
Identifiers: LCCN 2025028309 (print) | LCCN 2025028310 (ebook) | ISBN 9780881236682 (trade paperback) | ISBN 9780881236699 (ebook)
Subjects: LCSH: Jewish ethics–21st century.
Classification: LCC BJ1285.2 .S77 2025 (print) | LCC BJ1285.2 (ebook)
LC record available at https://lccn.loc.gov/2025028309
LC ebook record available at https://lccn.loc.gov/2025028310

Book interior design and typography by Scott-Martin Kosofsky at The Philidor Company, Rhinebeck, NY, www.philidor.com
Cover design by Barbara Leff
Cover art by Stuart Lutz. Used by permission of the artist.

Unless otherwise indicated, all translations of Torah are from The Torah: A Modern Commentary, *rev. ed. by W. Gunther Plaut (CCAR Press, 2005).*

Printed in USA
10 9 8 7 6 5 4 3 2 1

This publication has been lovingly dedicated by:

Anonymous
Michelle Anctil and Judith Smith
Romi and Jonathan Berck
Rabbi Cantor Jennifer Bern-Vogel
Judge Christy, *z"l*, and Jay Donenfeld
Joan and Michael Gittelsohn
Roberta and Philip Gold
Rachelle and Jeffrey Harmer
Chip Hogg
The Hordines Family
Bradley Hyman
Marlene and Gerald Jacobowitz
Renee and Michael Kress
Stacey Lazarus and Sherrill Murray-Lazarus
The Levinstein Family
Alyson and Jonathan Mehr
Gay Miller and Paul Pomerantz
Margie Orland
Toby and Sebastian Persico
Janet and Fredric Rabinowitz
David Rider
Nancy and Justin Rider
Mona and Ian Rieger
Barbara and Dr. Jeffrey Rubin
Laurie Schaffner
Ann and Asher Sheppard
Sally and Steven Sirota
Shauna and Walter Van Horn
Michele and Paul Zipperstein

Be ashamed to die until you have won some victory for humanity.
—HORACE MANN

The greatest evil perpetrated is the evil committed by nobodies, that is, by human beings who refuse to be persons.
—HANNAH ARENDT

Woe to our society if to be human becomes a heroic act.
—ELIE WIESEL

Contents

Foreword ix
Rabbanit Sara Tillinger Wolkenfeld
Acknowledgments xiii
Introduction 1
*Rabbi Douglas Kohn
and Rabbi Leah Cohen Tenenbaum, DMin, BCC-PCHAC*

Part I: Challenges from Within Us
1. Empathy, Power, and *Tzedakah*:
   Is Moral Justice at the Core of Humanity? 11
   Rabbi Sarah Bassin
2. The Human Question:
   Choosing Between Good and Evil 25
   Rabbi Lucy H. F. Dinner
3. Belonging: You Are Who You Are With 41
   Rabbi Jan Katzew, PhD
4. In Memory of the Wayward Son:
   Meditations in Queer Jewish Theology 61
   Rabbi Hilly Haber, PhD
5. The Feeling Being: Was the World Created for My Sake? 73
   Rabbi Ellen Lewis

Part II: Challenges from Beyond Us
6. Your Mercies Extend Even to a Bird's Nest:
   The Animal-Human Relationship 93
   Rabbi Alexandria Shuval-Weiner
7. Moving the Goalposts: Beyond the Beginning and End of Life 107
   Rabbi Jonathan K. Crane, PhD
8. When Artificiality Collides with Humanity:
   Can AI Develop a Soul? 119
   Rabbi Geoffrey A. Mitelman
9. From Creation to Creator: Humans Making Humans,
   Humanoids, Cyborgs, and Clones 135
   Rabbi Douglas Kohn

10. Medium, Message, and Humanity
   in the Newest Information Age 153
   Rabbi Dan Medwin

Conclusion: Tensions Between the Good and the Perfect . . . 169
   Rabbi Leah Cohen Tenenbaum, DMin, BCC-PCHAC

Contributors 179

Foreword

Rabbanit Sara Tillinger Wolkenfeld

כַּד קוּדְשָׁא בְּרִיךְ הוּא, בָּעֵי לְמִבְרֵי עָלְמָא, אִסְתַּכַּל בְּאוּמָנָא... אַקְדִּימַת אוֹרַיְיתָא תְּרֵין אַלְפֵי שְׁנִין לְעָלְמָא, וְכַד בָּעָא קוּדְשָׁא בְּרִיךְ הוּא לְמִבְרֵי עָלְמָא, הֲוָה מִסְתַּכַּל בָּהּ בְּאוֹרַיְיתָא, בְּכָל מִלָּה וּמִלָּה, וְעָבֵיד לָקֳבְלֵהּ אוּמָנוּתָא דְעָלְמָא. בְּגִין דְּכָל מִלִּין וְעוֹבָדִין דְּכָל עָלְמִין, בְּאוֹרַיְיתָא אִינּוּן. וְעַל דָּא קוּדְשָׁא בְּרִיךְ הוּא הֲוָה מִסְתַּכַּל בָּהּ, וּבָרָא עָלְמָא.

When the Holy Blessed One resolved to create the world, God looked into the plan . . . for the Torah preceded the creation of the world by two thousand years; and so, when God resolved to create the world God gazed into the Torah, into its every word, and fashioned the world correspondingly; for all the words and all the actions of all the worlds are contained in the Torah. Therefore did the Holy Blessed One look into it and create the world.[1]
—*Zohar, T'rumah 61*

For six days the Divine Creator brought new things into being: light and dark, water and dry land, celestial beings, plants and animals. Though each created being is itself a world, worthy of study and deserving of appreciation, ultimately, in Jewish thought, the world becomes the setting for the grand drama of human life. Humans are at the center of Creation, but what it actually means to be human—what makes us uniquely deserving of our role as the starring cast against the backdrop of God's intricately created universe—is a question that has engaged Jewish thinkers from Abraham until today.

Just as the Divine gazed into the Torah to find details of how to fashion the world, so too, Torah remains the blueprint into which the Jewish people gaze as we approach the big questions of our day. At a time of unprecedented ethical and technological change, when the challenges that face humanity threaten to overwhelm us, we reach for our ethical blueprint to help us make decisions. Just as the Torah's intricate details allowed the Divine to create a universe of beauty and complexity, we trust that the Torah's wisdom will guide us as we strive to navigate our changing world.

When I began working at the intersection of Torah and cutting-edge technology over a decade ago for Sefaria.org, the online digital library dedicated to bringing the Jewish canon into the digital age, the future of the digital age seemed to hold great promise. The internet had opened up access to knowledge in ways the world had never before seen: New tools were emerging to take advantage of that knowledge and use it to improve our world. While Torah—broadly construed as centuries of Jewish works surrounding Scripture and Talmud—has been digitized and put online, the broader context for the work has been changing dramatically.

The human obsession with technology has intensified to the point of deifying our own peers and their creations. Media outlets now routinely refer to the CEOs of large tech companies as the "gods" of Silicon Valley; indeed, their powers are vast and growing as they create ever more powerful computers and robots, as well as political influence. Machines are valued for all that they can do and for all that they might do within a few short years. Our era's rapid technological advancement is threatening the certainty we once felt that humans represent the pinnacle of Creation. Artificial intelligence is a new blow to human pride. Copernicus, Darwin, and Freud respectively removed humanity from the center of the universe, the center of the animal kingdom, and the center of their own mind, in turn. Now AI threatens to push humanity to the side of human civilization. The capacity to answer questions that a person might pose, to teach, to write essays, or to create works of art—all until recently the sole province of human beings—are now within the ambition of AI.

Among other things, religion is a technology for navigating uncertainty, and Judaism, with its promise of eternal relevance, was literally built for this moment. Millennia of evolving legal codes, rich ethical discussions, and layer upon layer of discussion and debate combine to guide our paths and remind us of ways to infuse our lives with meaning. Despite all the obstacles we face, Torah is, as it always has been, a blueprint: a framework for thinking about how we might build lives of meaning, purpose, and sanctity.

The scholars whose chapters comprise *Striving to Be Human: Jewish Perspectives on Twenty-First-Century Challenges* are answering the call of the moment, posing questions that speak to the social and political pressures of the modern world. How do we exercise our capacity for moral choice in the face of rapid change, and how do we ensure that we are choosing the side of justice when larger forces in the world push back? How and why do we connect with others, and how do we ensure that our true identities are being expressed in those interactions?

These scholars also grapple with the many technological changes that are pushing us to rethink morality and power. How do we navigate questions of medical ethics sparked by technologies our Sages could not have imagined or the challenges of what it means to have a new "artificial" intelligence to compare and contrast with the human mind? The information that we value is transmitted in new ways; how do changes in information technology change the ways we want to communicate?

Responding to any one of these challenges could produce an entire book's worth of thoughts. These questions emerge from the accelerating complications of modernity, threatening to overwhelm us with their vastness and their urgency. But Rabbinic sources also have suggestions for dealing with that which is overwhelming.

The Talmud in *Chagigah* 14b tells the story of Rabbi Akiva and three friends, who famously "entered the *pardes*"—the great orchard of esoteric Torah study. The details of what ensued are not available to us, but of the four, only Rabbi Akiva emerged whole and at peace. Discussing this story, the Rabbis ask the obvious question: What skills or aptitude did Rabbi Akiva possess that made him uniquely suited to avoid being overwhelmed by this thicket of deep spiritual knowledge? Rabbi Akiva, they answer, knew how to process information. He was capable of taking a deep breath and waiting, of pausing his collection of knowledge so that he could sit back, process, and sort out the various things he had learned. In the rush toward progress, in the thickets of everyday life, we forget the need to process what we know and articulate what we do not. *Striving to Be Human* represents precisely the deep, meditative pause that we need as we take stock of our situation and of the horizon ahead.

As the title of this volume expresses, and as Rabbi Leah Cohen Tenenbaum writes in her conclusion, all we can ever do is strive to be human—not to be perfect, necessarily, but to be "very good," as God proclaims after creating human beings. The midrash (*B'reishit Rabbah* 9:7) understands God's approval of all that was created as the beginning of a new stage in cosmic history. Before this time, "the glory of God was in concealment."[2] From this point on, glory is to be found in "investigating a matter," and the Torah is available as a tool for that investigation.

This book is a human-centric, "very good" attempt to grapple with the many existential questions raised by the twenty-first century. Each of these thinkers uses Torah as a blueprint and as a tool for inquiry, pushing us to delve more deeply as a community into our tradition, ourselves, and our values. I look forward to the conversations that will develop around this book and the learning that will ensue as a result of the authors' brave willingness to engage with these profound questions. No one has all of the answers, even when we engage with the fullness of our humanity and use Torah to guide us. Even as humanity faces the threat of marginalization from its own civilization, we must strive to be human.

NOTES

1. Translation adapted from *The Zohar* from 1933 Soncino Press edition (license: CC0, https://creativecommons.org/publicdomain/zero/1.0/), found on Sefaria (sefaria.org).
2. Translation from *The Sefaria Midrash Rabbah*, 2022 (license: CC-BY, https://creativecommons.org/licenses/by/3.0/), found on Sefaria (sefaria.org).

Acknowledgments

WRITING AND EDITING a book is a team effort. This is especially true when undertaking a complex and challenging volume on striving to be human, which addresses edgy themes that are both multi-directional and advancing swiftly—even faster than paragraphs could be penned. Thus, it required a substantial team. Initially, however, this book germinated and sat hopefully and expectantly alone in Rabbi Douglas Kohn's thoughts for over a decade, until Rabbi Leah Cohen Tenenbaum entered and partnered in the process, and the volume emerged and took form. Ours has been a healthy and exciting collaboration through various phases for over two years, as ideas would suddenly blossom, questions would stir unexpected insights, and we learned to rely on one another.

Soon the team would become much larger. Together, we deeply appreciate the many people who devoted immeasurable hours, wisdom, and talent to this book. We recognize the outstanding support and professionalism of CCAR Press and its editorial team, and we offer them our total and thorough thanks. Rafael Chaiken, director of the Press, brought both eagerness and well-considered prodding to every phase of the project, often sending us links to new books, seminars, and webinars, which continually broadened our perspectives. Rabbi Annie Villarreal-Belford, editor at CCAR Press, cheerfully and carefully read every word and nurtured the best in every sentence. Rabbi Hara Person, chief executive of the CCAR, was the rock behind this effort, and we salute her leadership. We thank the superb staff at CCAR Press, including Chiara Ricisak, assistant editor, Raquel Fairweather-Gallie, marketing and sales manager, and Deborah Smilow, CCAR Press operations manager. We also thank copy editor Debra Hirsch Corman, proofreader Michelle Kwitkin, and book designer Scott-Martin Kosofsky. We offer much appreciation to the CCAR Press Council and its chairperson, Rabbi Don Goor, for their confidence in this volume and their early suggestions, and we offer deep acknowledgment to the Editorial Advisory Committee, whose members are listed in the front matter and who seriously considered the scope and possibilities of this endeavor, stamping it with their imprimatur. A heartfelt thank you is extended to artist Stuart Lutz, a gifted talent and a product of the Reform Movement, for his original art that adorns the book cover and which suggests the themes and complexity of the pages within.

Our contributing authors deserve special praise. This was not an easy book to craft, and neither was it an easy book to write. Striving to be human is a vast, fluid theme. As much as we envisioned the volume, our writers enriched it immeasurably and added personal genius, texture, and vital suggestions. Together, without collaborating among themselves, they fulfilled one aspiration of this project: to foster a community discussion on what it means to strive to be human, and to face both ongoing and new challenges to this enterprise. Additionally, many other rabbinic colleagues and academicians were consulted on various themes, and though they did not write chapters, their thoughts and inspiration are in the fabric of the text. Each contributor is a busy professional with full plates of other demanding duties, and we are indebted to each for joining this project and adding their expertise. As editors, we only can do so much; our contributing authors shouldered the task of intellectual curiosity and collective wisdom. This is their book too.

Rabbi Douglas Kohn

I first imagined this book and began researching and designing it around 2008. I then detoured when I was asked to consider editing a volume addressing Judaism and dementia, for which some of this book's research could be applied, and that volume, *Broken Fragments*, appeared in 2012. Shelved, yet not forgotten, was this abiding question of *hishtadeil lih'yot ish*—what is striving to be human?

Periodically, I would pick up the outline, refine it, and again reshelve it. The book, and I, needed a partner.

She was found in Jerusalem, in 2023, at the Central Conference of American Rabbis annual convention. A midrash teaches that Jerusalem is the *tabur haolam*, the umbilical center or belly button of the universe, and that all gestation and wisdom emanates from Jerusalem (*Midrash Tanchuma, K'doshim* 10). It may be so. During that week of the conference, uncannily and repeatedly I shared sessions and programs with Rabbi Leah Cohen Tenenbaum. We spoke daily, and it was clear that she was the partner that this book and I had been seeking. She is a sensitive hospital chaplain, a careful intellect, a penetrating writer, and a genuine partner who also pondered what it means to be human. I am so appreciative that Leah agreed to share this book project, and her thinking is found from cover to cover. She nudged me, I nudged her, we nudged and strove together. Leah has become an enduring partner and more—a trusted, abiding friend.

My appreciation is extended to the members of the congregation I proudly serve as rabbi, Temple Beth Jacob in Newburgh, New York. They braved hearing my percolating thoughts, and they surrendered me to my writing and editing. Yet, their love and encouragement buttressed me, and I thank them.

Many colleagues and friends listened to ideas and offered advice and encouragement, and I mention Rabbi Andy Sklarz, Rabbi Jeff and Mindy Glickman, Rabbi Andy Straus, Rabbi Lon Moskowitz, and Rabbi Jacob Rosner. Some, I hoped, might write chapters for this book, but focus, economy, and scale did not allow every theme to be included. That does not diminish my wonderful respect and esteem for each of you.

I thank Sally Sirota, a congregant and friend with a background in public health, obstetrics, and gynecology, who reviewed the chapter on cloning and reproduction.

As mentioned above, Stuart Lutz created the dramatic art for the cover of this book. Stuart and I date our friendship to 1970s youth group years in Michigan State Temple Youth and to our teaching Hebrew school in Los Angeles in the 1980s. We have shared each other's difficult moments; it is a wonderful treat for Stuart's work to grace our cover.

I first used ChatGPT sitting at my father's desk in Silicon Valley in 2021, when he asked the AI to write an essay for this book. A healthy nonagenarian, my dad, Marvin Kohn, richly understands the intersections of technology and Judaism, as he lives them both every day. His thinking inspires mine.

Lastly, but truly firstly, this book shared day-to-day life with those whom I love the most and whose patience I had to indulge all too often when ideas or calls demanded my attention. Adoring thanks are due to my beloved wife, Cindy, and our collective children and grandchildren. If I enjoy creative, intellectual sparks in my life, it is due to the inspiration you stir every day and the permission you grant. This book has emerged because of the joy we share. With abundant love and appreciation!

Rabbi Leah Cohn Tenenbaum, DMin, BCC-PCHAC

Marge Piercy, in her poem "To Be of Use," struck a chord in me the first time I read it that has stayed with me ever since. What does it mean to be of use? I remember the expression "What a tool!" from my younger years as an insult to be flung (usually just in my mind). Fast-forward a few decades, and I hear these days of the fear that we are all becoming tools—how advances in technology are turning the users into the used, how survival in fields ranging from politics to finance, from education to health care, rests on the ability to be perceived as useful to one wielding greater power than yourself. Still insulting, but somehow more normalized and less personal than the "tool" of my youth.

Between then and now, I had the great fortune to have been ordained at Hebrew Union College–Jewish Institute of Religion, at the Cincinnati campus, twenty-five years ago. I was told on that day, "Yes, you are in fact a tool! You are now all *k'lei kodesh*, instruments of the Holy One. Go forth and be useful!"

This book was written by a bunch of tools, which I say with the utmost respect and admiration. As Marge Piercy wrote in describing her passion for purpose-driven people, "The people I love the best jump into work head first."[1] In my partner, Rabbi Douglas Kohn, I have found one who does just that—and persists, ponders, and plays in a relentless style that matches my own. Doug is a visionary, a collaborator, a thinker, and a writer. I have learned so much from him and am so honored to share this journey with him.

I am grateful for my teams at Yale–New Haven Hospital—the Palliative Care Team, the Department of Spiritual Care, and the Ethics Committee. As Hillel taught, you are living examples of what it means to *strive to be human*. Every day, you inspire and comfort me with your humanity, compassion, and care.

I was recently invited to take a deep dive into a place that describes the other half of Hillel's teaching, *in a place where there is no humanity*. I am so inspired by the unflinching work of the Fellowships at Auschwitz for the Study of Professional Ethics (FASPE) and by my colleagues whose dedication to shedding light in this dark space is humbling and transformative.

Acharon, acharon chaviv, the sweetest for the last—my precious family. To my loved ones who have gone before me, you are with me always. To my family members who walk with me still, you bring me so much joy and hope. And to Howard, my chosen one, your patience, technical savvy, and abundant love are written all over these pages. You are my rock and my heart's nest forever.

Finally, we dedicate this book to our teacher and thinker, the late Rabbi Stanley Davids, *z"l*, who died as this book was nearing completion; he was one who continually modeled striving to be human in his rabbinate, his love of the Jewish people and the Land of Israel, and his tremendous will to live, to write, and to make living meaningful.

NOTE

1. Marge Piercy, "To Be of Use," in *To Be of Use: Poems by Marge Piercy* (Doubleday, 1973), 49.

Introduction

Rabbi Douglas Kohn
and Rabbi Leah Cohen Tenenbaum, DMin, BCC-PCHAC

בְּמָקוֹם שֶׁאֵין אֲנָשִׁים, הִשְׁתַּדֵּל לִהְיוֹת אִישׁ.
In a place where there is no humanity, strive to be human.
—*Pirkei Avot* 2:6

WE TAKE BEING HUMAN for granted. It is a given. We think and do not even notice that we are doing so, even as Rene Descartes famously penned, "I think, therefore I am." We use our nimble, opposing thumbs to make and manage tools, thus separating humans from lower humanoids, and we transform our environment—for better or for worse—making us appear the masters of our fate. Yet, do we sufficiently or even periodically ponder what it means to be human? Is being human as simple as being endowed with the capacity to think, create, love, and feel, or is it something greater? Essentially, what does it mean to be human, and what challenges us as humans in the twenty-first century?

The prescient text of Rabbi Hillel from *Pirkei Avot* 2:6, "In a place where there is no humanity, strive to be human,"[1] is powerfully latent with meaning and teaching. The text comes to us from the earliest post-Biblical code of Jewish law, the Mishnah (dating to circa 200 CE), edited by Rabbi Y'hudah HaNasi, which commonly contains short legal instructions for conducting life in accordance with the dictates of Torah. The Mishnah is organized into six sections, called orders, each bearing Rabbinic teachings on various themes, including religious life and festivals, interpersonal life, damages and torts, sacrifices, and purity. Within those primarily legal sections, however, there is one tractate called *Pirkei Avot* ("The Teachings of the Sages"), which offers moral and ethical instruction, rather than legal prescriptions, commonly rendered "wisdom literature." *Pirkei Avot*'s brief, clever snippets promote guidance toward how to listen and learn, basic kindness, honor, hospitality, humility, and loving and serving others. Many of its beloved teachings have been set to music for synagogues and Jewish camps. Thus, it is a text from *Pirkei Avot* that inspires this volume: "In a place where there is no humanity, strive to be human."

Over millennia, this text has born various meanings. In the Talmud, the sixth-century successor to the Mishnah, it was argued that this verse means that where there is lacking a man—likely connoting community leadership—then be that man (Babylonian Talmud, *B'rachot* 63a). Rashi, the eleventh-century French Torah commentator par excellence, argued in his commentary on this Talmudic passage that in a place where people are not studying Torah, one should step up and do so. The brilliant twelfth-century Spanish philosopher Moses Maimonides suggested in his commentary on the same passage that the teaching urged one to accustom one's soul to pursuing virtue. For this volume, we render the text quite simply: Where humanity appears wanting, we are to strive to bring humanity. However, the nature of humanity and the endeavor of striving are open questions. Those concerns stir our curiosity and enliven our chapters.

It very well could be argued that this admonition constitutes the single most basic mitzvah articulated by our Rabbinic Sages: *Be human!* According to our tradition, we are not the Creator but the creation, albeit a very special, gifted, and unique creation. Humanity is endowed with an extraordinary gift: that of being human itself and of stretching ourselves to the boundaries of our imagination, even encroaching on the domain of the Creator. Early in the Book of Genesis, human beings strove to build a ziggurat to the heavens, the Tower of Babel, to demonstrate that we were more than human—that we could imagine and craft our way to the heavenly realm. It was an attempt to abandon the limitations of humanness, and it failed. But in its attempt, and in its very endeavor near the outset of the human enterprise, Torah demonstrated not only that we were "little less than divine" (Psalm 8:6), but that we aspired to the next threshold. We questioned humanness and challenged its boundaries in our very first communal undertaking and have been doing so in various manners ever since.

Concomitantly, Rabbi Hillel's admonition asserts that in a world that apparently was, and likely remains, somewhat absent of humanity, we are to fill it with something better. We are to fill it by and through striving. The striving that Hillel proposed is not to encroach on the Divine, but rather to embrace the fullness of our own humanness. Unlike the builders of the Tower of Babel, who failed to overcome the gravity holding humanity grounded in our place, Hillel directed us to soar because of and through our very humanity. To Hillel, there is no shame or limitation in "being only human"; rather, it is the springboard to human potential and greatness. Yet, if we do not ponder what humanness implies or demands, especially in the face of shifting moral foundations and advancing technological innovations that nibble at or could possibly devour the boundaries of humanity, how do we know we are fulfilling Hillel's charge? How do we even know how to fulfill it in the first place?

Being human, our tradition asserts, makes us little less than divine. But that is not our failing; rather, it is our glory. In the Torah's opening Creation mythology, after God has crafted the first human beings, Genesis 1:31 asserts: *Hineih tov m'od*, "It was very good!" We were created both very good and to be good. It was not enough for humanity to merely be acceptable; nor were we created as perfect or with the goal of striving to be perfect. Being "very good" ultimately was reserved only for humans after the entire corpus of Creation was finished. Thus, humanity, from the outset, was set on a unique path with the expectation toward "very goodness." Although we have spent millennia considering and questioning the nature of the Divine, have we devoted the same time and effort to considering the nature of being human and to being very good at being human? After all, the Tower of Babel narrative demonstrates that we are consigned to living in the domain of the human, not that of the Divine. Thus, it behooves us to study and understand the meaning and challenges of being human. Moreover, per the words of Rabbi Hillel's instruction to "strive to be human," we discover that we are continually in a condition of striving, becoming, or aspiring to our own humanness, or "very goodness." It is not yet achieved in our own generation and was not in ages past. Hence, we must consider the ever-evolving nature of being human.

Humanness requires our attention, especially in the early twenty-first century, when challenges to humanity abound from nearly every direction—from within us and from beyond us, from moral forces and from advancing technology—essentially, from ourselves and our creations. Technology appears nigh on supplanting elements of what uniquely had belonged to the human being, and interestingly this technology is invented and crafted by the very human enterprise that then becomes challenged or even threatened by the devices that we fashion. Artificial intelligence, advanced robotics, technology to conquer the beginning and the end of life, mechanisms of communicating, and the capacity to re-gender the individual human being and redefine gender itself are swiftly shifting us from being the creation to infiltrating the domain of the Creator. Are we building a new ziggurat? Are ethics apace with the speedy advancements of technology and potential applications? It is both an exciting time and a time of terrible unknowns when technical abilities and human appetites are running far ahead of ethical, reflective, and spiritual considerations. As we face challenges to being human, how are we to function in an advancing world that we do not fully comprehend and may not have been created to inhabit?

In the second century, the illustrious Rabbi Akiva was imprisoned for defying a Roman edict prohibiting teaching Judaism, but he continued to teach his fellow Jewish prisoners, even while in jail awaiting his horrible execution and at the peril of greater torture. Rav Papos, a fellow captive, confronted the great sage, imploring Akiva, "Even here? Even here?" Akiva replied with a compelling parable: He told a story of fish who were threatened by fishermen's nets and who complained about the hazards and their fears for their lives. A fox on the riverbank overheard the fish's grievances and suggested that they depart the water and come up on dry land, where they could avoid the nettings and traps of the fishermen. "No," exclaimed the frightened fish. "If we are afraid in our own environment, how much more threatened we will be in a place we do not know!" (Babylonian Talmud, *B'rachot* 61b). Akiva taught that we can thrive only in the place where we are intended to thrive; for the Jew, this is in a world of Torah, and for humanity, it is in the human world.

The human enterprise presently stands on this precipice. Our environment—intellectual, spiritual, social, moral, and physical—is undergoing rapid and uncertain change and redefinition, so much so that unlike the fish of the parable, we may not even recognize it as the place of our own comfort. And our place within it is subject to continual reconsideration. In this volume, we seek to initiate a conversation toward that consideration through the lens of Jewish wisdom.

Being human and striving to be human are uncertain categories. Moreover, as academia, medical ethicists, and the popular press regularly report on new insights, capabilities, and competencies in science, computing, rocketry, medicine, and even the arts, the wider public responds with both incredulity and disconnect, hope and excitement. It is incredible: Today machines can write poetry, term papers, or hit pop songs, and rockets are aiming to establish human civilization on other planets or destroying it on our own. While this may render us detached, the average individual has little or no relationship with these advances or advancing technologies. Moreover, the increased politicization, polarization, and polemicizing witnessed in recent years in America and elsewhere have shaken our social foundations and disrupted vital discussions about critical issues that impact the human experience, turning ethical inquiry into contentious debate instead of meaningful discourse. Such social pressures are not insignificant in our discussion of what is a human being, today and tomorrow. They render vital deliberations more difficult. We need a pause, as Rabbanit Sara Wolkenfeld taught in her foreword, to better understand who we are as humans, what it means to strive to be human, and the challenges that we are facing. Thus, we might recenter ourselves and our context in the changing world around us.

Notwithstanding present-day questions of what may be achieved by new human-esque technology, our ancient texts still ask vital questions. What does it mean to strive? To be human? To be good? Where is the place in which there is no humanity? Why does that place demand extra diligence? What is the nature of humanity when we become creators, or when we once again endeavor to craft towers to new or godly domains? How do we understand and manifest our constraint to be "only" human? Does striving demand that we achieve the elusive goal of being human and being very good, or is simply striving sufficient? Do we have to be perfect, as may be the requirement of the machine or the artificial human? Or is "very good"—as God describes in chapter 1 of Genesis—good enough?

Jewish philosophy and theology ought to undergird the nature of humanity today. Our task is to best understand the human world before we aspire to trespass the divine domain or futuristic worlds. This task is especially pressing in our post-Holocaust era, which more than ever requires rethinking and clarification of the meaning of humanity, and especially in the face of technologies of terror and warfare that can destroy not only all humanity, but any humanness that might remain in humanity. The complexity and under-evaluated meaning of humanity is the reason we conceived of this book. In this volume, we gather some of today's most thoughtful and creative minds to ponder the question "What is meant by striving to be human?"

Inspired by Rabbi Hillel's instruction "In a place where there is no humanity, strive to be human," our discussion includes established Jewish views and wisdom, with Jewish texts punctuating each chapter. The authors offer perspectives on today's challenging ethical questions while attempting to peer into the future and its rapidly approaching frontiers. This volume investigates our question via two key perspectives, each concerned with present and future challenges to humanity.

In Part I, "Challenges from Within Us," we consider gripping issues arising from ethical questions and challenges to humanity derived from within ourselves: our wider society, our inner drives and fears, our discourses, political pressures, public press, and academic institutions, which raise perspectives on living today. Chapter 1, by Rabbi Sarah Bassin, raises ethical questions regarding the role of justice in the human experience. Does being human require magnanimity and empathy, and is justice incumbent on being human? Rabbi Bassin explores the treatment of displaced persons as a timely example of both Jewish and wider intersections of morality and power. Chapter 2 examines choice and choosing within the human experience, wherein Rabbi Lucy H. F. Dinner dissects Jewish texts regarding the concept of moral choice: Is choice itself essential to humanity? In chapter 3, Rabbi Jan Katzew, PhD, addresses being social animals. Does the tendency toward grouping, cliquing, or clubbing define us as humans, and does it harm or help us? Rabbi Katzew reveals that belonging is not a distant concept; it is intimate, personal, and compelling, an essential aspect of being human. In chapter 4, Rabbi Hilly Haber, PhD, explores current questions regarding gender, re-gendering, and transgendering, as well as queer and transgressive theologies that offer a candid recontextualizing of the nature of gender in human beings. Lastly, the human being is a feeling, emotional being. In chapter 5, Rabbi Ellen Lewis, a practicing psychologist, guides the reader on a journey of the realm of feelings that encompass the human experience.

Part II offers attempts to glimpse beyond the present horizon, wrestling with "Challenges from Beyond Us." Chapter 6, by Rabbi Alexandria Shuval-Weiner, considers our human relationships with animals, which Genesis teaches were created just before humans emerged as the crown of Creation. Rabbi Shuval-Weiner addresses moral obligations that compel and constrain us as humans relative to other life. Chapter 7, by Rabbi Jonathan K. Crane, PhD, discusses medical ethics and the migrating goalposts at the beginning and end of life. Rabbi Crane explains these ethical dilemmas and examines an under-addressed theme in rabbinic literature: the unwanted life and lives that lack life. Chapter 8, by Rabbi

Geoffrey A. Mitelman, discusses AI and robotics. Few new technologies have been more misunderstood, yet are more challenging to the human being, than the possibilities and potential of artificial intelligence. Rabbi Mitelman maneuvers questions around AI, how it is a new intellectual technology, as well as the fears, uncertainties, and hopes AI evokes. In chapter 9, Rabbi Douglas Kohn discusses human reproduction and cloning technologies. The possibility of an artificial humanoid begs many questions as we stand to become the creator rather than the creation. Finally, at the edges of technology are further inroads in information systems, which Rabbi Dan Medwin reviews in chapter 10, offering both possibilities and cautions. Will humans become subject to systems that make us part of the network itself? Lastly, in our conclusion, Rabbi Leah Cohen Tenenbaum considers the relationship of the "good," the "very good," and the "perfect," while offering insights on humanity from the social and political milieu.

Moreover, the order of our ten chapters reflects an intentional ontology itself, essentially a theology of the nature of humanity. We offer ten rungs akin to Maimonides's ladder of *tzedakah*, in which the twelfth-century Sephardic sage posited eight successive steps of generous giving, each progressively higher in virtuosity (*Mishneh Torah*, Laws of Gifts to the Poor 10:7–14). Similarly, in this volume, we suggest a perspective on humanity in which we advance from the basic to our most perplexing, in our striving to understand what it means to be human and its present challenges. Commencing with moral justice, we contend that the human being innately aspires toward the better, the just, and the good, à la Plato. Thereafter, we introduce choice and assert that the human is more than an instinctual being, but one who exercises a godly privilege to choose within life—*uvacharta bachayim* (Deuteronomy 30:19). Deuteronomy's powerful admonition is commonly translated, "Choose life!" However, translating the text literally, one can render the assertion as "Choose within life." This emendation adds the moral imperative to be a choosing being. Thereafter, choosing begs belonging; we are social creatures, and John Donne's bell tolls for us all, together. Yet, we also are individual beings, reflected in gender and the inner identities that guide our relationships and yearnings. Finally, we conclude Part I with the observation that humanity is grounded in empathy, compassion, and relationship, recognizing our own and others' feelings and spiritual and emotional needs.

Part II continues the intentional ontological development. Opening with a discussion of our animal relationships, we recognize that we are part of a larger biosphere and are related both phylogenetically and socially to all living creatures. We realize that we can adjust and construct limits in the spectra of life itself—that our intellect and tools have empowered us to shape human life. Our next discussions advance to even greater artificiality: We can build machines, creatures, and features that transcend or supersede elements of humanity, including artificial intelligence and lifeforms themselves. Finally, we complete Part II by considering that humans connect or disconnect—communicate and transmit information—demonstrating further shifting in the balance or imbalance of life and machine.

Essentially, in this volume we offer a conceptual construct of humanity and open a conversation regarding what it means to strive to be human at a time of massive and accelerating change.

Jewish texts, history, and conversations have circumnavigated these themes for millennia. In fact, it very well could be deemed the central conversation of Jewish life: What does God expect of us? The simple Jewish answer has been that we are to perform the mitzvot, the commandments. However, a deeper answer is that God wants us to be fully human, as the twentieth-century luminary scholar and Holocaust refugee Rabbi Abraham Joshua Heschel brilliantly taught: God is searching for humanity (*God in Search of Man: A Philosophy of Judaism*). So, too, are we. Now, with humanity again on a potential threshold of destroying itself—starting decades ago with unchecked atomic power and continuing to our day via machines overtaking our humanity—we have to know who and what we are so that we might both thrive and seek to fulfill our role and expectations. Essentially, we have the opportunity to develop a meaningful understanding of our humanness and the prospect to fulfill the godly expectations set for us in Jewish tradition. To do so, we heed Hillel's admonition: "In a place where there is no humanity, strive to be human" (*Pirkei Avot* 2:6).

NOTE

1. Numbering of all quotes from *Pirkei Avot* follows Shmuly Yanklowitz, *Pirkei Avot: A Social Justice Commentary* (CCAR Press, 2018).

Part I

Challenges from Within Us

CHAPTER 1

Empathy, Power, and *Tzedakah*: Is Moral Justice at the Core of Humanity?

Rabbi Sarah Bassin

"STRIVE TO BE HUMAN," Rabbi Hillel charged back in the first century BCE. Jewish tradition still demands this of us today. It's a clear moral message about how we want to be in the world. In a place where no one is acting human, strive to act human.

In my role as rabbi in residence at HIAS, the world's oldest refugee protection organization, a window has opened for me to peer at the best and worst of humanity. Since the late nineteenth century when HIAS was founded in the United States to help waves of Jewish immigrants escaping poverty and pogroms in Eastern Europe, the organization's mission has expanded to help people of all backgrounds fleeing persecution and harm in more than twenty countries around the world. I have witnessed much of this need and this work in our own backyard. I have heard the testimony of a woman assaulted and left for dead once she reached the streets of El Paso. I have encountered a young man nearly killed and permanently disabled in a fire at a migrant detention facility in Ciudad Juarez where the cells remained locked as the building burned. I have sat with a young mother of two in Tijuana awaiting the return of her husband's body after he was murdered on their journey north. Their stories are far from unique. Profound inhumanity has overrun America's borders and the journeys people take to reach them.

There exist so many stories of people fleeing situations in which far too few are acting human. Parents leave everything behind so their children might have a chance at a future and evade being forced into violent gangs, raped, or murdered. These crises span the globe, impacting Sudanese, Rohingya, Uygurs, Afghans, Ukrainians, Venezuelans, Palestinians, and countless others. Often those fleeing face immense danger on their journey even as they seek to leave that danger behind. We presume that many start out knowing the risks. Yet, they make the calculation that the danger ahead is not as bad as the danger they seek to escape. As one of my colleagues put it, a 1 percent chance of hope is better than certain death.

My time at HIAS has taught me a *davar acher*—an alternative interpretation—of what it means to strive to be human. I now read the precept not only as a moral message but as an existential one. Coming from circumstances in which there is a shortage of human dignity, these people exemplify stories of striving to be—to exist—as a human. Their struggle to hold onto their humanity is a struggle simply to live.

When Jewish tradition orders us to strive to be human, our ears are trained to hear an inherently optimistic outlook on human nature—that when we are what we are intended to be, we are good. Acting human is an admirable objective. We are, after all, created in God's image, according to the opening chapter of our most sacred text. And yet, the instruction "to be human" comes precisely "in a place where no one is acting human." Strive toward humanity, the Sages tell us, when humanity has abandoned its task of stewarding God's project of Creation. Jewish tradition affirms in the same breath both our potential as God's executors *and* the possibility not only of individual misstep, but of complete societal failure. We are instructed to aspire to be human even though we know that we are *only* human.

It is a sober, almost defiant declaration. By claiming that the default orientation of humanity strives toward goodness, Jewish tradition takes a firm stand in its worldview. We would rather face the world with optimism in our potential than succumb to the notion that we are unable to rise above our flaws. We lean into hope.

The early stories of the Bible dance in this same tension, initially optimistic about our ability to live out our intended purpose as partners in the creation of a just and moral world. But the narrative almost immediately reflects the need to recalibrate just how much guidance and constraint we require in our striving to be human.

One might assume that the act of eating the fruit from the Tree of Knowledge of Good and Evil in Eden was our first failing. Indeed, Christianity interprets this act as the original sin for which humanity will always be indebted and in need of salvation. That line of thinking has never gained traction in Judaism.

Perhaps Jewish tradition found it unreasonable to demand moral accountability without the preexisting ability to distinguish right from wrong. It is only through the act of eating from the Tree of Knowledge of Good and Evil that we become moral beings. How could we be fully created in God's image if we lacked God's sense of moral justice? The eating of the fruit caused us to acquire awareness and conscience—a sense of our place in the world and in relation to each other. It was almost as if God's setup of the Tree of Knowledge of Good and Evil pushed us toward this last step of cocreating ourselves into moral agents. We opened our own eyes and took a step closer to the image of God.

Only once we acquire conscience as the basis for moral accountability does the language of sin enter the human story. Shortly after humanity's expulsion from the Garden of Eden, the text follows the lives of Adam and Eve's children. Their son Cain suffers disappointment and rage when God rejects his sacrifice and accepts his brother Abel's offering. In witnessing Cain's reaction, God issues him a cautionary warning:

> "Surely, if you do right,
> There is uplift.
> But if you do not do right
> *Sin* couches at the door;
> Its urge is toward you,
> Yet you can be its master." (Genesis 4:7)[1]

In its first appearance in the Jewish account of the human story, sin presents as a significant, though manageable force. And yet, humanity fails this first encounter. Cain murders his brother Abel out of jealousy, then lashes out against God with the famous retort, "Am I my brother's keeper?" (Genesis 4:9).

While God never answers that question directly, the expectation is clearly "yes." God replies that Abel's blood cries out from the ground, thus modeling the concern that had been anticipated from Cain. Morally capable beings rely on empathy. We most readily demonstrate our ability to distinguish right from wrong in our ability to display care for the other and treat them as beings worthy of dignity like ourselves. Empathy is the primary expression of the conscience we acquired when we ate the fruit. Conscience is also a powerful moral tool. If we were sufficiently in tune with the needs and feelings of others and responded accordingly, we would live in utopia. The blueprint of society first laid out in Genesis rests upon the premise that empathy is enough. The instructions seem simple. But the execution has proved much more difficult.

A few verses later, Cain's empathic failure appears endemic to humanity as a whole: "The Eternal saw how great was the wickedness of human beings in earth, that the direction of their thoughts was nothing but wicked all the time" (Genesis 6:5). Empathy alone did not prove to be a sufficient guarantor of moral action, much to God's chagrin. As a result, God reset the project by choosing Noah to survive and rebuild society with new safeguards in place. According to the Sages of the Talmud, God issued seven laws to establish a baseline of morality in the aftermath of the Flood, to guide us to be our brothers' and sisters' keepers. These would be seven laws for which all humanity would remain obligated: "The Sages taught: The descendants of Noah, that is, all of humanity, were commanded to observe seven mitzvot: the mitzvah of establishing courts of judgment; and the prohibition against taking God's name in vain; and the prohibition of idol worship; and the prohibition against forbidden sexual relations; and the prohibition of bloodshed; and the prohibition of robbery; and the prohibition against eating a limb from a living animal" (Babylonian Talmud, *Sanhedrin* 56a).[2]

This particular list of seven reflects some Rabbinic priorities that may not fully align with our own. However, the first among these commandments provides the key to any list of precepts: the establishment of the courts. God's relaunch of humanity could only follow a righteous path if a power to enforce and even coerce empathy was in place. Perhaps this societal configuration in which power undergirds empathy would prove sufficient in creating a world of moral justice.

Accountability in the form of law certainly adds a layer of protection, but it also becomes clear that law itself would need to be an iterative process. Seven laws and human courts were not enough to prevent our dehumanization as a people. Many generations after the Flood, in the aftermath of the Israelites' slavery and wholesale oppression in Egypt, our ancestors welcomed the opportunity to expand upon the Seven Noachide Laws by accepting the yoke of Torah. Perhaps more law would build a more just society. The additional regulations were intended to make us a holier people, so we embraced the raising of the bar from 7 to 613 commandments.

Still, we discovered gaps in the system—subsets of people who fell through the cracks due to how and when the law was constructed and enforced. The widow, the orphan, and the stranger (among others) found themselves on the periphery of the ancient Israelite legal code. So we implemented and culturally embraced *tzedakah*—charitable giving rooted in a sense of what is just and right—to be a responsive mechanism, simultaneously mandated and discretionary. Collective funds to which everyone gives are allocated to the greatest needs. Intentionally incomplete harvests allow those in need to help themselves. The framework of *tzedakah* functions as a safety net when empathy lacks compulsion and the power of law lacks sufficient coverage. *Tzedakah* establishes a baseline of human dignity even for those not centered in the code.

The prophet Isaiah explained the relationship between *tzedakah* and societal stability when he declared, "For the work of *tzedakah* shall be peace, and the effect of *tzedakah*, calm and security forever" (Isaiah 32:17). He understood that the calm and security of a functioning society are the product of investment in the well-being of the most vulnerable at the margins of that society.

The tool kit for a moral and just world came to rest on three legs instead of two: our empathy-fueled conscience, the power of legal accountability, and the safety net of *tzedakah*. It is an ancient system of checks and balances that still stands today. Whenever one element fails or comes under assault, another exists as a backup means of ensuring human dignity. While this three-pronged approach certainly has its flaws and has often failed at upholding human dignity, this remains our tool kit for moral justice in the world—at least until new revelation or insight expands what is currently at our disposal. And so, we continue to tweak and tune the tools that we have.

We were able to anticipate some of the pitfalls early on. The Torah posited the possibility of corrupt judges and built safeguards accordingly. For example, Deuteronomy 16:19–20 advises, "You shall not judge unfairly: you shall show no partiality; you shall not take bribes, for bribes blind the eyes of the discerning and upset the plea of the just. Justice, justice shall you pursue, that you may thrive and occupy the land that the Eternal your God is giving you." Still, the potential for corrupt judges was only the start of the possible misapplication of the law. Some of the early Rabbis questioned an overreliance on legal tradition and its continued expansion as the most robust tool for perfecting moral justice. They noted that when unconstrained by the other parts of our tool kit, the law could permit injustice.

The Jerusalem Talmud shares the story of Shimon ben Shetach, a poor rabbi scraping by who came into fortune at the expense of a non-Jew:

> Shimon ben Shetach was dealing with flax [as his profession]. His students said to him, "Master, leave it behind and we will buy you a donkey and you won't need to work so much," and they bought him a donkey from an Arab, and it had a jewel hanging from it[s neck]. They came

> to him and said, "From now on you won't have to work again." He said to them, "Why?" They said to him, "We bought you a donkey from an Arab, and it had a jewel hanging from it[s neck]!" He said to them, "Did the owner know?" They said to him, "No." (Jerusalem Talmud, *Bava M'tzia* 2:5)[3]

According to the plain reading of Jewish law, Shimon ben Shetach was not obligated to return the gem because it was not required for Jews to return lost property to gentiles. Yet he was appalled by the notion that he would keep the gem simply because the law allowed it. The text continues, "[Shimon ben Shetach] said to them, 'Go return it. . . . What, do you think Shimon ben Shetach is a barbarian?'"

Shimon ben Shetach was outraged by the idea that he would not return the lost gem, declaring how poorly it would reflect on Jews' morality. He understood the inadequacy of law as a stand-alone moral tool, especially when ungirded by the empathy of our conscience.

Likewise, the Babylonian Talmud blames the destruction of Jerusalem on an overreliance on legalism: "Rabbi Yochanan says: Jerusalem was destroyed only for the fact that they adjudicated cases on the basis of Torah law in the city. The Gemara asks: Rather, what else should they have done? Should they rather have adjudicated cases on the basis of arbitrary decisions? Rather, say: That they established their rulings on the basis of Torah law and did not go beyond the letter of the law" (Babylonian Talmud, *Bava M'tzia* 30b).[4]

The medieval scholar Nachmanides gave name to this phenomenon of the moral indifference of law in his commentary on Leviticus 19:2. He described one whose actions are legal but not moral as *naval birshut haTorah*—"a scoundrel with the permission of Torah": "Thus he will become a sordid person within the permissible realm of the Torah!"[5]

Law, whether religious or secular, can not only permit immorality but can be a source thereof. The project of modern nation-state building led to some of the worst atrocities sanctioned by elaborate legal systems that lost the anchor of human dignity. Slavery, colonialism, and genocides have all been carried out not in spite of the law but with its aid. Nazi Germany's Nuremberg Race Laws, which laid the legal groundwork for the persecution of Jews, were inspired by American Jim Crow laws. Yet the Holocaust was not the first genocide enacted with the moral perversion of law. "Ottoman Empire leadership employed policy mechanisms in order to legally legitimize the genocide of the Armenian population in

1915."[6] The "Doctrine of Discovery" provided legal authority for British colonialism and enabled sovereign, property, and commercial rights over indigenous populations.[7] Entire populations have been subjugated or eliminated with the permission and at the behest of legal code. People of conscience were either absent or overpowered, and civil charitable infrastructures were insufficient or impotent. Empathy and *tzedakah* hardly stand a chance at upholding a safety net for human dignity when law is intentionally weaponized to undermine it. It is as if someone ripped one leg off a stool and used it to whack down the ones that remained intact.

When a nation-state loses the thread of human dignity and becomes the source of abuse rather than of restitution, with the complicity of the governed, there exists no recourse for justice. The only viable option is for at-risk people to flee to another jurisdiction where law is a source of protection, not harm. But in a world with clear, controlled borders of nation-states, there arises a new problem: For the first time in human history, there is often no place to flee.

In this world premised on the supreme authority of the nation-state, forcibly displaced people simply fall beyond the scope of moral or legal consideration. Unsafe within their own borders, they are unclaimed by other countries. There are different subsets—the stateless, the refugee, the asylum seeker, the enslaved, and the trafficked—all of them trying to flee places that cannot protect them, will not protect them, or actively seek to harm them because of who they are. They lack recourse in any jurisdiction outside the one that failed or attacked them. In our own collective historical experience, the global indifference toward Jews fleeing Nazi oppression is well-documented and most exemplified in the Evian Conference of 1938, where thirty-two countries stared at the existential crisis facing Jews and refused to open their doors.

The great post-Holocaust philosopher Hannah Arendt framed the fundamental flaw of a world with the sovereign nation-state as the ultimate authority: "This calamity [of displacement] is far from unprecedented; in the long memory of history, forced migrations of individuals or whole groups of people for political or economic reasons look like everyday occurrences. What is unprecedented is not the loss of a home but the impossibility of finding a new one. . . . This, moreover, had next to nothing to do with any material problem of overpopulation; it was a problem not of space but of political organization."[8] As a refugee herself, Arendt declared, "We are not born equal."[9] Her declaration is not so much a rejection of the notion that all people are deserving of dignity and empathy, but rather a sober acceptance of the fact that equality (God-given or not) exists only within the framework of human enforcement. In a world of the sovereign nation-state, the three-pronged system of checks and balances to ensure human dignity—empathy, *tzedakah*, and law—is fundamentally reduced to two for forcibly displaced populations. In addition, it is often the case that a mass crisis can quickly overwhelm our capacity for empathy and *tzedakah*, especially when that crisis is ongoing. Absent a power over the nation-state, indifferent or xenophobic whims of a country codified into law can prove devastating to the forcibly displaced.

Arendt goes on to declare the most fundamental of human rights is "the right to have rights."[10] She understood that those unprotected or attacked by their state lack any real ability to claim these supposed universal human rights. The rights of the forcibly displaced hinge upon acknowledgment of their existence as a group and a global commitment to uphold those rights.

It is not surprising in the wake of the nineteenth and twentieth centuries that there arose a global skepticism of a nation-state's law as a source of or enforcer of moral justice. In the aftermath of the Holocaust, with this shortcoming laid bare, a global consensus emerged affirming transnational legal obligations to those who have been forcibly displaced. The 1951 Refugee Convention responded to the failure of global accountability in affirming human rights after the Holocaust. The "stateless," as they were known, became a group no longer beyond the scope of moral or legal obligation.

The convention created the formal definition of the term "refugee" and outlined the rights and the international legal standards of treatment for their protection. It established the right to apply for asylum and have cases heard while remaining safe. As with all law, some people are still left at the margins. Today, many climate refugees and those too impoverished to survive in their places of origin fall outside the established definitions of refugee and asylum seeker in international law that would afford them protection, even though they too flee conditions no less deadly than war or persecution.

The establishment of international law beyond the nation-state is an imperfect answer to uphold this "right to have rights" that Arendt named. Not exactly a novel revelation, the addition of international law to the law of sovereign nation-states nevertheless has created a more robust system of checks and balances. This is especially true for those moments when national law loses touch with the constraints of conscience.

For decades since in the United States, the embrace of these international legal standards blended into the dominant national story Americans have told themselves: The United States is a nation of welcome and integration. It is an oversimplified narrative, to be sure, given the many periods of backlash against refugees and immigrants. Still, the bipartisan embrace of this international law welcoming the refugee was significant and, most importantly, codified. Beginning in 1980, for nearly four decades, American presidents across the political spectrum set out to welcome tens of thousands of refugees per year. It was a source of national pride and strength. The United States was not alone in this global ethos. In 2015, the chancellor of Germany, the country once responsible for the greatest refugee crisis of the twentieth century, stood in a refugee camp as her nation accepted more than a million Syrians displaced by civil war and declared, *"Wir schaffen das"*—"We can do this." In recent years, Canada wagered its future on the welcome and integration of large numbers of refugees. Canada overtook its neighbor to the south in raw numbers of refugee resettlement in 2018. Yet many of these countries in the West that once touted the benefits of immigration in general and refugees in particular have walked back their commitments in response to prevailing political winds. A narrative of scarcity painting immigrants, refugees, and asylum seekers as agents of cultural change and competitors for jobs and housing has replaced the story of the newcomer as an essential contributor to economic stability and growth, especially in industries like agriculture, hospitality, and caretaking. It should also be noted that a country's wealth is rarely the best indicator of whether it embraces the international responsibility of welcoming refugees. Chad hosts more than a million refugees in a country of fewer than 20 million people. Lebanon hosts more than 1.5 million with a population of under 5 million.

Yet with increasing distance from the horrors of the Holocaust, competing national priorities, and a global backsliding toward authoritarian-tinged nationalism, many countries once again face historical winds that lay bare the fragility of our three-legged tool kit for a morally just society to ensure the dignity of all people. The international law embraced in the aftermath of the Holocaust may have articulated obligations of nation-states; it did not, however, come equipped with the power of enforcement that traditionally accompanies law. In this way, international law often feels more akin to *tzedakah* than it does to law. Its main mechanism of implementation is often peer pressure of fellow nations, not the actual power of enforcement. When nations and their leaders abandon commitments to the forcibly displaced for political calculations, there are few consequences.

Moreover, the method by which international law ensures the dignity of the forcibly displaced has built-in vulnerabilities. The right to request asylum is initiated through the act of stepping foot onto that country's soil. Recent US policies and procedures have been implemented to prevent people from exercising this right—barring them from presenting at ports of entry to actually step onto American soil. In their desperation to touch American ground and initiate the process of requesting asylum, they go between ports of entry—cross rivers and deserts and razor wire, wait in orderly lines, then turn themselves over to the custody of American officials. This approach is now punished with expedited removal and a ban of reentry, with few exceptions. When exercising the legal right under international law to seek asylum becomes exceedingly complicated, byzantine, and Kafkaesque, it ceases to function as a right.

There are amoral pragmatic arguments to be made about the importance of potential host countries embracing refugees and asylum seekers, such as the futility of deterrence as a tactic, the economic benefit brought to countries with aging demographics, and the global instability that will be fueled by ignoring a record crisis of forcible displacement. However, while these arguments may be useful tactics to attempt to reclaim a culture of welcome, ultimately our North Star must remain our commitment to build society on a foundation of moral justice. Jewish tradition compels us to reclaim the narrative of what makes us human—our empathy-driven conscience, our willingness to use the power of morally grounded law, and the construction of *tzedakah* safety nets that all combine to ensure human dignity. Through these mechanisms, we carry out the moral imperative to be one another's keepers. The totality of Jewish tradition provides a road map toward this North Star. It is no exaggeration to say that the Torah is teeming with the experience of migration and the imperative established from that memory. From the story of Noah escaping the Flood, to Abraham and Sarah's life of migration, to the Israelites wandering for forty years in pursuit of a home while under constant threat of attack—the stories we tell ourselves about our identity center on the memory of displacement. We direct our ire toward those who took advantage of us at our most vulnerable and celebrate those who provided aid. To reduce the centrality and moral orientation of the refugee experience in Jewish tradition to a singular verse, story, or commandment would be to ignore its ubiquity.

This is true in other traditions as well. In *A Theology of Migration*, Father Daniel Groody shines a light on the centrality of the refugee in Christianity—in the figure of Jesus himself and those he cared for.[11] The Muslim calendar begins counting at *hijrah* (emigration), when persecution forced Muhammad and his followers to flee. The memory of forced displacement is integral to the worldviews that undergird our cultures. Yet, when a fish swims in the ocean, it can forget that it is surrounded by water. We exist in a historical moment of great headwinds against moral justice for the most vulnerable populations in our midst, in which law has become a cudgel of injustice rather than a tool for dignity.

Even so, in this milieu, herculean efforts exist that remind us what a moral society looks like. I have witnessed it at HIAS, at Annunciation House in El Paso, and at Jewish Family Services in San Diego, where literal poor, huddled masses yearning to breathe free find their first respite, safety, and kindness in months. It is *tzedakah* in its purest form—existing to fill the gaps left by the way government has structured itself. It is extraordinary, holy, human work. Organizations like these embody the precept to strive to be human in settings where no one is acting human. They harness the power of religious tradition to reclaim and recenter our societal norms around human dignity in places where society has abandoned its obligation. They model what it means to take seriously a call to moral justice. It is on us to take that call seriously as well. In an era when their holy work is constrained by law and policy increasingly hostile to human dignity, it is on us to take that call even more seriously.

Our sustained ability to push for policies of dignity and build up support for the networks of charity depends more than anything on not losing sight of our own moral compass. Times of moral challenge can alter our own sense of what is acceptable and just. In these moments of ethical disorientation, we find ourselves reaching for the most primal tool in our pursuit of moral justice—our empathy. As the post-Holocaust American theologian Harold M. Shulweis declared in his book *Conscience: The Duty to Obey and the Duty to Disobey*, "Although conscience may be dismissed as merely human, it is nevertheless all we humans have. . . . If conscience is a fence, it is erected to protect the gullible from succumbing to all forms of totalitarianism, religious as well as political."[12]

We must choose to be anchored by the vision of humanitarian groups and not pulled by the shifting political winds that value life only when it is politically expedient.

It is a hard moment not to feel despair as we stare down the fragility of the checks and balances of the moral justice we have painstakingly cultivated over the centuries. Yet herein lies the genius of Jewish tradition: Its wisdom speaks to us at the moment in which we find ourselves on the brink of giving up. At the moments in which the headwinds seem greatest and we seem most skeptical of our collective capacity for moral justice, our Sages remind us that acting human is still an admirable aspiration. Throughout history, we have often found ourselves in a place where no one is acting human. However, in every era, we commit again and again to strive toward our humanity no matter how limited or flawed our tool kit for moral justice. In this way, we remind ourselves of our capacity for goodness and our ability to rise above our flaws and that when we are what we are intended to be, we are good.

Notes

1. Translations from Biblical sources are from *The JPS Tanakh: Gender-Sensitive Edition* (Jewish Publication Society, 2023), found on Sefaria (sefaria.org). Emphasis added.
2. Translation adapted from the William Davidson digital edition of the *Koren Noé Talmud*, with commentary by Adin Even-Israel Steinsaltz (license: CC-BY-NC, https://creativecommons.org/licenses/by-nc/4.0/), found on Sefaria (sefaria.org).
3. Translation of the Jerusalem Talmud is adapted from the merger of the translation and commentary by Heinrich W. Guggenheimer (Berlin, De Gruyter, 1999–2015) and Sefaria Community Translation (license: CC-BY, https://creativecommons.org/licenses/by/3.0/), found on Sefaria (sefaria.org).
4. Translation adapted from the William Davidson digital edition of the *Koren Noé Talmud*, with commentary by Adin Even-Israel Steinsaltz (license: CC-BY-NC, https://creativecommons.org/licenses/by-nc/4.0/), found on Sefaria (sefaria.org).
5. Translation from *Commentary on the Torah by Ramban (Nachmanides)*, by Charles B. Chavel (Shilo Publishing House, 1976) (license: CC-BY, https://creativecommons.org/licenses/by/3.0/), found on Sefaria (sefaria.org).
6. Marie Miller, "Genocide Under the Ottoman State: Nationalistic Co-Optation of Classical Legal Paradigms and Responses to Western Interference," *Columbia Undergraduate Law Review*, May 9, 2024, https://www.culawreview.org/journal/genocide-under-the-ottoman-state-nationalistic-co-optation-of-classical-legal-paradigms-and-responses-to-western-interference#:~:text=Instigated%20by%20fear%20of%20foreign,the%20legal%20status%20of%20religious.

7. Robert J. Miller, "The Doctrine of Discovery," in *Discovering Indigenous Lands: The Doctrine of Discovery in the English Colonies*, ed. Robert J. Miller, Jacinta Ruru, Larissa Behrendt, and Tracy Lindberg (Oxford University Press, 2010).
8. Hannah Arendt, *The Origins of Totalitarianism* (Meridian Books, 1951), 293–94.
9. Arendt, *Origins of Totalitarianism*, 301.
10. Arendt, *Origins of Totalitarianism*, 296.
11. Daniel P. Goody, *A Theology of Migration: The Bodies of Refugees and the Body of Christ* (Orbis, 2022).
12. Harold M. Schulweis, *Conscience: The Duty to Obey and the Duty to Disobey* (Jewish Lights, 2008), 67.

CHAPTER 2

The Human Question: Choosing Between Good and Evil

Rabbi Lucy H. F. Dinner

CHOICE FRAMES the raison d'être of human existence. From Torah's earliest teachings to the essence of democracy, we learn that stripping people of choice eviscerates what makes them human. Choice is the defining feature that separates humanity from all other creatures. The ability to discern and make decisions based on that discernment separates human action from animal, instinctual response. The choices one makes, from the simplest to the most consequential, build the moral compass of the individual and reflect upon the essential character of humanity. As well, the centrality of choice to Judaism and of the responsibility that accompanies our choices suffuses the totality of Jewish civilization. It frames the covenant that connects Jewish belief to a purposeful and meaningful existence.

From the earliest teachings in the Torah to the undergirding of generations of Jewish theology and practice, choice stands at the center of living a Jewish life. At the conclusion of the Torah's opening Creation story, God willed dominion over future creations to Adam and Eve, and through them to all subsequent generations. Every choice a person makes plays a role in diminishing or adding to Creation. Thus, at the end of the Torah we read, "I call heaven and earth to witness against you this day: I have put before you life and death, blessing and curse. Choose life—if you and your offspring would live" (Deuteronomy 30:19).

A midrash on Creation teaches that the differentiating feature of God's creation of the universe was the unique creation of human beings and their ability to choose. The early Rabbis indicate that this world was not the first one God created:

> Rabbi Y'hudah bar Simon said, "'It will be evening' is not written here, but rather, 'it was evening'—from here we learn that there had been an order to time even beforehand." Rabbi Abahu said, "This teaches that God continuously created worlds and destroyed them, until God created the current one, and said: 'This one pleases Me, those did not please Me.'" Rabbi Pinchas said, "The source for Rabbi Abahu is: 'God

saw everything that God had made, and behold, it was very good' (Genesis 1:31)—this pleases Me, those did not please Me." (*B'reishit Rabbah* 3:7)[1]

This midrash dives deeply into the importance of each word and phrase in the Creation story, filling in the gaps left by unwritten words. If this was the first world, why did time already exist? If God beholds this Creation as "very good," then previous creations must not have met that standard. Moreover, the Rabbis are probing for the reasons why this Creation is considered "very good." What choices did God make?

This phrase at the end of God's Creation—"behold, it was very good" (Genesis 1:31)—refers on the one hand to the totality of Creation; specifically, however, it comes after the creation of humanity. Why do humans merit the superlative "very good," while all the creations of the previous days are deemed only "good"? The answer lies in the unique responsibility God assigns to humans, differentiating humans from all other living beings. God declares, "Let them hold sway over the fish of the sea and the birds of the sky, over the beasts, over all the earth, over all that creeps upon the earth. So God created human beings in [the divine] image" (Genesis 1:26-27). Adam and Eve were given dominion over God's creations and endowed with the ability to choose the fate and future of Creation.

The entirety of the Creation narrative points to the theological ideology and responsibility of human choice. Created from dust from the four corners of the earth, Adam's very essence is intertwined with the essence of the earth. Adam and Eve are given dominion over the earth, sealing their obligation to care for the substance from which they were created. Every generation inherits that obligation; each person bears responsibility for the ongoing symbiotic relationship between the sustenance of the earth and the sustenance of humanity. And yet, the earth screams out at human neglect. Wildfires consume the land. Plastic particulates pollute the water. Fossil fuels that we burn with abandon fill the air with toxins. Humanity is failing the earth; without quick action, the earth will inevitably fail humanity.

Adam and Eve inherited a world that contained all the necessary components for human sustenance; today, the number of people presently suffering from hunger, homelessness, and poverty is staggering. There is enough food in the world to end world hunger today, if only people made the choice to distribute it rather than to hoard and waste it.

Stable housing has a direct impact on all other paths to end poverty. The National Low Income Housing Coalition reports, "Research shows that increasing access to affordable housing is the most cost-effective strategy for reducing childhood poverty and increasing economic mobility in the United States."[2] In spite of the benefits to society as a whole and specifically to those facing poverty, civilizations persist in ignoring the welfare of an alarming percentage of their inhabitants.

Surpassing the neglect humans perpetuate, it appears people are bent on destroying one another. Racism poisons one generation to the next, with its impact evident in every segment of society from health, wealth, imprisonment rates, and access to education and employment. The proliferating number of guns in America exceeds the population of the country. For many, the right to bear arms is more important than the right to life itself. The Centers for Disease Control and Prevention notes an alarming rise in children killed by guns from 2019 to the early 2020s and ranks guns as the leading cause of death among children and teens.[3] Surely, this cannot be what God labeled as "very good" after creating humanity. Are these the choices God wanted from us?

This power of human beings to choose and control the fate of God's creations sparked debate among the early Rabbinic interpreters of Torah. The divinely ordained ability to choose endows humans with the unique authority to control the course of their own lives and to have dominion over all other creations. The early Rabbis foresaw inherent danger in leaving the future of Creation in the hands of Adam and Eve and the generations to follow. As Moses warns the Israelites, with choice comes the power to impact life and death. Through the midrash, the Rabbis imagine an angelic debate on the advisability of creating humans:

> Rabbi Shimon said, "When the Holy One, blessed be God, came to create Adam the first human, the ministering angels divided into various factions and various groups. Some of them were saying, 'Let them not be created,' and some of them were saying, 'Let them be created.' That is what is written: 'Kindness and truth met; righteousness and peace touched' (Psalm 85:11). Kindness said, 'Let them be created, as they perform acts of kindness.' Truth said, 'Let them not be created, as they are full of lies.' Righteousness said, 'Let them be created, as they perform acts of righteousness.' Peace said, 'Let them not be created, as they are all full of discord.' What did the Holy One, blessed be God, do? God took Truth and cast it down to earth. That is what is written: 'You cast truth earthward' (Daniel 8:12). The ministering angels said before

the Holy One, blessed be God, 'Ruler of the universe, why are You demeaning Your very seal? Let Truth ascend from the earth.' That is what is written: 'Truth will spring from the earth' (Psalm 85:12)." ... Rav Huna, the rabbi of Tzippori, said, "While the ministering angels were busy deliberating with one another and engaging with one another, the Holy One, blessed be God, created [Adam] and said to them, 'Why are you deliberating? Humanity has already been created.'" (*B'reishit Rabbah* 8:5)[4]

The midrash implies that human beings are created precisely because of our unique ability to make choices and thereby define the values and course that will shape the continuing evolution of God's creations. The Rabbis recognized that much evil—"lies" and "discord"—will come from choice, an ageless observation that haunts people to this day. Why do these evils pervade civilization? Does the human propensity to choose love and justice outweigh our inclination to falsehood and discord—or vice versa? God ignores the debate of the angels, casts Truth to the ground as witness, and persists in creating humanity. As Truth will attest, the choices we make will determine which of the angels were right about humanity.

Humanity offers God something that neither celestials nor the sum of all other living creatures can tender. Cognition and the ability to think, analyze, and engage in the process of change constitute the heart of what it means to be human. They make for the continuing, dynamic transformation of people and the earth. Each individual decision moves the needle either toward building goodness and instituting justice or toward destroying God's world.

Western culture frequently refers to belief in God as a leap of faith, yet it takes an even larger leap of faith for God to place the choice between good and evil in human hands. After all, Creation could have been complete without the addition of human beings. The earth would still spin on its axis. The planets would circle the sun in predictable repetition. Seasons would come and go. Plants and animals would grow and mature, reproduce, and die. The world would still exist, with the exception that there would be no one here to witness, acknowledge, and add to its glory.

The possibility that the creation of the human species could add to the world also required a divine leap of faith on the part of God. Hearing fully the argument of the angels, God created Adam and Eve for more than an instinctual response in the ebb and flow of Creation. Instead,

God left the future of Creation to Adam and Eve and their descendants. Ceding choice to humanity endows humans with unbridled possibility. The ability to choose is the crowning jewel of all Creation: It gives humanity vast authority to reign over the earth and transfers both power and responsibility into the hands of mortal beings.

However, human beings pose the greatest hope and the gravest threat to God's creations. The gift of free will, God's greatest leap of faith, challenges people to make their lives count. It raises ultimate questions about the purpose of life and demands consideration of how the choices one makes add to or detract from the universe.

At its best, this unique lens of choice motivates humans to make meaning of their time on this earth. It creates that quest for higher purpose and fosters goals that bring personal and existential meaning. The quest to achieve, the desire to leave a legacy to the next generation, the drive to compete—all are derived from the ability to choose. History is replete with examples of individuals who directed their choices toward the greater good.

In the early nineteenth century, Sojourner Truth's quest for human rights began with her fight for the right to her own freedom and became her steadfast, lifelong mission. Born into slavery, Truth endured harsh abuse, eventually making the choice to run away to the protection of an abolitionist family in New York, a year before New York passed a law abolishing slavery. She not only won a fight to retrieve her young, enslaved son, but she also traveled the country boldly demanding human rights for all. Her efforts drew the attention of President Abraham Lincoln, who invited her to the White House. After the abolition of slavery she continued her quest, helping those freed find employment and rebuild their lives.

Jane Goodall laid the groundwork for her concern for the environment with her best-known work with primates. Not only does Goodall work for the protection of endangered species, but she also uses her focus on primates as a springboard to the greater responsibility of the protection of the earth. Goodall sees the struggle with climate change as the key to protecting and restoring the earth for all creatures.

Congressman John Lewis helped establish the Student Nonviolent Coordinating Committee, organizing against segregation in the South. In 1965, Lewis led the civil rights march across the Edmond Pettus Bridge in Selma, Alabama. As riot police beat marchers, they cracked

Lewis's skull. Lewis's televised pleas after the march stirred President Lyndon Johnson to urge Congress to expedite passing the Voting Rights Act. John Lewis continued his struggle for societal change, eventually working within the system as a US congressman representing the State of Georgia and becoming Congress's standard-bearer for protecting civil rights for decades. The choices that Lewis made long reverberate in the tapestry of American culture.

Ruth W. Messinger links her activism to her Jewish roots. "I feel like I've been an activist my whole life," she says. "I was raised to care about social justice and to believe that problems existed, that change was possible and that we all had to do our part to help heal the world. My parents suggested that it was a fundamental Jewish obligation—and our main purpose for being on this earth."[5] Her leadership spans a career that led to her assuming the presidency of the American Jewish World Service (AJWS). Through her vision at the helm of the AJWS, she reached the poorest around the world with reforms in food aid, with small business grants for women, and by defending against genocide. Through one grant, one meal, one light shining on a rising oppressor, the AJWS is bringing change to the most impoverished people in the world.

These individuals represent but a drop in the bucket of the countless people who use the uniqueness of human choice for the advancement of the human condition and the betterment and continuation of the world in which they dwell. The blessings of human creation continue through the zealous and brave choices of these exemplary leaders, as do the infinitesimal, unrecognized efforts of one recycled can, one dollar for a beggar, one kind word.

As much as some individuals dedicate their lives to the betterment of the world, many use their ability to choose toward the world's detriment. Human choice complicates the fate of the world because the future depends on the composite of independent decisions made by individuals. The evil choice of one can so easily wipe away the decision of scores who want to preserve and add to God's creations. Fear and threats too often subvert the process of choice. The examples of leaders ruling with egocentric disdain for anyone or anything beyond themselves abound. Indeed, for every anonymous act of goodness, the headlines roar with the perpetration of the cruelty of one human being against another. At its worst, history records those whose quests to achieve, to compete, and to establish a legacy lead them to raze everything and everyone that gets in their way. They embrace narcissism as their North Star, bulldozing a path of destruction in their wake. Every generation has its Hamans, the evil ones bent on annihilating the other. Delphine LaLaurie, an established nineteenth-century New Orleans socialite, tortured and massacred enslaved people. American cult leader Charles Manson brutally enlisted his followers in terrorizing and murdering victims across California. Osama bin Laden orchestrated the 9/11 attacks with calculated acts of mass murder that have upended the world to this day. Pol Pot, the Cambodian prime minister, led the execution of 25 percent of his own country's population. Hitler orchestrated the murder of six million Jews, over three million Soviet prisoners of war, countless gypsies, people with handicaps, and political dissenters. Add to these the untold millions who abuse children, maltreat workers, and defraud the vulnerable, wantonly employing the privilege of choice for destruction.

The angels were right: Their warning to God about the human capacity for evil foreshadowed evils stretching through time. Human beings exploit the ability to choose, spurning the inheritance of God's creations time and again. People falter whether by accident or intent, failing again and again to meet the divine will. Nonetheless, they also rise in ways that surpass understanding and keep the flame of hope alive. Freedom to choose absent responsibility and accountability leads to turmoil and chaos.

That is the crux of God's message after the creation of humanity. "God then surveyed all that [God] had made, and look—it was it very good!" (Genesis 1:31). After giving humans dominion over all creations, God declares: *Tov m'od*, "Very good!" This is both a proclamation about Creation and a directive to humanity: The proclamation accentuates God's satisfaction with this Creation as opposed to all the previous ones that God destroyed; the directive is for humanity to use our authority to improve the greater good—to make it *tov m'od*. The text implies that humans not only have the capability to choose, but also have the obligation to choose for the good. Rabbi Simcha Bunam of Pzhysha used to teach, "Everyone must have two pockets, so that he can reach into one or the other, according to his needs. In his right pocket are to be the words: 'For my sake was the world created,' and in his left: 'I am but dust and ashes.'"[6] Rabbi Dan Levin illuminates the teaching: "We must always be reminded that while we are only dust and ashes, we must shoulder the responsibility for a world that was created for our sake."[7]

What the Creation story implies, the Redemption and Revelation narratives codify: Freedom comes with responsibility. While the siddur orders the prayers Creation, Revelation, and Redemption, the Torah orders the story Creation, Redemption, then Revelation. Thus, as our choices evolve, they progress from Creation to Redemption, and finally Revelation. Redemption opens the possibility, while Revelation leads us to join together in making choices that add goodness to the world.

Through the process of redemption, God assigns Moses a dual role—to convince both the Israelites and the Egyptians that God has a purpose for the world that transcends any ruler. The Egyptians need to accept that enslavement of the Israelites is neither sustainable nor right. The Israelites need to believe that they can relearn what it means to be free, gain the freedom to make their own choices, and have the self-confidence to direct their own destiny. Redemption means uprooting those people and systems that perpetuate oppression. Whether it be enslavement by force, discrimination rooted into laws, or cultures that subvert the law to their own classism, oppression rears up repeatedly throughout human history. The lessons of the Biblical Redemption story instill the ideal of ensuring that those oppressed in every generation are redeemed.

The familiar refrain "Let My people go" becomes the tagline of the Redemption story. Repeatedly, Moses demands of Pharaoh, "Let My people go." Freedom is the right; freedom is the universal privilege; freedom is for one and all. Freedom's supreme value underlies the redemption from the ancient times of Torah to democratic civilization today. The establishment of the United States of America is based on freedom for all: "We hold these truths to be self-evident, that all men are created equal, that they are endowed by their Creator with certain inalienable rights, that among these are life, liberty and the pursuit of happiness."[8] These words codify the purpose of democracy. As redemption from Egyptian slavery resets freedom for the Israelites, the United States Declaration of Independence reinforces the redemptive features of American democracy and freedom.

When God sends Moses to Pharaoh to redeem the Israelites, Moses's exhortation always contains a purpose: "Let My people go that they may worship Me" (Exodus 7:26). As familiar as a call to freedom is "Let My people go," the second part of the verse holds the crux—"that they may worship Me." The Hebrew word for slave, *eved*, and the Hebrew word for worship, *avodah*, derive from the same root, meaning "to serve." The enslaved Israelites serve their taskmaster, and the freed Israelites serve God in word and deed.

In the Redemption narrative, God does not reclaim control over human choices; rather, God asks for acknowledgment in the form of worship, emphasizing to the Israelites that human choice is a gift. No individual or ruling party has the right to usurp the rights of others. As God cannot control the choices one makes, even more so, no person or governing authority has the right to usurp the freedom of another.

The choices one makes define who one serves. Some serve only themselves, seeing others as either obstacles to or opportunities for their own aggrandizement. Others lose their sense of self entirely, hitching their choices to outside demands. No matter who or what directs the decisions one makes, ultimately, as the great singer Bob Dylan instructs, "You're going to have to serve somebody / Well, it may be the devil or it may be the Lord / But you're going to have to serve somebody."[9]

The Israelite's redemption remains a defining point in the maturation of the Jewish people. It symbolizes the process each person goes through in their development and growth. Breaking free of the confines of childhood and the walls of one's environs shapes personal redemption. The realization that one has the ability to make a difference liberates and motivates. What people do with that ability defines their character, impacts their surroundings, and composes the opus of their existence.

Throughout history, individuals and groups have embraced this transformation process to bring about seismic change to uphold freedom for one as freedom for all. The Reverend Martin Luther King Jr. created the road map for redemption in the civil rights movement of the twentieth century. King paired nonviolence with a passionate call to equality. He utilized communal organizing, protests, and civil disobedience, alongside negotiations with political leaders, to demand the overthrow of the oppressive Jim Crow laws permeating the South. King's activism extended well beyond interest for the Black churches he pastored in Montgomery, Alabama, and Atlanta, Georgia. He channeled his oratory charisma to galvanize the masses for civil rights and workers' rights, to protest the Vietnam War, and to eradicate poverty. His guiding principle—that all people regardless of color or creed are members of the human family, with equal rights to dignity, respect, and unencumbered life—underscored every cause King championed.

King's nonviolent civil disobedience galvanized Americans well beyond the Black community. Christians and Jews from all walks of life were inspired by King to join the movement against racism. Kivie Kaplan, a social justice advocate in his own right and leader in the national Union of American Hebrew Congregations (now the Union for Reform Judaism), played a critical role in the civil rights movement. He served as president of the NAACP from 1966 to 1975. Kaplan's civil rights activism was ignited by an antisemitic sign he came across at a Florida country club and his Black driver's comment that Blacks weren't listed on the sign because it was assumed they were not welcome.[10] Kaplan made it his personal mission to expand the membership of the NAACP, so he traveled the country soliciting new members and grew the organization from 221 to 51,000 members.[11] Kivie, a successful businessman, donated the historic building where the Civil Rights Act of 1964 and the Voting Rights Act of 1965 were drafted to the Religious Action Center of Reform Judaism.[12] Kaplan's generosity ensured that his legacy of work for racial justice and his commitment to the prophetic call of Reform Judaism would endure in the work of the Reform Movement for decades to come. In the twenty-first century, the Reform Movement has committed to a new initiative to fight racial injustice, keeping alive Kivie Kaplan's Jewish vision and devotion to human rights.

Over half a century after the civil rights movement of the 1960s, the prevalence of discrimination and oppressive practices toward people of color ignited the zeal of the Reverend Bishop William Barber II to employ nonviolent civil protest, renewing the call to end racism, classism, and a myriad of other wrongs. Barber's redeeming work started locally, aiming at rooting out racism. Early on he gathered a group of interfaith leaders in Raleigh, North Carolina, for a press conference held at Temple Beth Or, where he called out the covert attempts by the newly elected school board to resegregate the largest school system in the state. Those efforts led to a broader effort, the Moral Monday Movement, which demanded that North Carolina's legislators address inequities in education, health care, job access, racism, and more. Eventually, Barber's activism morphed from local and state to the national stage, as he became cochair of a new Poor People's Campaign built on the principles of King's March on Washington and the civil rights movement's original Poor People's Campaign. Reverend Martin Luther King Jr., Kivie Kaplan, and the Reverend William Barber II demonstrate how to make choices toward the ideals of redemption. They teach how to part the seas and stand for the oppressed. The marches, rallies, organizing, and protests inject energy and raise attention to the issues of the day. They open the door of possibility, they instill hope, and they motivate people to act. They unfasten the shackles that have held back generations. In each age, bold people choose to rise up in the face of the wrongs of their day. They are the ones who heed the call, give voice to the oppressed, and agitate the system for change. They exemplify redemption in modernity.

Where redemption opens doors, revelation lays out the steps to create a viable path for the specific needs of the times at hand. Though people have the inherent ability to freely choose, unbridled freedom leads to destruction and chaos. The Israelites had barely made it across the sea to freedom before they started complaining. Freedom, with no boundaries, direction, or instruction felt almost as weighty to the Israelites as the cruel labor that Pharaoh thrust upon them. Revelation, the receiving of Torah, provided the path that reassured the Israelites. Revelation gave them a guide. Torah frames human decisions with respect, ethics, and purpose. Through the lens of Torah, morals and values come into focus as the lens through which choice takes place, both for individuals and for building community and social structure.

The Revelation of Torah provides a road map not only for the ancient Israelites, but for all future generations. The words of Deuteronomy reiterate the inclusivity: "You stand this day, all of you, before the Eternal your God—your tribal heads, your elders, and your officials, all the men of Israel, your children, your women, even the stranger within your camp, from woodchopper to water drawer. . . . I make this covenant, with its sanctions, not with you alone, but both with those who are standing here with us this day before the Eternal our God and with those who are not with us here this day" (Deuteronomy 29:9–11, 29:13–14). These words apply to men, women, and children, from the highest-ranking leaders to the stranger, to those of future generations who are yet to stand to receive its words. It is the ancient Biblical equalizer for time eternal.

Revelation guides the journey for more than the bounds of self-direction and choice. It calls upon every individual to choose wisely, honor the gift of Creation, and add to its blessings. It emphasizes the power for good and evil inherent in free choice. Hearkening back to the debate of the angels at Creation, who argued that humans could and would choose evil, Revelation offers a guide to direct humanity to choose good not only for themselves but for the people with whom they dwell and the land in which they live. A Talmudic midrash (*Shabbat* 88b) posits that at the time of Revelation, like at Creation, the angels again try to intervene. How easy it would have been for God to appoint the angels as gatekeepers over the world, using the Torah to continue to advance God's vision. The angels object vigorously that they are the rightful protectors of God's sacred Torah:

> Rabbi Y'hoshua ben Levi said: When Moses ascended on High to receive the Torah, the ministering angels said before the Holy One . . . : "Master of the universe, what is one born of a woman doing here among us?" The Holy One . . . said to them: "He [Moses] came to receive the Torah." The angels said before [the Holy One]: "The Torah is a hidden treasure that was concealed by You . . . before the creation of the world, and You . . . give it to flesh and blood? . . . Rather, 'God our Eternal, how glorious is Your name in all the earth that Your majesty is placed above the heavens' (Psalm 8:2). The rightful place of God's majesty, the Torah, is in the heavens."
>
> The Holy One, blessed be God, said to Moses: "Provide them with an answer as to why the Torah should be given to the people. . . ." Moses said before God: "Master of the universe, the Torah that You are giving me, what is written in it?" God said to him: "I am the Eternal your God who brought you out of Egypt from the house of bondage" (Exodus 20:2). Moses said to the angels: "Did you descend to Egypt? Were you enslaved to Pharaoh? Why should the Torah be yours?" Again, Moses asked: "What else is written in it?" God said to him: "You shall have no other gods before Me" (Exodus 20:3). Moses said to the angels: "Do you dwell among the nations who worship?" Immediately, each and every one of the angels became an admirer of Moses.[13]

Where redemption addresses breaking free, Revelation compels taking responsibility to uphold that freedom not just for the individual, but for all humanity. Revelation seals the covenant not person by person, nor generation to generation, but for an entire people. That covenant sets the guide for choosing within a context, wedding individuals to community. Revelation requires responsibility by the community for the community and for the world. Revelation teaches that freedom comes with responsibility and obligation that is greater than the individual. The pathway that Revelation lays out leads us to choices that reverberate horizontally across the world and vertically through generations to come.

The idea that freedom comes with responsibility establishes the core of free and democratic societies from Biblical times to this day. People are responsible to one another and to the world beyond any individual's personal choice. A midrash explains this principle in the form of a parable. Commenting on Numbers 16:22—"When one member sins, will You be wrathful with the whole community?"—Rabbi Shimon bar Yochai taught, "This is analogous to people who were sitting in a ship. One of them took a drill and began drilling a hole. His counterparts said to him: 'What are you sitting and doing?' He said to them: 'Why do you care? Am I not drilling under myself?' They said to him: 'Because the water will rise and flood the ship we are on!'" (*Vayikra Rabbah* 4:6).[14]

Free choice is not free when it drowns our fellow humans. Revelation strengthens freedom by ensuring that individual choices do not overpower the world. It sets cornerstones on which to continue to build upon the creations that humanity inherited. Those cornerstones make up the core values of human civilization: that every person is created in the image of the Divine, that you shall not destroy, and that you shall not oppress the widow, the orphan, or the stranger. These values frame the choices people make with dignity and respect.

Moses's final sermon, the Book of Deuteronomy, teaches, "I call heaven and earth to witness against you this day: I have put before you life and death, blessing and curse. Choose life—if you and your offspring would live" (30:19). "Choose life"—the choices one makes constitute the critical difference between a life worth living and one that wallows as a listless curse. Those choices make for a holy world worthy of life or for a world of chaos that wholly swallows life.

Our world is ripped apart by inequities that attest to the depths to which human choices reach. This need not be the case. The imperative of Revelation demands choices that recognize that "whoever saves a single life is considered by Scripture to have saved the whole world" (Babylonian Talmud, *Sanhedrin* 37a).[15] It is upon places of worship, community centers, and universities—every place where people gather—to unite to save imperiled human life. Though no one act can feed the vast number of children going to bed hungry each night, the collective actions of people committed to food banks, meals-on-wheels, communal farms, and international hunger relief can end hunger in this decade. Though no one person can conquer the depravity of racism infecting the public arena, the voice of one, plus one, plus one can drain the hatred and replace it with compassion, understanding, and opportunity. Though one tutor cannot teach the entire world to read, a community of tutors can transform a village of the disenfranchised into a city of hope.

In order to transform the world, it will take more than a myriad of random individual good choices. Moving the needle toward good requires organized, coordinated choosing. It means uniting for the purpose of *tikkun olam*, "repairing the world." It is the highest call of human responsibility. The choice to leave the world a better place than we found it is more than "a nice thing to do." It is not only an obligation; it is the gateway to breaking free of self-centered desire and to linking one's days to purpose and meaning.

The covenant of Revelation was made with the Israelites as the unifying force that transformed the covenant with Abraham and his descendants into the formation of a people with a mission and purpose. Revelation elevates individual random choices for the good to a pathway toward cohesive civilization. Working together with a mission and vision for the benefit of all not only brings meaning to the lives of those united, but also engenders a culture that preserves, protects, and defends the freedom of choice so dear to humanity.

The challenge remains how to coalesce communities to choose good, when voices scream to choose evil. These voices trade in fear and scarcity, insisting on making the choice to hoard power, money, and resources for the benefit of a select few and at the peril of many. In every generation Hamans and Pharaohs rise up, so in every generation we must unite for universal good. We must unite for a good that lifts every person's rights and work as a community toward healing the painful rifts in our world. Where evil trades in fear and scarcity, the greater good operates from a place of abundance. There is enough food on this planet to feed every hungry person, if the collective will of the world chooses to make it so. There is enough land and enough resources in the world for Ukrainians, Russians, Israelis, Palestinians, Chinese, and Tibetans to exercise sovereignty on their own piece of the rock we call earth, if only we exercise the political choice to make it so.

Of course, as soon as one problem is solved, the choices of others will create another that needs solving. That is why it is integral to understand the Creation-Redemption-Revelation process not as what happened once upon a time but what happens every day. As the cycle continues to unfold, as societies create chaos, peoples united can make redeeming choices, following the path revealed for a thousand generations. As *Pirkei Avot* teaches, "You are not required to complete the work, yet you are not free to desist from it" (2:21).

From Creation, to Redemption, to Revelation, from childhood, to youth, to maturity, the choices one makes define the character of the individual and the course of the world. Without the human ability to choose, the earth is just another trophy on God's mantle, another of the worlds created and destroyed. God implanted free will in Adam and Eve as the defining characteristic of humanity. Free will is honed through redemption—whether by revolution or evolution—as each person breaks free and embraces their choices as their own. The covenant of Revelation elevates individual choice, harnessing the power of choice through organized community that collectively builds a better way of life and a better world. In so doing, one transforms from self-absorbed to self-fulfilled. In so doing, random individuals evolve from isolated beings doing random acts of good to purposeful communities uniting with vision and principle to build upon the continuing chain of evolution of this earth. In so doing, choice is elevated from the will of the one to the good of the world.

Notes

1. Translation adapted from *The Sefaria Midrash Rabbah*, 2022 (license: CC-BY, https://creativecommons.org/licenses/by/3.0/), found on Sefaria (sefaria.org).
2. "Why Do Affordable Homes Matter?," National Low Income Housing Coalition, https://nlihc.org/explore-issues/why-we-care#:~:text=Research%20shows%20that%20increasing%20access,inside%20and%20outside%20the%20classroom.
3. Glenn Kessler, "Is Gun Violence Really the Leading Cause of Death for Children?," *Washington Post*, February 7, 2024, https://www.washingtonpost.com/politics/2024/02/07/is-gun-violence-leading-cause-death-children/.
4. Translation adapted from *The Sefaria Midrash Rabbah*, 2022 (license: CC-BY, https://creativecommons.org/licenses/by/3.0/), found on Sefaria (sefaria.org).
5. "Ruth Messinger's Story," American Jewish World Service, https://ajws.org/stories/ruth-messingers-story/.
6. Martin Buber, *Tales of the Hasidim: Later Masters* (Schocken Books, 1961), 249–50.
7. Dan Levin, "Dust and Ashes—and Holy," ReformJudaism.org, https://reformjudaism.org/learning/torah-study/torah-commentary/dust-and-ashes-and-holy.
8. Declaration of Independence, United States, 1776.
9. Bob Dylan, "Gotta Serve Somebody," track 1 on *Slow Train Coming*, Muscle Shoals Sound Studios, 1979.
10. Gabriel Sands, "Why Civil Rights Are Everyone's Problems—and What You Can Do," Refinery29, January 18, 2016, https://www.refinery29.com/en-us/kivie-kaplan-martin-luther-king-civil-rights.
11. Sands, "Why Civil Rights Are Everyone's Problems."

12. Jonah Dov Pesner and Yolanda Svage-Narva, "Announcing the Launch of the Reform Movement's 2021 Racial Justice Campaign: What You Need to Know," Religious Action Center, April 6, 2021, https://rac.org/blog/announcing-launch-reform-movements-2021-racial-justice-campaign-what-you-need-know.
13. Translation adapted from the William Davidson digital edition of the *Koren Noé Talmud*, with commentary by Adin Even-Israel Steinsaltz (license: CC-BY-NC, https://creativecommons.org/licenses/by-nc/4.0/), found on Sefaria (sefaria.org).
14. Translation adapted from *The Sefaria Midrash Rabbah*, 2022 (license: CC-BY, https://creativecommons.org/licenses/by/3.0/), found on Sefaria (sefaria.org).
15. Translation by the author.

CHAPTER 3

Belonging: You Are Who You Are With

Rabbi Jan Katzew, PhD

I AM AN ADOPTED CHILD and an adoptive parent. I grew up hearing people say that I did not physically resemble either of my parents, and then as an adult, I had the experience of hearing people say that one or both of our children looked like me or my spouse. I now understand better why these seemingly mundane, innocuous observations were much more salient than I had realized. I belonged with the only family I ever knew growing up. I was being recognized and affirmed as a member of the Katzew family, not only by a judge in family court, but also by society's informal, but very real, court of appeals. As Jewish thinker Mara Benjamin, PhD, writes:

> The drive to connect parents and children as the "same" is expressed in the most prosaic of ways. New parents and their kin, for instance, routinely remark that the baby "looks like" biologically related family members. More than confirming an objective reality, this "resemblance talk" is a means of seeking out, affirming, and creating a sense of belonging that mitigates the otherness of one's child. The symbolism of belonging, of which resemblance talk is just one example, is both something that parents feel as one element of their relationships with their children and something they may feel compelled to feel. When both biological and non-biological parents look to a familiar gesture or a verbal expression, they are seeking to establish and affirm a common participation in a shared and recognizable reality, in which "you belong with me and I with you."[1]

You are who you are with! I understand Dr. Benjamin as claiming that you are with whom you belong (association), which aligns with her claim that you are who you are with (identity). In other words, life is a team sport. According to Rabbi Isaac Luria, a leading exponent of the Jewish mystical tradition, even God, the One, *Echad*, decided it was better to be together with imperfect, mortal beings, than to remain alone.[2] Humans are the product of a network that begins with our parents, who teach us what love is by loving us, who care for us when we are unable to care for ourselves, who show us what it means to belong. Alone, each of us is partial—incomplete and biased—a limited being in search of connections that are complementary, compassionate, and caring. Although we may protest to the contrary, humans are not independent beings; rather, we are *interdependent* beings. Like pieces in a mosaic, we seek to fit in a larger whole, confirming our individual identity by "finding ourselves" within a group. We need each other to be fully human. Our lives are principally defined by the quality of our relationships with other people.

The Talmudic statement *Kol Yisrael areivim zeh bazeh*, "Every Jew is a guarantor for one another"; Babylonian Talmud, *Sh'vuot* 39a) means that when someone is guilty, all are responsible.[3] To belong with someone is to accept responsibility for them, to realize that your individual actions reflect on the perception of the whole group. To belong is to implicate and to be implicated. "At the very core of Jewish tradition is the idea that we are responsible for one another—and more than that, that we are implicated in one another's deeds. Fundamentally, there is no self that is fully prior to or independent of human relationships. We are not isolated monads but ever-connected members of families and communities. I am my parent's child and my child's parent before I am my own person. Disturbing as it can be—and it can be very disturbing indeed—the notion of corporate responsibility reflects something true, and crucial about human selfhood."[4]

The subject of this chapter is the lifetime pursuit of a person to belong, from the intimate to the ultimate: from a family to a friendship, from a team to a cohort, from a tribe to a community, from a people to all humanity, from humanity to divinity. "Belong" is the intensive form of the word "long." Therefore, at its core, to belong is to be connected *longer* than the norm, to associate over time with a person or a group, to be in a lasting relationship, to be a durable, enduring member of a community. To belong is to be noticed, not only seen; to be listened to, not only heard; to be cared for; not only to be the one caring; to be counted on, not only counted.[5] To be sure, associations, memberships, friendships, partnerships, and other types of relationships can and do evolve, devolve, and end, yet each of us can reflect and assess with whom we belong. The preposition that follows "belong" matters. To belong "to" someone or some group suggests a form of possession, as expressed in a prophetic verse that frames the distinction between a covenantal partnership and property ownership in relationship to God: "And it shall be on that day—says *Adonai*—that you shall say, 'my Spouse' and shall no longer say to Me 'my Master'" (Hosea 2:18).[6] To belong "with" someone or some group implies mutuality and reciprocity, and perhaps a shared mission, vision, values, history, destiny, and from a moral perspective, shared responsibility. While acknowledging the legitimacy of the question "To whom do I belong?" the focus of this chapter will be associative belonging—belonging with—rather than possessive belonging—belonging to.

In its fullest expression, "to belong" is to be at home, to be with people who recognize you and affirm you. As the prophet proclaims, "Then my people shall dwell in peaceful homes, in secure dwellings, in untroubled places of rest" (Isaiah 32:18).[7] To be at home need not only be in relation to a particular place; it can also mean to be at home in relation to a person or group.

Looking at the people of Israel through a particularistic lens offers a prime example of how complicated it can be to belong with a group. To belong with the people of Israel, who over time have become known as the Jewish people, has been the subject of enduring, perhaps endless, debate. The boundaries of Jewish peoplehood testify to the truth of the paradoxically cogent claim that two Jews can hold three opinions. The question "Who is a Jew?" is an ongoing Jewish (and non-Jewish) preoccupation.[8] In the Bible, Israelite identity was patrilineal. Joseph and Moses, for example, married non-Israelite spouses, and their children were Israelites. During the early Rabbinic period, however, Jewish identity became matrilineal, and it was confirmed as such in authoritative codes of Jewish practice such as the *Mishneh Torah*, by the twelfth-century rabbi Rambam. "This is the general principle: When a child is born from a servant, a gentile, a maid-servant, or a female gentile, [the child] is like his mother. We are not concerned with the father."[9] In 1983, the CCAR adopted a resolution that stated, "The child of one Jewish parent is under the presumption of Jewish descent."[10] In addition to belonging with the Jewish people by birth, one can also choose to belong with the Jewish people by a process often termed "conversion," which is not surprisingly also a problematic and controversial construct. Rambam devoted an entire chapter of the *Mishneh Torah* to the topic.[11] Since 1983, the CCAR has articulated an alternative perspective on the requirements for a person who chooses to belong with the Jewish people, one that presumes a Jewish identity of a child with one Jewish parent as long as the child is raised exclusively as a Jew and concretizes that identity with public acts of Jewish identification.[12] Another factor in determining one's Jewish identity involves a person who wishes to dissociate from the Jewish people. "Rabbi Abba Bar Zabda teaches: Even when Israel [a Jew] sins, one is still Israel" (Babylonian Talmud, *Sanhedrin* 44a).[13] Hence, once a person belongs with the Jewish people, through an ascribed identity or a chosen identity, that person is always considered a Jew.

In keeping with the evolving, protean definition of a Jew, no one position is final or determinative. The State of Israel originally enacted the Law of Return, which grants the right of every Jew to live in Israel, in 1950. It was later amended in 1954 and again in 1970 to make explicit that "every Jew has a right to come to this country as an *oleh* [an immigrant who can claim expedited citizenship]. 'Jew' means a person who was born of a Jewish mother or has converted to Judaism and who is not a member of another religion."[14] Jewish identity is a hybrid composed of religious, ethnic, and cultural elements. To belong with the Jewish people can be a product of chance and/or choice. No human authority or body has the power to determine the definitive response to the question "Who is a Jew?" although in Israel the Chief Rabbinate wields enormous political power in matters of personal status.[15] *Pirkei Avot* 5:20 teaches, "Every dispute that is for the sake of heaven is destined to endure."[16] I believe the question "Who is a Jew?" or "Who belongs with the Jewish people?" is a prime example of a worthy, if not holy dispute—one that I hope to preserve.

Judaism is perpetually countercultural. When Abraham introduced himself to the Hittites as he prepared to bury his deceased wife Sarah, he said, "I am a stranger and a resident among you" (Genesis 23:4).[17] In this apparent contradiction in terms lies a profound truth about Jewish life and thought. Ever since Abraham and Sarah, the story of the Jewish people has unfolded by discerning when we were to be strangers and when we were to be residents, when we needed to swim upstream against societal norms and when we could join the cultural mainstream. Jewish identity is a hybrid identity, a both/and proposition. Paradoxically, Jews are both a part of general society and apart from general society.

McIntyre writes, "The story of my life is always embedded in the story of those communities from which I derive my identity. I am born with a past; and to try to cut myself off from my past, in the individualist mode, is to deform my present relationship. The possession of a historical identity and the possession of a social identity coincide."[18] Belonging is a diachronic construct that connects us to our past; it is a synchronic concept that connects us to our present and potentially to our future.

Reflecting on my being part of a multigenerational adoptive family, it is clear: To be with whom you belong is an honor and a responsibility, a delicate balance captured in Hebrew because they are essentially the same word—*kavod* means "honor" or "respect," and *koved* means "responsibility" or "weight." This balance is both personal and communal. For example, Reform Judaism's creation of a confirmation ritual was more than an attempt to ascribe greater meaning to the holiday of Shavuot; it was a statement that the confirmands have made the conscious choice to identify and be identified as Jews, to accept the honor and the responsibility of Jewish life.

When I have been asked why I became a rabbi, I share a story from my childhood. I grew up in Brockton, Massachusetts, where our family belonged with Temple Israel, a sacred community that no longer exists. After spending time at the synagogue one day when I was in elementary school, I told my parents that I hoped to become a rabbi. An engineer and a doctor, respectively, they were amused and curious enough to ask me how I had come to this realization. My response then, and ever since, was "I belong there." "I am at home there." I hesitate to state that I was "called" to be a rabbi, but I am comfortable with language suggesting that as much as I chose to become a rabbi, the rabbinate chose me. I am a rabbi, and because I too am partial, I will be drawing upon Jewish sources to uncover and illuminate the concept of belonging. I choose to belong with the Jewish people.

The story of the Jewish people began before there were any Jewish people—before there were any people at all—with the words "When God was about to create heaven and earth" (Genesis 1:1). What was the rationale for devoting the entire first of the Torah's five books plus the next eleven chapters of the second book essentially to prologue? If the Torah intended to narrate the particular relationship between God and the Jewish people, why not begin the story with the first commandment addressed specifically to the people of Israel? This conundrum led Rabbi Shlomo ben Yitzchak, known by the acronym Rashi—the greatest rabbinic commentator on the Torah and the Talmud, who lived in eleventh-century France—to wonder why the Torah did not begin with Exodus 12:2, which is the first mitzvah explicitly directed to the Jewish people.[19] He explained, "Should the peoples of the world say to Israel, 'You are robbers, because you took by force the lands of the seven nations of Canaan,' Israel may reply to them, 'All the earth belongs to the Holy One of Blessing. God created it and gave it to whom God pleased. When God willed, God gave it to *them*, and when God willed, God took it from them and gave it to *us*.'"[20] In contrast to the universality of God, Rashi asserted the tribalism of humanity by pitting *us*—the people of Israel—against *them*—the rest of the world. Nearly a millennium has passed since Rashi wrote his Torah commentary, which remains as timely as it is timeless.

Belonging can be a blessing to those who belong, just as it can be a curse to those who do not. Human history, from its ancient myths to its contemporary acts, testifies to the enduring truth that belonging is a veritable double-edged sword. One who belongs feels at home, seen, proud, protected, safe, joyful, empowered, supported, and loved. One who does not belong feels alienated, invisible, persecuted, impotent, alone, depressed, othered, and hated. The Bible opens with a universal lesson about belonging—what it means to belong to the human family, to have the power to create and to destroy human life, powers that we have continued to refine through science, powers that ultimately respond to an eternal question: Should humans have been created?[21] After a series of creations by divine fiat epitomized by "'Let there be light'—and there was light" (Genesis 1:3), God enacts a different strategy for human creation, the first Biblical use of the first-person plural. God engages in some sort of consultation.

"God now said, 'Let us make human beings in our image, after our likeness; and let them hold sway over the fish of the sea and the birds of the sky, over the beasts, over all the earth, over all that creeps upon the earth" (Genesis 1:26). This verse has been grist for the mill of Biblical commentators. Who is "us"? With whom or what does God engage in consultation that results in human creation? What does it mean to create a human in the image of the Divine, especially a Divine that has no physical, tangible image? These questions persist as we struggle to define the capacities for humans to realize our potential for good, for growth, for love, and for life. Although humans may trace our origins to a single source, divine or hominid, we are a divided humanity, knowing that by belonging to and with some groups, we are also deciding that we do not belong to and with others. There are significant lessons about belonging worth learning from religion and science, from theology and biology. Both fields deal with "us" and "them," friends and foes, healthy cells that grow and malignant cells that metastasize.[22] Belonging is an amoral concept. From Adam and Eve humans have transformed belonging into a cardinal virtue that creates and sustains life, and yet from Cain and Abel we continue to demonstrate that not belonging can be a cardinal vice that ends and destroys life. With whom to belong or not to belong is quite literally a matter of life and death.

The first account of human creation in the Torah makes our need for relationships into a theological axiom. "God created human beings in [the divine] image, creating [them] in the image of God—creating them male and female" (Genesis 1:27). This remarkably pregnant verse has justly deserved its veritable library of commentary. The ambiguous, polysemous nature of language allows for multiple interpretations. However, God's initial human creation is a "them"—perhaps an intersex person, perhaps two (or more) individual humans, who are immediately given the command to procreate (Genesis 1:28).

The second account of human creation in the Torah makes the need for relationships an ethical principle. This time God creates a male human from the soil (humus) and "blows into him the breath of life" (Genesis 2:7).[23] The second Creation story projects vastly different roles and ultimate fates for humanity: responsibility for being environmental stewards, pain in childbirth, patriarchy, a lifelong struggle to earn a living, and death. This time a male human is created first, but God makes an ethical judgment whose significance echoes throughout human history. God says, "It is not good that the man be alone—I will make him a helpmate" (Genesis 2:18).

It is not good for a person to exist alone. We now live in the most connected world in human history, yet loneliness is a pandemic. Solitary confinement is an extreme form of punishment, a dehumanizing last resort. It is not good for a person to exist alone. The only other time the words "it is not good" appear in the Torah is when Moses's father-in-law, Jethro, observes Moses acting as the sole arbiter of disputes among the Children of Israel and says, "What you are doing is not good; you are going to wear yourself out, you too and this people that is with you. This is too heavy for you. You cannot do it alone" (Exodus 18:17–18).[24] Moses learns from a wise, caring adult that it is not good leadership practice to lead alone or behave as though a particular person is indispensable. It demonstrates poor judgment. Millennia have passed, and yet the wisdom of Jethro continues to be honored in the breach by leaders who insist that only they can save the people they purport to serve. These leaders refuse to delegate authority along with responsibility, and as a result they suffer from delusions of grandeur and create an unsustainable reality for everyone else.

The Rabbinic authors of the Babylonian Talmud derive profound inferences from the creation of the first human being, among which is the belief that every human belongs to and derives from the same parents, and therefore belongs to the same family. "Adam, the first [hu]man, was created alone.... This was done due to the importance of maintaining peace among people, so that one person will not say to another: My ... progenitor is greater than your [progenitor]" (*Mishnah Sanhedrin* 4:5).[25] Nevertheless, it did not take long—exactly one generation—for the family to devolve and essentially dissolve as a result of fratricide, a narrative we continue to rewrite and tragically to relive. The Rabbis expand on the mishnah quoted above:

> In cases of capital law, if one testifies falsely, the blood of the accused and the blood of [any] offspring ... is ascribed to the witness's false testimony until eternity. The proof for this is as we found with Cain, who killed his brother, as it is stated concerning him: "The voice of your brother's blood [*demei*] cries out to Me from the ground" (Genesis 4:10). The verse does not state: Your brother's blood [*dam*], in the singular, but rather: "Your brother's blood [*demei*]," in the plural. This serves to teach that the loss of both his brother's blood and the blood of his brother's offspring are ascribed to Cain.... The court tells the witnesses: Therefore, Adam the first man was created alone ... so that one person will not say to another: "My ... progenitor, is greater than your[s]...." Since all humanity descends from one person, each and every person is obligated to say: "The world was created for me," as one person can be the source of all humanity and recognize the significance of their actions. (Babylonian Talmud, *Sanhedrin* 37a)[26]

God's human creation was capable of reproduction through an act of sexual relations, the Hebrew word for which is *ladaat* ("to know")—to have intimate, direct (in this case, carnal) knowledge of a person. Consider the people you know—colleagues, neighbors, acquaintances, service providers, friends, family members, classmates, teachers, students, partners, teammates, roommates, and other categories of human connection.

How many of these people would you claim to recognize—*really know*—in terms of their fears, flaws, passions, vulnerabilities, needs, gifts, priorities, character, and soul traits? Your response will give you a sense of what it means to be you, because your identity is formed through your relationships with other people, how well you know them and how well they know you.[27]

We may have learned from our Rabbinic Sages that one who has saved a life is as though one has saved a whole world. That is true, but not the whole truth. There are two versions of this text—a universalist reading adopted by the Jerusalem Talmud, and a particularist reading adopted by the Babylonian Talmud, which adds the words *nefesh achat miYisrael*. This renders the teaching as "One who saves a Jewish life, a Jewish soul, it is as though one has saved the whole world" (Babylonian Talmud, *Sanhedrin* 37a). The perspective flouts our humanist, universalist sensibilities. The tension between particularism and universalism in Jewish texts, as in Jewish life, transcends time and space. Hillel the Elder, a Rabbinic sage known for his profound yet accessible wisdom, lived most of his life during the first century BCE. In *Pirkei Avot*, a compilation of Rabbinic epigrams, Hillel posed three timeless questions about human character. He asked first and foremost, "If I am not for myself, who will be for me?" Only then did he posit, "And if I am only for myself, what am I?" and then, finally and poignantly, "And if not now, when?" (*Pirkei Avot* 1:14). The order of Hillel's questions makes all the difference. In our ever-expanding world of concentric circles, Hillel, the quintessential Rabbinic representative of caring, empathy, and compassion, teaches that we begin with ourselves and then reach out to others. Yes, thirty-six times the Torah repeats a variation of the mitzvah to love the stranger, the innocent victim, because we have memories of being strangers—but we can fulfill this mitzvah only after we have triumphed over our enemies and lived to continue our story. Only a member of a living people can remember what it was like to have been a stranger. In his exquisite book *Judaism Is About Love*, Rabbi Shai Held writes, "Jewish ethics allows us—indeed it requires us to prioritize concern for those near and dear to us over concern for others who are more distant. . . . But at the same time, Jewish ethics demands that we not stop there: family first . . . must not be allowed to devolve into—family only."[28]

Jewish particularity is perpetually in tension with human universality. A debate in the Jerusalem Talmud makes it clear that this tension is not new, although it is holy: "Rabbi Akiva taught: *Love your neighbor as yourself*" (Leviticus 19:18). This is the greatest principle of the Torah.' Ben Azai says: 'I know a more fundamental principle than that. *This is the written record of the human line from the day God created human beings, making [them] in the likeness of God* (Genesis 5:1)" (Jerusalem Talmud, N'darim 30b). In this text, Ben Azai, who was not a rabbi, offers a critique of Rabbi Akiva: What if you do not love yourself? If you relate to your neighbor as you relate to yourself, you will make a sadist out of a masochist. It will mean that someone who is miserable will make others miserable. Another implicit criticism is challenging Akiva on how he defines a neighborhood. Who counts as a neighbor? Someone of the same race? The same nation? Gender identity or sexual orientation? Political party, socioeconomic class, or religious community? Ben Azai argued that being human, and therefore having been created in the image of God, is sufficient to warrant our respect and care, if not our love. Nearly two millennia may have passed since Rabbi Akiva and Ben Azai faced off, but we are still caught on the horns of a dilemma struggling to span the ethical distance between particularism and universalism—loving ourselves, loving neighbors, loving strangers, all of which are interrelated with loving God.

One Biblical perspective on the relationship of the Jewish people to the rest of humanity is epitomized in a perplexing, problematic statement ascribed to a non-Israelite prophet named Balaam, who is charged by Balak, the king of Moab, to curse the Israelites. The king brings the prophet to a hill overlooking the Israelite encampment, where he proclaims, "As I see them from the mountain tops, gaze on them from the heights, there is *a people that dwells apart, not reckoned among the nations*" (Numbers 23:9) (emphasis added). The verse continues to present a social and political challenge to and for the Jewish people. Medieval rabbinic commentators chose to interpret the verse as a virtue, a divine compliment. For example, "If it is a people content to be alone, faithful to its distinctive identity, then it will be able to dwell in peace. But if Jews seek to be like the nations, the nations will not consider them worthy of respect."[29] Furthermore, as the sixteenth-century Italian commentator Ovadia Sforno taught, "In the final analysis, they are the only people who will eventually populate the earth. This concept is repeated by Moses: God alone will guide them (Deuteronomy 32:12). It will be impossible to destroy them."[30] The meaning of Balaam's words is that "just as I see them now dwelling alone, so will they forever *dwell in safety, the fountain of Jacob alone*, and they will always be at the head, for no nation will [ever] prevail over them [and cause them to perish], and they will never become assimilated to them [i.e., other nations]."[31]

The medieval exegetes did their utmost to wrest victory from calumny, but the thrust of the prophetic vision nonetheless still hurts when we consider the history and the continuing story of the Jewish people. Although it is an honor and a blessing to belong with the Jewish people, if it means not to be reckoned among the other peoples, not to belong with the rest of humanity, then the prize may not be worth the price. An enduring, if not eternal, dilemma of the Jewish people inheres in the concept of belonging to a people that dwells apart—a separate people, a holy people, a treasured people, all of which are Biblical monikers for the Children of Israel. Ironically, the most common description of the Israelites in the Torah—*am k'sheih oref* ("a stiff-necked people")[32]—may be the least controversial. A stiff-necked people is obdurate, like an ox—and therefore difficult to yoke, even for God. Jewish history attests to its cogency. It would be hard to argue against the claim that the Jewish people is a stubborn people.

The greatest medieval Hebrew poet, Y'hudah HaLevi, wrote a book in the form of a Platonic dialogue, best known as the *Kuzari*, in which he sought to explain what it means to belong to and with the Jewish people. The *Kuzari* is an apologetic work; its subtitle is "a rejoinder and proof for a despised religion."[33] HaLevi sought to persuade a spiritual seeking king that he should join the Jewish people and that by doing so he would enrich his life and elevate his status—if not in the eyes of humanity, then in the sight of God:

> THE HAVER [member of the Jewish people]: Israel amidst the nations is like the heart amidst the organs: it is the sickest and the healthiest of them all.... The heart is visited without interruption by all sorts of diseases, as sadness, anxiety, envy, wrath, enmity, love, hate, and fear. Its constitution changes continually according to the vigor and weakness of respiration, inappropriate meat and drink, movement, exertion, sleep or wakefulness. These all affect the heart, whilst the rest of the limbs rest uninjured.
>
> THE KHAZAR KING: I understand how far it is the sickest of the organs. But in what sense is it the healthiest of them all?
>
> THE HAVER: Is it possible that in the heart there should settle a humour producing an inflammation, a cancer, a wart, etc., as is possible in

other organs? . . . The [heart's] sensibility and feeling expose it to many diseases, but they are also the cause of expulsion of the same at [their very inception], before they have taken root. The relation of the Divine Power to us is the same as that of the soul to the heart. For this reason, it is said: "You only have I known among the families of the earth, therefore I will punish you for all your iniquities" (Amos 3:2).[34]

The *Kuzari* extols the unique virtues of the Jewish people, its history, and its destiny, as well as the superiority of the Land of Israel and the Hebrew language. When HaLevi wrote the *Kuzari* in the twelfth century, the Jewish people was politically, economically, and militarily powerless, subject to forced conversion, exile, and in too many instances, murder. Nine hundred years later, the sovereign State of Israel is the most powerful nation in the Middle East, and it has among its allies the United States, the most powerful nation on earth. The historical context in which HaLevi composed the *Kuzari* helps to explain why he may have had to resort to hyperbole to keep a sense of pride in a Jewish community that was suppressed, oppressed, and depressed. He could justify his overt claims for Jewish superiority as an attempt to prevent a loss of faith and hope that could lead to hemorrhaging by a defeated people being treated like pawns in a human chess game, liable to be sacrificed at any time to achieve greater leverage by the local hegemon.

Echoes of HaLevi's triumphalist perspective on Jews and Judaism reverberate through Jewish time. The ideas that the Jewish people constitute the beating heart of humanity, that the Land of Israel with Jerusalem at its center is the spiritual and ethical axis around which the world turns, and that the Hebrew language is the holiest of the languages may be centripetal forces that have sustained the Jewish people, but they also are ideas that have made the Jewish people an anathema to others. They foster a social asymmetry in which the Jewish people, despite their relatively miniscule quantity, somehow counterpoise the weight of the rest of humanity. It is one thing to be particularist and emphasize distinctive aspects of belonging to or with a group; it is another thing entirely to proclaim the superiority of that group and the dependence of everyone else upon its benevolence. HaLevi's gambit has withstood the test of time as a worthy work of medieval thought, but we need to acknowledge that we now live in a modern or perhaps postmodern world, and therefore we can assert our uniqueness as a people without proclaiming our intrinsic superiority.

Rather than deride or dismiss HaLevi out of hand as an anachronism or worse, I believe his voice is worth redeeming, if only because he offers timeless insights into Jewish spirituality. Y'hudah HaLevi's philosophy may be anachronistic and irretrievably bound to twelfth-century Spain, but his theology, as expressed in the following poem, transcends time and space: "God, where shall I find You? Your place is lofty and secret. And where shall I not find You? The whole world is full of Your glory! You are found in a human's innermost heart, yet You fixed earth's boundaries. You are a strong tower for those who are near, and the trust of those who are far. . . . I have sought to come near You, I have called to You with all my heart; and when I went out towards You, I found You coming toward me."[35] God is a nonbinary being, who defies simple categorization—neither imminent nor transcendent. God is both intimate and ultimate, "Wholly Same" and "Wholly Other." To the extent that humans are created in the divine image, we can learn to be both alike and unlike, universal and unique at the same time.

For nearly 250 years Jews have received invitations to belong to modern, Western secular society. The invitations have come at different times and in different places, under a variety of conditions, from cordial and genuine to grudging and half-hearted. The Jewish responses have also been along a spectrum, from thrilling acceptance to reticence, ambivalence, or outright rejection. The following four texts—from the French Revolution (1789), the Pittsburgh Platform of the Central Conference of American Rabbis (1885), the prophetic proponent of political Zionism (1896), and a Jewish partisan who became one of the great Israeli poets of the twentieth century—illustrate the range of responses by Jews facing the challenges embedded in entering modernity.

On the cusp of the nineteenth century, in the context of the French Revolution, the Jews were given the choice to belong with France as individual Jews or to belong elsewhere as a Jewish community. "We must refuse everything to the Jews as a nation and accord everything to the Jews as individuals. They must be citizens individually; it is repugnant to have a nation within a nation."[36] Accepting the invitation to join the project of Emancipation and Enlightenment—that is, to participate in the modern, Western world—meant that the Jews needed to compromise their status as a separate nation. The prize of citizenship was acquired by Jews who were willing to relinquish their claim to peoplehood. Belonging became an either/or proposition, a zero-sum game. Belong with the

Jewish people or belong with the French, British, Canadian, or American people. We are still living with the consequences of the choice between individual Jewish personhood and collective Jewish peoplehood.

Reform Jews and early Zionist leaders made opposing fateful choices toward the end of the nineteenth century. Fully embracing the spirit of the Emancipation and their understanding of prophetic Judaism, American Reform rabbis proclaimed, "We recognize, in the modern era of universal culture of heart and intellect, the approaching of the realization of Israel's great Messianic hope for the establishment of the kingdom of truth, justice, and peace among all men. *We consider ourselves no longer a nation, but a religious community*, and therefore expect neither a return to Palestine, nor a sacrificial worship under the sons of Aaron, nor restoration of any of the laws concerning the Jewish state."[37]

The "spiritual father" of political Zionism, as he is called in Israel's Declaration of Independence, Theodor Herzl, asserted that the Jews constitute a distinct people and therefore deserve a nation:

> We have honestly endeavored everywhere to merge ourselves in the social life of surrounding communities and to preserve the faith of our fathers. We are not permitted to do so. In vain are we loyal patriots, our loyalty in some places running to extremes; in vain do we make the same sacrifices of life and property as our fellow-citizens; in vain do we strive to increase the fame of our native land in science and art, or her wealth by trade and commerce. In countries where we have lived for centuries we are still cried down as strangers.... If we could only be left in peace.... But I think we shall not be left in peace.[38]

The philosopher Yuval Noah Harari offers a counternarrative:

> Contrary to common wisdom, nationalism is not a natural and eternal part of the human psyche, and it is not rooted in human biology. True, humans are social animals through and through, with group loyalty imprinted in their genes. However, for hundreds of thousands of years *Homo sapiens* and its hominid ancestors lived in small intimate communities numbering no more than a few dozen people. Humans easily develop loyalty to small intimate groups such as a tribe, an infantry company, or a family business, but it is hardly natural for humans to be loyal to millions of utter strangers. Such mass loyalties have appeared only in the last few thousand years—yesterday morning, in evolutionary terms—and they require immense efforts of social construction.[39]

David Brooks acknowledges the perpetual challenge involved in preserving the unique identity of an individual and the shared identity of a group:

> The challenge in seeing a person, therefore, is to adopt [a] kind of double vision. It means stepping back to appreciate the power of group culture and how it is formed over generations and then poured into a person. But it also means stepping close and perceiving each individual person in the midst of their lifelong project of crafting their own life and their own point of view, often in defiance of their group's consciousness. The trick is to hold these two perspectives together at the same time.... To see a person well, you have to see them as culture inheritors and as cultural creators.[40]

Ironically, the sacred unit of Jewish belonging, the minyan of ten people praying, derives from an egregious example in the Torah. When Moses appointed twelve agents to scout out the Land of Promise, ten of the twelve returned with a negative report: "The country that we traversed and scouted is one that devours its settlers. All the people that we saw in it are of great size" (Numbers 13:32). In a memorable, inspiring poem, Abba Kovner redeemed the concept of a minyan by capturing its spiritual essence:

> During my first week in the Land, I stood near the Kotel, the Western Wall.... I stood about a pace away from the wall, from the stones, and I felt like I did not belong, that my existence was rooted in a different experience, that I couldn't take that extra step. But somebody tugged at my sleeve and asked me to join in a *minyan*. I put on a hat and I joined the *minyan*. I said the *Minchah* prayer, and I arrived. This is something Jewish, something most particular to Judaism, about being one of a *minyan*. To know that the nine need a tenth, and that the one needs the nine. This may be the most meaningful thing in Judaism.... I pray that I will always be one of the collective, that my good words will join with the words murmured by the community.[41]

In 1995, the eminent political scientist Robert Putnam published an essay entitled "Bowling Alone: America's Declining Social Capital," which five years later grew into a sobering, seminal book—*Bowling Alone: The Collapse and Revival of American Community*.[42] Putnam argues that a seemingly benign common denominator—the national decrease in bowling leagues—resembles a canary in a coal mine, a harbinger of an antisocial disease with potentially disastrous consequences, a portrait of a society that is coming apart at the seams. Instead of being joiners, Americans have become loners. There have been significant efforts to redress the phenomenon of "bowling alone." The most powerful and profound of them are the efforts to create virtual communities, especially the launch of Facebook—a public corporation that boldly endeavors to create a global community—in 2004. Twenty-two years later Facebook has more than two billion members. Embedded in the transformation of the concept of "community" from actual to virtual is the redefinition of the word "friend," which for millennia has been exclusively a noun. "Friend" is now also a verb, as is its antonym, "to unfriend." This change is more than grammatical or linguistic; it is epistemological and ethical. The idea that a friend may be a person you have never met face-to-face is revolutionary, just as is the recent reality that you can belong to a community without ever having interacted previously with any of its members. We are participating, whether we like it or not, in a global experiment designed to reengineer what it means to be human, including what it means to belong with other humans. The power of social media and celebrity influencers is transforming the meaning of belonging to a group or community. Participating in a crowdsourcing activity or supporting a CaringBridge or joining a GoFundMe page are actions that are redefining belonging, for better or for worse.

Not all belonging is easy or natural. Some belonging, the kind that may be initially uncomfortable and inconvenient, requires learning and intensive ongoing effort. However, learning to belong has the potential of lasting benefits. Putnam trenchantly notes, "Ties that link you to people like yourself are called bonding social capital. . . . Bridging social capital is your ties to people *un*like yourself. . . . In a diverse society like ours, we need a lot of bridging social capital. . . . Bridging social capital is harder to build than bonding social capital. That is the challenge . . . of America today."[43] As the gaps grow between social groups, socioeconomic classes, political parties, and religious communities, bridging them becomes more difficult, urgent, and important. Instead of people learning to navigate diversities of thought, practice, and life experience, we are reliving the plot of *Romeo and Juliet*, and its contemporary counterpart *West Side Story*, as people "stick to their own kind,"[44] and thereby reinforce their own opinions and their own prejudices. Instead of building bridges between people who belong with different groups, we are erecting social fences and defenses, actual and virtual. The result of this erosion of the American social fabric yields people who are lonely, unable to see each other as whole human beings, dismissive of the perspectives of people who do not share their ideology, and whose relationships tend to be transactional and superficial, lasting only as long as they belong to the same group.

If *Bowling Alone* offered a diagnosis of the social disease affecting American culture, Putnam's next book, *Better Together: Restoring the American Community* offered a prescription. "People may go to the library looking mainly for information, but they find each other there."[45] Belonging—becoming a part of a group that recognizes and affirms oneself—is a powerful, magnetic human force for good; not always, but most often, belonging is worth the risk. As Dr. Mara Benjamin observes, "A sense of belonging and familiarity—even if it is only partial, episodic, and constantly subject to the irruption of difference—is inevitable for people who spend long periods of time helping children develop into themselves. Belonging and sameness, mystery and alterity: as distinctive as they are from each other, they can in fact only be articulated in relation to one another."[46]

I live in Plymouth, Massachusetts, but I am at home wherever and whenever I am with my spouse. I belong with her. I am most myself when we are together. In this sense, belonging requires both emotional and cognitive connections, feelings and actions that express caring and commitment, a relationship that begins with recognition and leads to affirmation, a relationship that elicits shared responsibility, shared memories, shared hopes, and optimally, shared love. Belonging can be a most intimate relationship, especially when it is reciprocal, mutual, endearing, and enduring.

You are who you are with.

Notes

1. Mara Benjamin, *The Obligated Self: Maternal Subjectivity and Jewish Thought* (Indiana University Press, 2018), 81.
2. The Kabbalist Rabbi Isaac Luria is best known for the doctrine of *tzimtzum* (contraction), when God, who took up all space, withdrew some of Godself in order to make room for Creation.
3. Abraham Joshua Heschel, "Religion and Race," January 14, 1963, as found on Voices of Democracy: The U.S. Oratory Project, https://voicesofdemocracy.umd.edu.
4. Shai Held, *Judaism Is About Love: Recovering the Heart of Jewish Life* (Farrar, Straus and Giroux, 2024), 276.
5. Nel Noddings, *Caring: A Feminine Approach to Ethics and Moral Education* (University of California Press, 1986).
6. Translation by this author.
7. Translation from *The JPS Tanakh: Gender Sensitive Edition* (Jewish Publication Society, 2023), found on Sefaria (sefaria.org).

8. See Baruch Litvin, *Jewish Identity: Who Is a Jew?*, 2nd ed. (Ktav, 2012), which reprints scholars' responses to a question posed by David Ben-Gurion about the identity of children of interfaith marriages. See also Lawrence Schiffman, *Who Was a Jew? Rabbinic and Halakhic Perspectives on the Jewish-Christian Schism* (Ktav, 1985); and Susan A. Glenn, "In the Blood? Consent, Descent, and the Ironies of Jewish Identity," *Jewish Social Studies* 8, no. 2/3 (Spring 2002): 139–52.
9. Maimonides, *Mishneh Torah*, Laws of Forbidden Intercourse 15:4. Translation of *Mishneh Torah* from the Sefaria Community Translation (license: CC0; https://creativecommons.org/publicdomain/zero/1.0/), found on Sefaria (sefaria.org).
10. CCAR Responsa 5758.11: "On Patrilineal Descent, Apostasy, and Synagogue Honors," available at https://www.ccarnet.org/responsa-topics/on-patrilineal-descent/. The details of the resolution are beyond the scope of this chapter, but they serve to amplify the significance of belonging to the Jewish people. Reconstructing Judaism shares the perspective of the CCAR on Jewish identity.
11. Maimonides, *Mishneh Torah*, Laws of Forbidden Intercourse 14.
12. CCAR Responsa 5754.15: "Atheists, Agnostics and Conversion to Judaism," https://www.ccarnet.org/ccar-responsa/tfn-no-5754-15-147-152/. While this responsum dates from the twentieth century, it references the earliest CCAR responsa on conversion.
13. Translation by the author.
14. Israel: Law No. 5710-1950, The Law of Return; and https://www.nbn.org.il/life-in-israel/government-services/rights-and-benefits/the-law-of-return/. An interesting case study is the Brother Daniel case, as described in Asher F. Landau, ed., *Selected Judgments of the Supreme Court of Israel* (Routledge, 1971), 1–34. Brother Daniel was born Oswald Rufeisen and was the child of Jewish parents. As a young adult, he served as a translator in a Polish town under German occupation and was responsible for saving Jews who were about to be deported. Eventually, his Jewish identity was discovered, and he was protected in a monastery, where he embraced Christianity. After the end of World War II, he was ordained as a priest. He decided to emigrate to Israel and live as a Carmelite monk; however, he was not granted citizenship under the Law of Return.
15. Noah Feldman, *To Be a Jew Today* (Farrar, Straus and Giroux, 2024).
16. Translation by the author.
17. Translation based on Joseph Baer Soloveitchik, "Confrontation," *Tradition*, Spring–Summer 1964, 5–29.
18. Alasdair MacIntyre, *After Virtue: A Study in Moral Theory* (Notre Dame Press, 1984), 281.
19. Exodus 12:2 includes the mitzvah to observe the month of Nisan, the month in which Passover falls, as the first of the months.
20. Rashi on Genesis 1:1, emphasis added. See also Psalm 24:1: "Of David: A Song. To the Eternal belongs the earth and its fullness, the world, and those who dwell within it."
21. See Babylonian Talmud, *Eiruvin* 13b, where the schools of Hillel and Shammai debated whether humans should have been created.

22. Siddhartha Mukherjee, *The Song of the Cell: An Exploration of Medicine and the New Human* (Scribner, 2022).
23. Translation by Robert Alter, from *The Five Books of Moses: A Translation with Commentary* (W. W. Norton, 2008).
24. Translation from *Metsudah Chumash* (Metsudah, 2009) (license: CC-BY, https://creativecommons.org/licenses/by/3.0/), found on Sefaria (sefaria.org).
25. Translation from the William Davidson digital edition of the *Koren Noé Talmud*, with commentary by Adin Even-Israel Steinsaltz (license: CC-BY-NC, https://creativecommons.org/licenses/by-nc/4.0/), found on Sefaria (sefaria.org).
26. Translation from the William Davidson digital edition of the *Koren Noé Talmud*, with commentary by Adin Even-Israel Steinsaltz (license: CC-BY-NC, https://creativecommons.org/licenses/by-nc/4.0/), found on Sefaria (sefaria.org).
27. David Brooks, *How to Know a Person: The Art of Seeing Others Deeply and Being Deeply Seen* (Random House, 2023).
28. Shai Held, *Judaism Is About Love*, 135.
29. Commentary on Numbers 23:9 by Netziv, *HaAmek Davar*.
30. Commentary on Numbers 23:9 by Ovadiah Sforno.
31. Commentary on Numbers 23:9 by Ramban (emphasis added).
32. For example, "[Moses] said, "If I have gained Your favor, O my lord, pray, let my lord go in our midst, even though *this is a stiffnecked people.* Pardon our iniquity and our sin, and take us for Your own!" (Exodus 34:9).
33. See the Hebrew translation from Judeo-Arabic by Michael Schwartz (Ben-Gurion University Press, 2017).
34. Y'hudah HaLevi, *Kuzari* 2:36, 38–40, 42, 44, in *Three Jewish Philosophers*, trans. Isaak Heinemann (Toby Press, 2006), 74–75.
35. Translation adapted from Judah Halevi, "Lord, Where Shall I Find You?," in *The Penguin Book of Hebrew Verse*, ed. T. Carmi (Penguin Books, 1981), 338.
36. Count Stanislas de Clermont-Tonnerre, "Speech on Religious Minorities and Questionable Professions," December 23, 1789, from Liberté, Égalité, Fraternité: Exploring the French Revolution, https://revolution.chnm.org/d/284/.
37. "Declaration of Principles—The Pittsburgh Platform," Central Conference of American Rabbis, 1885, https://www.ccarnet.org/rabbinic-voice/platforms/article-declaration-principles/. Emphasis added.
38. Theodore Herzl, *The Jewish State*, ed. and trans. Jacob M. Alkow (Dover, 1988), 76.
39. Yuval Noah Harari, *21 Lessons for the 21st Century* (Random House, 2018), 110.
40. David Brooks, *How to Know a Person*, 235–36.
41. Abba Kovner, "One of the Minyan," in *Al Hagesher Hatzar* (Sifriyat Hapoalim, 1981).
42. Robert D. Putnam, *Bowling Alone: The Collapse and Revival of American Community* (Simon and Schuster, 2000).
43. Lulu Garcia-Navarro, "Robert Putnam Knows Why You're Lonely," *New York Times*, July 13, 2024, https://www.nytimes.com/2024/07/13/magazine/robert-putnam-interview.html.

44. Stephen Sondheim, "A Boy Like That / I Have a Love," *West Side Story*.
45. Robert D. Putnam and Lewis Feldstein, *Better Together: Restoring the American Community* (Simon and Schuster, 2009), 49.
46. Mara Benjamin, *The Obligated Self*, 83.

CHAPTER 4

In Memory of the Wayward Son: Meditations in Queer Jewish Theology

Rabbi Hilly Haber, PhD

> *If a householder has a wayward and defiant son, who does not heed his father or mother and does not obey them even after they discipline him, his father and mother shall take hold of him and bring him out to the elders of his town at the public place of his community. They shall say to the elders of his town, "This son of ours is disloyal and defiant; he does not heed us. He is a glutton and a drunkard." Thereupon his town's council shall stone him to death. Thus you will sweep out evil from your midst: all of Israel will hear and be afraid.*
> —Deuteronomy 21:18–21

THE STORY of the *ben soreir umoreh*, the "wayward and defiant son," comes from a section of Torah that craves order and categories, rules and regulations:

> A woman must not put on man's apparel, nor shall a man wear woman's clothing [Deuteronomy 22:5]. . . . You shall not plow with an ox and an ass together. You shall not wear cloth combining wool and linen [Deuteronomy 22:10–11]. . . . If a man is found lying with another man's wife, both of them—the man and the woman with whom he lay—shall die [Deuteronomy 22:22].

This portion of Deuteronomy is one that seeks to confine and delimit, to categorize and separate, and to label those who defy categorization as deviants and criminals. It is a world composed of stark binaries, a fraught ethical terrain governing public and private behaviors from the mundane to the sacred. It is a world in which, in just four verses, the *ben soreir umoreh* is tried, found guilty, condemned to death by stoning, and executed before the entire community.

I have always felt a sense of queer kinship with the *ben soreir umoreh*, Deuteronomy's wayward and defiant son. Growing up, I lived in a world of binaries and boundaries—a world defined and divided by ethically charged notions of sexuality and gender. As hard as I tried to bend and mold and twist myself to fit these categories, I never managed to fit in.

As a child, I used to sneak into my younger brother's closet and borrow his clothes. I loved his plaid button-downs, his long jean shorts, and one particular white sweatshirt with a tiger on the front. Every gym class in the girls' locker room, every trip to the bathroom, every summer I slept in a bunk at camp, was a reminder that I was wrong. I was always ashamed and embarrassed. Like the *ben soreir*, I didn't fit into the world around me.

In *Radical Love: An Introduction to Queer Theology*, Dr. Patrick Cheng identifies three possible elements that mark theologies as queer: queer authorship, an explicitly transgressive bent, and that which erases or blurs socially constructed binaries.[1] Broadly defined, queer authorship encompasses LGBTQ+ people "talking about God," or theology done by and for LGBTQ+ people.[2] Transgressive theologies challenge social norms, especially those related to sexuality or gender. Transgressive theologies can also seek to upend or deconstruct existing power structures.[3] Finally, queer theologies seek to erase boundaries and blur the lines between binary categories of not only sex and gender, "but also more fundamental boundaries such as life vs. death, and divine vs. human."[4]

Though the *ben soreir*'s voice is absent in the Biblical account of his story, the Rabbinic interpretation of the *ben soreir umoreh*'s story identifies the ways in which his character upends legal and social norms within the text. Centuries after the Torah introduced us to the *ben soreir umoreh*, the Rabbis of the Talmud, in Tractate *Sanhedrin* (71a), reexamine his case, seeking to understand the exact nature of the boy's crime, his age, and the role his parents played in the story. Their critique surfaces several challenges to the veracity and morality of the verdict rendered in the Biblical account. Even if this boy drank and ate to excess, as the Rabbis imagine he did, stumbling through his life in ways that seemed reckless compared to his peers, nothing in the text itself suggests that he committed a crime worthy of capital punishment. Nor does the Deuteronomic text suggest that he had even reached an age of criminal responsibility.

Struggling to justify the boy's execution, one rabbi suggests that perhaps the rebellious son was executed at such a tender age to prevent future wrongdoing, so that he could die an innocent person. This explanation, however, is rejected, for how can we predict a person's future based on past behavior? Noting the lack of clarity surrounding the boy's age and his relationship to his parents, the absence of any judicial process, and the litany of missteps that potentially fall into the category of gluttony, none of which merit capital punishment, a majority of the Rabbinic voices determine that this case never actually happened; the *ben soreir* was never executed or perhaps did not even exist as portrayed in the Biblical account (Babylonian Talmud, *Sanhedrin* 71a).

In its emphasis on "the slipperiness of meaning and the transgression of categories and boundaries,"[5] the Rabbis' analysis of the text underscores the queer elements present in the *ben soreir umoreh*'s story. The uncertainty surrounding his age and the indefinability of his crime speak to a failure of the justice system to adequately render or understand this boy's character in a legal setting. Further, the wayward son rejects his parents' authority over him, subverting and transgressing the ethical and social norms within the world of the Biblical text. Beyond gender and sexuality, the Rabbinic analysis of this narrative opens the door to a multiplicity of possible futures for the *ben soreir* and others labeled as deviants. As Bible scholar and theologian Robert Shore Goss writes, "Queerness is bigger than GLBT lives; queerness is more than a linguistic reversal; and queerness is way deeper than merely 'odd.' Queerness is public solidarity in the struggle for sexual and gender justice and of irrepressibly making connections to other struggles for justice, compassion, and reconciliation."[6] Through their questions, the Rabbis push back on the ostensibly harsh nature of Biblical justice: What could a child have done to merit execution? Perhaps another future was possible for this child and others like him.

In reimagining the wayward son's fate, the Rabbis infuse the Biblical narrative with new possibility, paving the way for future readers to envision a future in which the wayward son survives and has the opportunity to narrate his own story. In an essay entitled "Queer Persistence: On Death, History, and Longing for Endings," Maia Kotrosits writes about the unique challenges inherent in queer continuity and survival. Those who survive their teenage years into adulthood or live with HIV, those "who have lost a lot, the ones making sense not of the past but of their presence, and their difficult place in the endurance of things,"[7] are left to write queer history. And as they write, they live into "a moment of haunted survival: [a] life that goes on after it should have ended; goes on haunted by terrible possibilities that never occurred, almost did, or still might; goes on despite itself in the face of other losses; or simply just goes on."[8] Haunted by the certainty of his death and continuity of his story, how would the wayward son reimagine the world around him to make sense of renewed and ongoing life? What are the theologies that would sustain him and enable him to flourish into adulthood?

Like queer theorists who "appl[y] 'queer' as a strategic method to deconstruct and expand the textual possibilities of cultural metanarratives—examining textual meshes, dissonances, absences, resistances, and disruptive potentialities,"[9] the Rabbinic understanding of this story functions as an act of queer resistance and of hope. The Rabbinic commentary exposes a lacuna in the Biblical text, a theological void between a life cut short and a life ongoing. To fill that gap requires theologies that hold space for messiness, transgression, and holiness all at once—theologies that shock. As Mark Jordan writes, "The jolt supposed to be produced by speaking of queer theology is roughly like the jolt of saying 'indecent theology' or 'the queer God.' It is the jolt of putting the stigmatized next to the holy. We are to imagine a stable or standard theology, a reigning orthodoxy, that is disrupted by the queer."[10] In essence, the Rabbis assert that the *ben soreir* was not executed; what was a life cut short in the Biblical text is now a newly opened future that offers a location from which to construct queer Jewish theologies that weave together and hold as sacred Jewish texts, queer lived experience, and the voices of queer theologians.

As I reflect on the story of the *ben soreir umoreh* and the ways in which Biblical and religious "clobber" texts have been used to condemn and dehumanize queer people,[11] I believe that another feature of queer theology is that which offers theological anthropologies of individual and collective change and evolution over time, recognizing that each of us deviates, transgresses, and evolves throughout our lives. The God of queer Jewish theology is one who meets us in moments of transgression and transformation with mercy, understanding, and compassion, resisting rigid constructions of identity and harsh conceptions of justice, and modeling a kind of grace that could have carried the *ben soreir* into adulthood.

What, then, would it look like for the wayward son to leave the landscape of binaries and boundaries, of night and day, and step into a world of twilight? In the Rabbinic imagination, twilight is a time of endless creative potential; as Rabbi Larry Hoffman articulates, it is "an anomalous time that gives rise to anomalous creation."[12] *Pirkei Avot* 5:8 teaches that God made ten seemingly supernatural aspects of Creation *bein hashmashot*, during twilight of the first Shabbat, including the manna (Exodus 16:15), the well that followed the Israelites in the desert (Numbers 21:16–18), the rainbow that served as the sign of the covenant between God and Noah (Genesis 9:13), the ram that saved Isaac (Genesis 22:13), and Moses's staff that performed wonders in Egypt (Exodus 4:2). According to *Pirkei D'Rabbi Eliezer*, a midrashic text composed in Italy during the ninth century, God taught Adam how to make fire during the twilight hours of the first Shabbat on earth (20:4). The God of twilight is a God of mercy, a God whose last-minute additions to Creation sustain and affirm collective and individual life.

We know the God of twilight by the name *HaMaariv Aravim*, the convenor of *erev*, the mixing hour: the God who seamlessly blends day into night, one season into the next. The *Maariv Aravim*, a prayer recited each evening, tells the story of a universe in constant motion, of a God who "thoughtfully alters the time and changes the seasons . . . rolling light away from darkness and darkness from light."[13] *Erev* is an hour of fusion, of mixing and mingling, of transformation and possibility.

Twilight walks between night and day. To see the world in twilight is to see a world filled with unique creation, a world that "strive[s] towards emphasizing difference and the margins, rather than sameness,"[14] a world made both exhilarating and, at times, terrifying by its uncertainty. The same mishnah that teaches us the lifesaving possibilities of twilight also teaches that demons were created in twilight (*Pirkei Avot* 5:8). Rife with possibility and ambiguity, twilight is a queer space in Jewish time, with "normative boundaries blurred, dualistic definitions refuted and the creation of permissive identities. It is in this space that we enter 'the kingdom of heaven,' a world without the confines of traditional, patriarchal structures, systems and roles."[15] Twilight recognizes the ways we all deviate, transform, and evolve throughout our lives, making room to reimagine new ways of walking in and shaping the world.

Twilight is the backdrop of queer Jewish theology. It is a time for crossing boundaries and transition—acts that define us as a Jewish people. We are the *Ivrim*, the Hebrews, or literally, "the boundary crossers."[16] We are also *Yisrael*, Israel, "those who wrestle or struggle with God." Both names inform us that we are in constant motion, unending transformation, and enduring transition.

The *Ivrim*: A Theology of Movement and Mercy

Abraham is the first person referred to by the Biblical text as an *Ivri* (Genesis 14:13). Guided by a divine promise, Abraham leaves his father's house and the land of his ancestors to build a new nation with his wife, Sarah. On Abraham and Sarah's departure, Bible scholar Avivah Zornberg writes, "An act of radical discontinuity is, it seems, depicted in the Torah as the essential basis for all continuity: for that act of birth that will engender the body and the soul of a new kind of nation."[17] Abraham's decision to cross a border and break from his father's story in order to begin his own is the first step toward realizing a new nation, a people with a distinct and unique identity in the world.

The implications for such an act of rupture play out in the names and on the bodies of Abraham and Sarah. Initially called Abram and Sarai in the Biblical text, Sarah and Abraham are renamed by God after leaving the place in which they are born and entering into a covenant with God. Sarah and Abraham are renamed for a moment of rupture. Further, Sarah is unable to conceive (Genesis 11:30). Zornberg notes that the Hebrew word for "barren" shares a common root with the Hebrew word for "uprooted."[18] Metaphorically and literally cut off from their respective lineages and places of origin, Abraham and Sarah begin the life of a new nation with an act that disrupts and reorders the world they both knew. As border crossers whose lives are disrupted and reordered by movement, Abraham and Sarah embody the temporal turn of queer theology, raising questions within the Biblical text about what constitutes a full and divinely blessed life.[19] By leaving their homeland and taking on new names, Sarah and Abraham resist the futures they were born into, choosing instead to break from the past and reimagine their world as it could be. In their movement, they embody a "queerness [that] is the longing that propels us onward, beyond romances of the negative and toiling in the present. Queerness [that] is that thing that lets us feel that this world is not enough."[20] This queerness is baked into the identity of the *Ivrim*, a people whose history is one of movement and longing.

As a people descended from Abraham and Sarah, we are called on to move across national and geographic borders and boundaries, across time and space—called on to relive a collective past and a shared memory in every act of ritual, in every reading of text, and in every moment of prayer. We are a people of multiplicity, a people with "multiple co-existing and overlapping identities, as opposed to a singular dominant identity."[21] This notion of overlapping identities is embedded in the divine blueprint for God's created world. In Genesis we read that God formed the first human being from the soil (2:7). The Sages derived an ethical precept from this verse, teaching that God gathered dust from all four corners of the earth with which to make human beings so that no person could tell another that they didn't belong or claim ownership over parts of God's created world.[22]

Jewish notions of justice and redemption reflect this queered understanding of what it means to be human. Perpetual punishment is a foreign concept in Jewish tradition. Unlike our criminal legal system in the United States, punishment is neither permanent nor an end itself, according to Jewish law and ethics. The purpose of punishment in Jewish tradition is *t'shuvah*: repentance, atonement, and return to community. Our Jewish sages teach us that when people are able to return to community and fully participate, our communities thrive and flourish.

In his legal compendium, the *Mishneh Torah*, the medieval sage Maimonides detailed the multilayered process of *t'shuvah*. When seeking to atone, someone who has caused harm must first make a verbal confession and ask for forgiveness from the aggrieved party.[23] These steps are followed by an expression of sincere remorse and a firm resolve to never repeat the offense again.[24] The person who transgressed must also make restitution or reparation as a means of healing the person or people they have hurt.[25] Finally, the test of true repentance is the ability to change one's actions if the same situation presents itself again.[26]

Inherent in Maimonides's steps of *t'shuvah*, the backdrop for atonement is community. Admission of guilt, repair, and healing are not projects of perpetual separation from the community, but rather rely on the presence and participation of those around you. The path of *t'shuvah*, of return, and of healing happens in conversation, in relationship. Justice in Judaism is not meant to be life-ending, but rather life-affirming, giving new life to communities and individuals through the repair of harm. Unlike the Biblical account of the *ben soreir*'s life and death, justice in Judaism functions restoratively.

In her book *How We Reckon: Violence, Mass Incarceration, and a Road to Repair*, Danielle Sered defines restorative justice "as a decision making process that involves those most directly impacted by a given harm in identifying the pathway toward repair—and then carrying out the actions to get there."[27] At their very core, restorative justice principles and Jewish tradition share a common understanding of what it means to be human. Paraphrasing from the *Mishneh Torah*: Throughout the entire year, a person should always look at themself as equally balanced between merit and sin and the world as equally balanced between merit and sin. If they perform one sin, they tip their balance and that of the entire world to the side of guilt and bring destruction upon themself.[28] In "Restorative Justice and the One Who Harms," Rabbi Jericho Vincent writes, "Restorative justice posits that there isn't a binary between those who cause harm and those who don't—we all cause harm, just at different scales. Restorative justice also assumes that restitution is possible. Even those who have caused grave harm have the potential to engage in the noble work of repair."[29] As Jews we walk the path of *t'shuvah* throughout our lives, honoring the humanity of all people who walk with us. As Danielle Sered writes, "We should acknowledge that even when the harm is great, even when it is massive, the humanity of the person who caused it, even then, is greater."[30]

The Children of Israel:
A Theology of Transition, Becoming, and Blessing

As Israel, we are a people named in struggle and embrace. In the Book of Genesis, the patriarch Jacob wrestles with a divine being (32:25–30). From nightfall to daybreak, the two are locked in what the medieval commentator Rashi describes as both embrace and struggle.[31] At sunrise, Jacob is blessed with a new name, a new way of being and walking in the world. Through this struggle with God, through an ultimate embrace of himself, Jacob and his descendants become Israel. Jacob's transition is memorialized in words of Biblical poetry and liturgy, echoing through sanctuaries across time: "How fair are your tents, O Jacob, your dwellings, O Israel" (Numbers 24:5).

Traditionally recited upon entering the sanctuary for the morning prayer service, the words of *Mah Tovu* come from the mouth of Balaam, a non-Israelite diviner and dream interpreter who is sent by Balak, the king of Moab, to curse the Israelite camp on the border of Moab. "Put a curse upon this people . . . ," orders the king. "Perhaps I can thus defeat them and drive them out of the land" (Numbers 22:6). Our Sages read into the king's command a desire not only to weaken the Israelite camp, but to eradicate them from the land entirely.[32] Beyond a military strike, the desire to curse the Israelites signals an existential threat, the intention of bringing an end to this people.

Balaam agrees and sets out for the Israelite encampment. On the way, he meets a divine messenger, who rebukes him and instructs him to speak only the words that God puts in his mouth. Balaam continues on, meeting Balak at the border of the encampment.

The two summit a peak overlooking the camp and gaze out across the mixed multitude of Israel. Imagine what they saw and what they heard as they looked down from their perch. We meet the Children of Israel in this moment, and we see them through the eyes of their enemies: a mass of formerly enslaved wanderers freshly mourning the death of Miriam, recovering from a rebellion in which hundreds of people were engulfed by a divine flame, and reeling from the news that after all of this, they will not enter the Promised Land.

To merely describe this people, to imagine their worn-out bodies and blistered feet, their hunched shoulders and backs bent under the weight of an uncertain future, is to envision them cursed, to speak a hopelessness into being. And yet, as Balaam gazes across the Israelite encampment, words of poetry and blessing fall from his lips: "How fair are your tents, O Jacob, your dwellings, O Israel" (Numbers 24:5). Our Sages teach in the Talmud that what Balaam originally meant to curse, he ultimately blessed. Though he sought to say that the kingdom of Israel would not endure, he instead said that it would endure forever: "Like winding brooks" (Numbers 24:6), which flow continuously (*Sanhedrin* 105b).[33]

As Audre Lorde, self-described Black, lesbian, mother, warrior, and poet, teaches us, words of poetry and praise are a means of survival, a way of speaking a future into existence, of singing hope into the world. In a 1977 essay entitled "Poetry Is Not a Luxury," Lorde writes about the deep human need for poetry:

> Poetry is not a luxury. It is a vital necessity of our existence. It forms the quality of light within which we predicate our hopes and dreams toward survival and change, first made into language, then into idea, then into more tangible action. Poetry is the way we help give name to the nameless so it can be thought. The farthest horizons of our hopes and fears are cobbled by our poems, carved from the rock experiences of our daily lives. If what we need to dream, to move our spirits most deeply and directly toward and through promise, is discounted as luxury, then we give up the core—the fountain—of our power ... we give up the future of our worlds.[34]

Poetry offers us an alternative way of seeing; it shows us a world that looks different from the one that's before us. It shows us a despised people lifted up to dignity, stronger than they ever suspected, enduring through the ages. It can show us new possibilities for the future, a better life that lies ahead, a way of embracing and loving our own imperfect selves. It can offer a vision of the way the world could be, and the power to keep fighting to bring that world about. It offers us the precious power of change and transformation. Imagination liberates and inspires; it is the path to survival; it is the very doorway to hope.

In the life-affirming words of *Mah Tovu*, including both "Jacob" and "Israel," I read a blessing for struggle and striving, for transition and transformation: a blessing for Jacob-becoming-Israel. This is a blessing that calls attention to the beauty of before and after, a blessing with the power to offer loving affirmation to those who are "not only exercising their freedom to cocreate their bodies but also, in turn, manifesting the process of God's self-revelation within transitioning bodies."[35] Jacob-becoming-Israel offers a sacred frame with which to coauthor one's body with God through the process of transition.

The God who wrestles with and embraces Jacob through the night is a God who defies the boundaries between divine and human realms, a God who partners with us in the ongoing work of Creation, a God whose "trans" characteristics mirror our own ever-evolving identities. As Rabbi Julia Watts-Belser writes, "Just as human genders come in a variety of expressions, divine gender is not a stable, reified finality ... *Ehiyeh Asher Ehiyeh*—the ultimate divine force that will be whatever it will be—has neither a womb nor a penis to tangle our thoughts."[36] To understand God as trans is not only to resist idolatrous and static constructions of God, but also to resist static and prescriptive notions of human identity and behavior. Like God, like Jacob, we are in a constant state of becoming, wrestling, and striving.

Conclusions: The *Ivrim*, Israel, and the *Ben Soreir*

Imagine if the *ben soreir* had lived. If on the day he was to be executed, his community instead walked with him into the twilight hour and together imagined a multiplicity of possible futures. What name would he take for himself? Which curses would he reshape into his (and our) greatest sources of strength? What lessons from his own life, from the mercy that stayed his execution, would he bring to enrich the *Ivrim*, Israel?

Writing from the void of his future allows us not only to imagine the theologies that could have brought him into adulthood, but also to reimagine and write queer Jewish theologies of mercy, resistance, and hope that are haunted by his memory and intended for today's wayward and rebellious children.

NOTES

1. Patrick S. Cheng, "What Is Queer Theology?," in *Radical Love: An Introduction to Queer Theology* (Seabury Books, 2011), 9–10.
2. Patrick S. Cheng, "What Is Queer Theology?," 9.
3. Patrick S. Cheng, "What Is Queer Theology?," 9.
4. Patrick S. Cheng, "What Is Queer Theology?," 10.
5. Hannah McCann and Whitney Monaghan, "Defining Queer Theory," in *Queer Theory Now: From Foundations to Futures* (Red Globe Press, 2020), 2.
6. Robert E. Shore-Goss, "Gay and Lesbian Theologies," in *Liberation Theologies in the United States: An Introduction*, ed. Stacey M. Floyd-Thomas and Anthony B. Pinn (New York University Press, 2010), 201.
7. Maia Kotrosits, "Queer Persistence: On Death, History, and Longing for Endings," in *Sexual Disorientations: Queer Temporalities, Affects, Theologies*, ed. Kent L. Brintnall, Joseph A. Marchal, and Stephen D. Moore (Fordham University Press, 2018), 138.
8. Kotrosits, "Queer Persistence,"139.
9. Shore-Goss, "Gay and Lesbian Theologies," 199.
10. Mark D. Jordan, "In Search of Queer Theology Lost," in *Sexual Disorientations: Queer Temporalities, Affects, Theologies*, ed. Kent L. Brintnall, Joseph A. Marchal, and Stephen D. Moore (Fordham University Press, 2018), 306.
11. "Clobber" passages are the Biblical passages typically used to justify LGBTQ+ exclusion in church life. See Chris Greenough, "Queer Bible," in *Queer Theologies: The Basics* (Routledge, 2020), 98.
12. Lawrence Hoffman, ed., *My People's Prayer Book*, vol. 9, *Welcoming the Night: Minchah and Ma'ariv (Afternoon and Evening Prayer)* (Jewish Lights, 2005), 7.
13. *Mishkan T'filah: A Reform Siddur*, ed. Elyse D. Frishman (CCAR Press, 2007), 6.
14. Hannah McCann and Whitney Monaghan, "Defining Queer Theory," in *Queer Theory Now: From Foundations to Futures* (Red Globe Press, 2020), 12.
15. Lewis Reay, "Towards a Transgender Theology: Que(e)rying the Eunuchs," in *Trans/formations*, ed. Marcella Althaus-Reid and Lisa Isherwood (SCM Press, 2009), 157.
16. Rachel Adler, "A Question of Boundaries: Toward a Jewish Feminist Theology of Self and Others," *Tikkun* 31, no. 3 (August 2016): 48–49, https://doi.org/10.1215/08879982-3628356.
17. Avivah Gottlieb Zornberg, *The Beginning of Desire: Reflections on Genesis* (Image Books, 1995), 77.
18. Zornberg, *Beginning of Desire*, 76–77.
19. Hannah McCann and Whitney Monaghan, "Temporality and Queer Utopias," in *Queer Theory Now*, 213.

20. Hannah McCann and Whitney Monaghan, "Temporality and Queer Utopias," 229.
21. Patrick S. Cheng, "Introducing Rainbow Theology," in *Rainbow Theology: Bridging Race, Sexuality, and Spirit* (Seabury Books, 2013), 89.
22. *Pirkei D'Rabbi Eliezer* 11:5; *Yalkut Shimoni*, Genesis 1:13.
23. Maimonides, *Mishneh Torah*, Laws of Repentance 1:1.
24. Maimonides, *Mishneh Torah*, Laws of Repentance 2:2.
25. Maimonides, *Mishneh Torah*, Laws of Repentance 2:9.
26. Maimonides, *Mishneh Torah*, Laws of Repentance 2:1.
27. Danielle Sered, *Until We Reckon: Violence, Mass Incarceration, and a Road to Repair* (New Press, 2019), 135.
28. Maimonides, *Mishneh Torah*, Laws of Repentance 3:4.
29. Jericho Vincent, "Restorative Justice and the One Who Harms," Sefaria, https://www.sefaria.org/sheets/335152?lang=bi.
30. Danielle Sered, *Until We Reckon*, 96.
31. Rashi on Genesis 32:25.
32. *Midrash Tanchuma, Balak* 4.
33. Translation of Numbers 24:6 is from the William Davidson digital edition of the *Koren Noé Talmud*, with commentary by Adin Even-Israel Steinsaltz (license: CC-BY-NC, https://creativecommons.org/licenses/by-nc/4.0/), found on Sefaria (sefaria.org).
34. Audre Lorde, *Sister Outsider* (Crossing Press, 1984/2007), 37–39.
35. Shore-Goss, "Gay and Lesbian Theologies," 193.
36. Julia Watts-Belser, "Transing God/dess: Notes from the Borderlands," in *Balancing on the Mechitza: Transgender in Jewish Community*, ed. Noach Dzmura (North Atlantic Books, 2010), 238–39.

CHAPTER 5

The Feeling Being: Was the World Created for My Sake?

Rabbi Ellen Lewis

IN 1988, eight years after I was ordained a rabbi, I began to study at a modern psychoanalytic institute. After my stint—first as an assistant, and then as an associate rabbi—at a large Texas congregation, I became a solo rabbi in a congregation of three hundred families. The more time I spent in congregational work, however, the less I understood why people behaved the way they did. I felt limited in my ability to help people. I felt equally limited in my ability to help myself. And so I took the slow route, signing up for one class at a time, drinking in the learning but not intending to finish the training and become a psychoanalyst—at least, not at that point.

While I enjoyed studying traditional texts in rabbinical school, my learning was lacking in what my new institute labeled "emotional education." Now I was attempting to integrate my prior intellectual learning with emotional learning. Although people respectfully addressed me as Rabbi Lewis (the institute was rather formal in how we addressed each other), my being a rabbi was treated at times as a curiosity and at times a detriment. The director of the institute asked me more than once, "When are you going to give up this rabbi stuff?" Her question reflected the historical antipathy between the worlds of psychoanalysis and religion, with some tracking the differences to Freud's dismissal of religion as an illusion and a collective neurosis.[1] For her, the choice was either/or: You could not ascribe to both analytical thinking and Jewish thinking.

The more I studied modern psychoanalysis,[2] however, the more I discovered the opposite to be true. I found more commonalities than differences between Judaism and analytical thinking. Each time I was exposed to a psychoanalytical theory, I immediately thought of a Jewish illustration. I realized that both disciplines strive to address the emotional complexities of what it means to be human. The two different approaches both attempt to answer these questions: What is our purpose? How can we use our feelings to live fuller, more meaningful lives? One of the elements that makes us human is our capacity to experience complex emotions.³ Having our feelings matters, not only for its own sake, but also because we have the capacity to choose what to do about those feelings. You might expect psychoanalysis to value feelings, but what of Judaism? We must dig deeper to find the answer to that question. Because traditional Jewish sources focus on behaviors over emotions, feelings get neglected. This was highlighted for me when I was a rabbinical student and was fortunate to participate in a program that placed us in mental health clinics at the University of Cincinnati. Five of us participated in an integration seminar led by psychologist Dr. Sophia Ralson. Her task was to help us understand the difference between being a therapist and offering pastoral rabbinic care. In one memorable meeting, she looked at us in exasperation and said, "The problem with you rabbis is you think that when someone comes in and asks you for a book, they want a book!" We were so academically oriented that we had a hard time "listening with the third ear."⁴ I learned from that seminar that attending to people's feelings matters as much as showing academic prowess.

The outside world doesn't often describe Judaism as feelingful. Early on, Christianity disparaged Judaism as a religion of law. Islam and others have called us "the People of the Book." Some have incorrectly categorized us as a race, others—most notably Rabbi Mordecai Kaplan—as a civilization. Other than race, we are all of the above. But those are largely descriptions from external sources. What does it mean to offer a view from the inside of Judaism as a relational religion? Whenever we start by asking what Judaism is or says, we first turn to the text, but Jewish text itself can be a problematic and limited source. Biblical and Rabbinic texts, if not composed exclusively by men, were redacted by men and interpreted by men. And so as we read the stories of our people, we also need to supply emotions from stories not told, the stories of "the Jew who wasn't there."⁵ Dr. Rachel Adler, writing on feminist methodological approaches to text study, suggests, "One crucial contribution will be the methodologies feminists have developed for understanding and using narrative. . . . As a method of vision, feminist narratives draw upon fantasies and desires, prophecies and prayers to imagine possible worlds in which both women and men could flourish. As a tool of critique, narrative can expose within abstract theories assumptions about the nature and experience of being human, what people know, how they love, what they want and what they fear."⁶ In other words, we need to look behind human behaviors to discover the feelings that consciously or unconsciously influence our actions. Judaism is at heart a relational religion, reliant on how our feelings guide our connecting with each other. Feelings and thoughts, emotions and intellectual learning go hand in hand in Jewish tradition.

We are not the first to infer feelings from the stories we have inherited. The Rabbis did it through midrash centuries ago when they found the Bible's emotional terseness wanting. They infer from Rachel's crying that she felt pain and from Rebekah's comforting Isaac over the loss of his mother that she felt compassion for him in his grief. They imagine Moses's jealousy at being replaced as leader by Joshua. We need supply less inference about feelings when we read how the Psalmist cries out from the depths and pleads for God's response to suffering. Since there is no systematic study of emotions in Jewish tradition, we work to imagine what our ancestors felt. And we base our assumptions on some identification with those who preceded us.

The rabbis could draw emotional inferences from earlier texts because they assumed their ancestors were like them, despite the intervening centuries. I remember the first time this idea occurred to me. I was a student in a Bible class taught by Rabbi Chanan Brichto, PhD, z"l. I do not recall the specific topic under discussion, but I do remember Rabbi Brichto's frustrated intervention. "Why do you all start from the premise that times were different then and people were different then?" he asked. "What makes you think people were so different in Biblical times? What if you assumed they were just like us?" I remember experiencing a feeling of revelation in that moment: We can imagine what they felt based on what we feel. I realized that I had been operating under certain false assumptions. I had been placing an unnecessary barrier between me and the humanness of my Biblical ancestors. Suddenly I saw a connection where before there had been only distance. They were people just like us. Their context may have been different, but what made them human was the same. They, too, lived with complicated feelings and had to make equally complicated choices.

While we may resemble our ancestors emotionally, we do live in a radically different time. We live in a time of incessant stimulation. We are glued to cell phones on which people can message us day and night. Streaming services offer a relentless visual of the world with all its suffering. The internet calls to us and consumes us. We still grapple with the aftermath of a worldwide pandemic. How can we avoid feeling overwhelmed? And how can we manage the feelings that come with being overwhelmed? Pauline Boss, in her work on ambiguous loss, advises, "When the outside world is unmanageable . . . learning how to manage one's inner world is helpful and stress reducing. One's subjective sense of control is more important than one's objective control of the situation. When the situation cannot be changed realistically, we can reinterpret it in such a way that it is no longer perceived as immobilizing; positive interpretation can change negative arousal. Shifting mastery from trying to control one's environment and the people in it to controlling one's inner self is a redefinition of mastery."[7]

Despite and because of these challenging times, we need to come to terms with our emotional limitations if we want to live lives of meaning. The interpersonal psychoanalyst Harry Stack Sullivan reminds us, "We are all much more simply human than otherwise."[8] The words of *Pirkei Avot* remind us, "[Rabbi Tarfon] used to say: You are not required to complete the work, yet you are not free to desist from it" (2:21). When our feelings are tender, we need to be intentional about creating personal boundaries and protecting ourselves. To paraphrase the British psychoanalyst John Bowlby, who studied evolutionary biology and ethology in addition to psychology: The optimal level of attachment is to experience the world of the other without being overwhelmed by it.[9] All of these thoughts are predicated on the most basic of human experience: We have complex feelings. Without understanding what that means, we cannot develop the boundaries and insulation we need to live as human beings in our challenging times.

And so we begin our exploration of what it means to be human by asking: Where do our feelings come from? I do not believe we come into the world with specific feelings. We are born with bodily sensations and what you might call a nascent self. Observing newborn babies, one notices how they express comfort and discomfort with their entire bodies. Babies can only experience pleasure and pain through their physical senses; they do not yet have the mental and emotional capacities to have feelings. It is only in relationship to our early caregivers that these sensations begin to become feelings. The British psychoanalyst Donald Winnicott famously said, "There is no such thing as a baby. . . . A baby alone cannot exist but is essentially part of a relationship."[10] There is only the baby in relationship with its caregiver. In other words, a feelingful self does not form in a vacuum; it forms in relationship. We impute feelings to infants based on what we observe about them. When babies cry, parents often intuitively mirror their distress and supply possible feelings: "Are you hungry? Are you angry that I waited too long to feed you? You're so tired. Do you need to go to bed?" Analytical literature is replete with discussions of early mirroring as a way in which babies turn sensations into feelings.[11]

While later life circumstances will also impact those early seeds of feeling, mirroring sets the tone for lifelong emotional development and continues to matter throughout our lives. Being seen emotionally offers us a fundamental experience that allows us to feel understood. "Under optimal conditions, children eventually are able to internalize this mirroring function, and emotionally experience the whole range of their psychic life. However, unless all of the child's moods and needs are 'seen' first by the parents, the child cannot feel completely real. In essence, what the parents fail to see remains invisible to the child as well."[12]

How might we describe Jewish ideas about where feelings come from? We can begin with the creation of human beings: "This is the written record of the human line from the day God created human beings, making [them] in the likeness of God" (Genesis 5:1). What does it mean to be created in God's likeness? "The Rabbis said, 'As God is merciful, so shall you be merciful; as God is just, so shall you be just.'"[13] If we know we were created in the likeness of God and we infer God has feelings, then having feelings is a way of emulating God. We hear further about being created in God's likeness from Shimon ben Azai, a second-century *Tanna* (a rabbi of the Mishnaic period), Rabbi Akiva, another great sage of the time, and Rabbi Tanchuma, a fifth-century *Amora* (a rabbi of the Talmudic period):

> Ben Azai said, "'This is the written record of the human line from the day God created human beings, making [them] in the likeness of God' (Genesis 5:1) is a great principle in the Torah."
>
> Rabbi Akiva said, "This is a great principle of the Torah: 'You shall love your neighbor as yourself' (Leviticus 19:18). Thus, one should not say, 'Since I am scorned, I should scorn my fellow as well; since I have been cursed, I will curse my fellow as well.'"
>
> Rabbi Tanchuma said, "If you act thus, realize who it is that you are willing to have humiliated—'the one who was made in the likeness of God' (Genesis 5:1)." (*B'reishit Rabbah* 24:7)

Being created "in the likeness of God" (*bidmut Elohim*; Genesis 5:1) becomes the foundation for how we are to treat each other, rather than loving your neighbor as yourself. Self-love is a fickle feeling; if we rely on it to dictate how we should treat our neighbor, we run the danger of maltreating our neighbor. Letting our own egos get in the way can prevent us from truly seeing the other person. Ben Azai's gentle reminder that we were all created in the likeness of God offers a better relational path. In tracing the derivation of human feelings back to Adam and Eve, the Rabbis assume the universality of human feeling. Adam and Eve were the first human beings, not the first Jews. Genesis describes the creation of the world as the formation of all humankind. The particularism of Jewish history does not begin until the narratives of Abraham and Sarah. While later development in Jewish history constructs a different and unique road to salvation for the Jewish people, Jewish tradition has retained the premise that there are many roads to human happiness. In the words of Maimonides, "The pious of the other nations have a share in the world-to-come."[14] Judaism is not prescriptive about belief, but rather recognizes our common humanity and our obligation to treat each other humanely. Rabbinic observations about human emotion and behavior are meant to apply equally to all human beings.

The Rabbis, as part of a conversation that is not systematic, do contribute additional ideas about the source of human emotions. We learn from them that human beings innately possess a *yetzer ra* and a *yetzer tov*, generally translated literally as an "evil inclination" and a "good inclination": "Rabbi Nachman said in Rabbi Sh'muel's name: 'Behold, it was good' refers to the good desire [*yetzer tov*]; 'And behold it was very good' refers to the evil desire [*yetzer ra*]. Can then the evil desire be very good? That would be extraordinary! But without the evil desire, no person would build a house, take a spouse, and beget children" (*B'reishit Rabbah* 9:7). In this midrash, the "evil" human inclination is necessary for existence and can also be used for the good. Rather than emphasizing the potential emotional conflict incurred by the two inclinations, we can also consider them a dialectic where they work together to foster human wholeness. For instance, in our liturgy, the *Sh'ma* tells us to love God with all our heart (Deuteronomy 6:5). The Talmud says this means we should love God with both our *yetzer tov* and our *yetzer ra* (Babylonian Talmud, *B'rachot* 54a). If we are to worship God with a whole heart, that means we aspire to worship with both *y'tzarim*, with our entire being.

While the history of the *yetzer* in Rabbinic literature is a complicated one, for our purposes I will use it psychologically and homiletically,[15] noting its superficial similarity to Freud's notion of a dual drive theory of aggression and libido.[16] I think of the dynamic relationship between the dual inclinations along the lines of a teaching by Jeffrey Spitzer: "*Yetzer hara* is not a demonic force that pushes a person to do evil, but rather a drive toward pleasure or property or security, which if left unlimited can lead to evil (see Genesis *Rabbah* 9:7). When properly controlled by the *yetzer hatov*, the *yetzer hara* leads to many socially desirable results, including marriage, business, and community."[17] Our *yetzer ra* and *yetzer tov* do not have to work in opposition to each other, as the Rabbis often picture, but can work together for a full emotional experience.

All feelings are necessary for a full human experience. To be human is to have and enjoy feelings of love and feelings of hate and whatever feelings fall between them. The Chasidic Rabbi Pinchas of Koretz confirms, "A person cannot be consciously good unless they know evil. No one can appreciate pleasure unless they have tasted bitterness. Good is only the reverse of evil and pleasure is merely the opposite of anxiety.... Without the evil impulse, a person could do no evil; but neither could they do good."[18] This is another way of saying that we cannot have just some of our feelings and still lead a full life. Feelings are an all-or-nothing game. While most of us are more comfortable with our loving feelings than with our aggressive feelings, all feelings are necessary to live a full life. Hard though it may be to believe, it is even possible to learn how to enjoy aggressive feelings. I think of a woman I know who was raised never to express anger (which, for a child, translates to not feeling anger). Her first reactions to finally allowing herself to feel anger—really feeling it—can only be described as joyful. The Rabbis see the enjoyment of feelings—at least, the positive ones—as a human mandate. The Mishnah quotes Ben Zoma, who asks, "Who is rich?" He answers, "The one who is happy with one's lot" (*Pirkei Avot* 4:1). What might this mean? "Rabbi Hezekiah and Rabbi Cohen both taught in the name of Rabbah: In the eschatological future, a person will have to give an account concerning everything in which their eye delighted, but the enjoyment of which they nevertheless denied themself" (Jerusalem Talmud, *Kiddushin* 4:12).[19] Human "wealth" equates to enjoying our lives.

Yet certainly you can also find in Jewish tradition the idea that feelings can be dangerous and must be managed or suppressed. While the Rabbis saw that the *yetzer* could be a productive force, they are also wary of the negative behavior the human *yetzer* might inspire. Thus, they admired the one who could *koveish et yitzro*, who could "control one's urges": "Ben Zoma said, 'Who is strong? One who subdues one's base instincts'" (*Pirkei Avot* 4:1). We can read this text in various ways. I imagine that the Rabbis were concerned less with feelings than with the potential for impulsive (often sexual) behavior. Sometimes we confuse impulse with emotion, but we need to understand them as separate and distinct. Rabbi Dr. Abraham Twerski was a Chasidic rabbi and psychiatrist who specialized in the treatment of addiction. I once heard him speak to a group of predominantly Orthodox rabbis.[20] He told the story of how his family was accustomed to meeting his Jewish recovery patients, whom he routinely invited to his home for Shabbat dinner. One day, he needed a plumber and found one in his recovery group. As the plumber was working in the bathroom, Rabbi Twerski's daughter noticed that the plumber was wearing a cross and said in astonishment, "I didn't know non-Jews could be addicts!" Indeed, when I was a child, one frequently cited (positive) stereotype was that "Jews don't drink." While there is a study that links a Jewish DNA mutation to lower rates of alcoholism, it is not empirically true that Jews don't drink.[21] Rabbi Dr. Twerski knew that everyone, Jew and non-Jew alike, has feelings that can lead to impulsive and addictive behavior. He also believed that all people are created *b'tzelem Elohim* (in God's image) and did not distinguish between them based on race, religion, or gender. In one of his many books, he comments on a statement by the Baal Shem Tov, "It is commonplace to pray for protection from our enemies. We should also pray to be protected from ourselves. Sometimes we can be our own greatest adversaries."[22] The rabbis in the room where he spoke that day argued with him about the value of twelve-step programs as the primary path to curing addiction. Their position was that if you want to solve addiction, you should study more Torah. His position was that you must deal with people's humanity first before studying Torah will make any difference. Twerski, as one of the most orthodox of rabbis, saw no distinction between human need and religious practice.

As human beings, we need to guard against equating feeling and action. I remember some years ago when President Jimmy Carter gave a controversial interview to *Playboy* magazine.[23] He was quoted as saying, "I've looked on a lot of women with lust. I've committed adultery in my heart many times." The general American public reacted in widespread shock; the Jews I knew just shrugged and said, "What's the big deal? He didn't *do* anything." I believe that response was influenced by the Jewish distinction between feeling and behavior. We are taught we can have a feeling, consider the consequences of our behavior in advance, and choose whether this is the moment to act. I might love you, but that does not mean I should automatically throw my arms around you. I might hate you, but that does not entitle me to hurt you. This knowledge can work in both directions, either letting a feeling guide us not to act or letting a feeling direct us toward action.

Feelings can be contagious, particularly strong feelings. We can easily be induced to have the feelings of the person we are with. If we spend time with someone who is deeply depressed, we ourselves often begin to feel depressed. When I work in supervision with therapists, we often observe how the therapist can be feeling just fine until a particular patient enters the room. If that person is feeling agitated, the therapist, too, can begin to feel agitated. If the therapist returns to a normal feeling level after that person leaves the room at the end of a session, that is a clue that the therapist was experiencing the patient's feelings. Understanding this phenomenon of induced feelings can be helpful in a therapeutic context because it can build empathy between therapist and patient. Lack of awareness of induced feelings, however, can be dangerous in other situations. We have seen from history how emotional contagion can drive forces like the Crusades to wreak destruction. Mob behavior, like that of the Ku Klux Klan, can result from emotional contagion. We have seen that people in groups sometimes behave in ways they normally would not had they been alone. This knowledge reinforces the necessity of distinguishing between feeling an emotion and acting on that emotion. Only once we become aware of our feelings can we choose whether to act on them. Actually letting ourselves have the feeling, paradoxical as that might seem, is what can allow us to discern whether or not to take action.

The awareness that our feelings can and will change allows us to wait before acting. What feels imperative in a moment will often pass if one stops and takes a breath. The wisdom of this knowledge is found in a folk tale about King Solomon: "King Solomon once searched for a cure against depression. He assembled his wise [advisors] together. They meditated for a long time and gave him the following advice: Make yourself a ring and have thereon engraved the words 'This too will pass.' The King carried out the advice. He had the ring made and wore it constantly. Every time he felt sad and depressed, he looked at the ring, whereon his mood would change, and he would feel cheerful."[24] Anything can be lost at any time. Happiness can pass in an instant, and so can sadness. Human feelings can only exist in the moment. When we understand how feelings can change, we can appreciate the moment that much more just because we know it is impermanent.

It is almost impossible to make good choices if we do not know what we feel, and yet at times it is hard for us to access our own feelings. What stops us from knowing? As we grow up, we learn to protect ourselves emotionally by repressing or suppressing feelings. We do so to be able to survive our environment. Our feelings do not disappear, however; they live in our unconscious, unavailable to us, and sometimes are expressed in our bodies as a remnant of infancy. Childhood trauma can still manifest in our bodies long after it has ended.[25] We are taught by Rabbi Sholom Rokeach of Beltz, "There are three types of exile and they are of increasing severity. The first is when Jews are in exile among other nations, the second is when Jews are in exile among fellow Jews, and the third and most severe is when a Jew is alien to himself—for then he is both captor and captive, in exile within himself."[26] Behaving in ways we do not understand usually occurs because we have no access to the feelings behind our behavior. We are in exile from ourselves.

How, then, do we gain access to what we feel? It is almost impossible to do it ourselves. We need help. Both Jewish and psychoanalytic thinkers believe in the value of telling our story in the context of a relationship. We might frame this as the oral tradition of both Judaism and psychoanalysis. The Torah tells us that the answer lies not in the heavens but in our hearts and mouths (Deuteronomy 30:12–14). The Hebrew word *Haggadah* literally means "telling"; we are to retell our story and relive the emotional journey of our ancestors as we share our Passover seders. Our liturgy reminds us every day that the world was created out of speaking: *Baruch she-amar v'hayah haolam*, "Blessed is the One who spoke the world into being."[27] When we speak in the right context, we call our own emotional worlds into being. The very telling of one's story to another person is what allows our deeper feelings to surface. In the same vein, the Talmud relates a story about a time when Rabbi Chiya bar Abba was sick:

His teacher Rabbi Yochanan went to visit him and said to him, "Are your sufferings dear to you?" Rabbi Chiya replied, "Not them and not their reward." Rabbi Yochanan said, "Give me your hand." He gave him his hand, and he stood him up and restored him to health. Similarly, when Rabbi Yochanan was sick, Rabbi Chanina went to visit him and asked, "Is your suffering dear to you?" He replied, "Not them and not their reward." Rabbi Chanina said, "Give me your hand." He gave him his hand and he stood him up. The Gemara asks: Why did Rabbi Yochanan wait for Rabbi Chanina to restore him to health? The Gemara answers: A prisoner cannot free themself from prison but depends on others to release them from their shackles. (Babylonian Talmud, *B'rachot* 5b)

There are things we as human beings cannot do alone; we rely on others for our emotional well-being. The philosopher Martin Buber speaks of an I-Thou relationship in which two people are fully emotionally present to each other.[28] He came to his thinking in part as a result of a meeting with "a young man who had come to him for advice. Buber recalled being less than fully attentive to the young man's 'unasked question': whether he should enlist. When the young man did enlist and was killed at the front, Buber took his death as a thunderous judgment."[29] Buber believed that the self is found in relationship to others. He spent the rest of his life trying to be fully present in his relationships.

Another frame for feelings from within Jewish tradition lies in how we understand the heart. In our culture, when we see a heart, we automatically think "love." The heart represents more than love in Jewish tradition. It encompasses both emotions and thought. "In Jewish tradition the heart is also the seat of all emotions. There is a midrash that lists over sixty emotions of the heart. Among these emotions: 'the heart sees, hears, speaks, falls, stands, rejoices, weeps, comforts, sorrows . . .' (Ecclesiastes *Rabbah* 1:16). In Judaism, our hearts are the vessels of both our feelings and our wisdom."[30] The heart was the seat of wisdom; as the Psalmist wrote, "Teach us to number our days that we may attain a heart of wisdom" (Psalm 90:12).

There is also a relationship between our hearts and the hearts of others. Empathy is a fundamental Jewish value. Empathy does not require having the same feelings as someone else; rather, out of our first knowing what we feel, we come to appreciate what the other person is feeling. The reminder that we were slaves in Egypt undergirds Jewish tradition. Every year at Passover seder, we not only recite but relive the words, "In every age and generation, the task is ours: To see ourselves as if we had come out of Egypt." If we can reexperience the pain of slavery, we can empathize with others who are enslaved. Our particular Jewish experience allows us a universal empathy with those who have yearned for freedom. Relating with empathy can matter even more than study. A story is told of Rabbi Shneur Zalman of Liadi, who was once studying upstairs in his son's home. On the floor below, his grandchild slept while his son studied nearby. The baby started crying, but the son—seated only a few feet away from the crib—was so involved with his study that he did not hear his own child crying. Shneur Zalman of Liadi descended the stairs, calmed the baby, then sternly addressed his son by reminding him that one cannot reach the holy if one cannot hear the cry of a baby.[31] There are times when we are called to choose between the heart and the head.

At times, our feelings overwhelm us. In those moments, we require the emotional resilience that comes as a result of having all our feelings. Resilience is a tool that can help us adapt to difficult situations. Although each generation faces its own challenges, we know that our ancestors felt overwhelmed at times by their unique circumstances. Where they might have been immobilized by feelings, there were times when some among them managed to think clearly. In Jewish history, for example, we know that the destruction of the Second Temple was devastating and overwhelming. It was the greatest of national tragedies, a stressor beyond all stressors. When all seemed hopeless, Yochanan ben Zakkai was smuggled out of Jerusalem in a coffin so he could ultimately establish a center of learning in Yavneh (Babylonian Talmud, *Gittin* 56a–b). Despite the emotional devastation we can assume he experienced, he was able to adapt to circumstances and construct a new model of Judaism. In his system, study replaced sacrifice, the home replaced the Temple, and the individual became a priest in their own home. This resilient approach allowed the Jewish people to survive sure destruction. As an heir to Ben Zakkai, Rabbi Abraham Joshua Heschel reminds us, "We as a community are committed to the principle that learning is our daily bread, compassion is the essential sign of becoming human. We are a community that maintains that a table in the home is an altar, that we must start each day with an act of celebration, that the conclusion of each day is a moment of self-examination."[32]

Every generation experiences its own overwhelming stressful moments. When human beings are under stress, we tend to regress back to childhood times when we experienced deep emotions. The feelings reawakened in us can be so intense that they lead us to regressive behaviors. As I write, we live in the shadow of an ongoing war in Gaza. In the United States, I have been struck by the level of reactivity to the October 7 violence by Hamas against Israel and the subsequent retaliation by Israel in Gaza. I know of one person who refuses to set foot in a synagogue that has an Israeli flag on the bimah. I know of one rabbi who was fired for being too Zionist and another who was fired for not being Zionist enough. Some members of synagogues feel personally rejected if their synagogue's official position on the conflict does not match their own. Others quit the synagogue if they feel that their personal position is not shared by fellow members. The emotional power of this moment has led people to a regressive behavior: I cannot be seen or understood unless my feelings are reflected in yours. When we want people to read our minds, we are reliving an intrapsychic return to those early moments of life when our every need felt anticipated. "Before I formed thee in the belly, I knew thee," says God to Jeremiah (Jeremiah 1:5).[33] God knew our needs before we were born without our ever needing to speak them aloud, but human beings do not read minds. Having our feelings can lead us to communicate our feelings directly; we stand a better chance of getting our needs met if we can speak our wishes.

It is easy to become overwhelmed by hopelessness and feel incapable of making a difference in the world. How do we develop boundaries that guard the self? In psychoanalytic circles, we would say we learn to mentalize, to develop "an awareness that thought and feelings are lodged internally in the mind and a capacity to think about and reflect upon one's thoughts and feelings and also to realize that others also have thoughts and feelings, beliefs and desires."[34] That way, we can relate to each other while respecting each other's differences. In a similar Jewish frame, we might turn again to *Pirkei Avot*: "They said: . . . Make a fence for the Torah" (1:1). Our tradition derives from a teaching of Rabbi Shimon ben Elazar that each person is a Torah (Babylonian Talmud, *Mo-eid Katan* 25a). We are allowed—perhaps even required—to make a fence around ourselves, to protect ourselves, as long as that protection remains porous and lets us live in the world. We are taught that every sanctuary must have a window so that even in our moments of deepest prayer, we do not forget the needs of the outside world (Babylonian Talmud, *B'rachot* 34b). And so we return to where we began, asking: What does it mean to be a human being? Adam Phillips expands our question by asking, "What do we depend on to make us feel alive or real? Where does our sense come from, when we have it, that our lives are worth living?"[35] The answer lies in the complexity of being human, of having feelings, of being uniquely emotionally different from one another and yet the same. The Mishnah teaches us, "If a human being stamps several coins with the same die, they all resemble one another. But the Ruler of rulers of rulers, the Holy One, praised be God, stamps all human beings with the die of the first human; and yet not one of them resembles the other. Therefore, every human individual is obliged to say: For my sake was the world created" (*Mishnah Sanhedrin* 4:5).

What does that mean, to believe that the world was created for my sake? Listen again to the words of Rabbi Yechiel Michal of Zloczov, as quoted by Martin Buber: "Every person should know and consider the fact that you, in the particular way that you are made, are unique in the world, and no one like you has ever been. For if someone like you had already been, there would be no reason for you to be in this world. Actually, everyone is something new in this world, and here we must work to perfect our particular being, for because we are still imperfect, the coming of the Messiah is delayed!"[36]

Each of us is a whole world. Having our feelings does not just make us unique; having our feelings makes us whole. That human wholeness is as close to divine as we can get. Rachel Naomi Remen says, "We don't serve with our strength, we serve with ourselves. We draw from all our experiences: our wounds serve, our limitations serve, even our darkness serves. The wholeness in us serves the wholeness in the other, and the wholeness in life."[37] If we can have our feelings—the feelings that make each of us truly unique—then we can fulfill not just our personal mission on earth but also the prophetic mission of using our whole selves to serve others and bring peace to our world.

NOTES

1. "Religion is comparable to a childhood neurosis"; Sigmund Freud, *The Future of an Illusion*, in *The Standard Edition of the Complete Psychological Works of Sigmund Freud*, ed. and trans. James S. Strachey, vol. 21, 1927–31 (Hogarth Press and the Institute of Psychoanalysis, 1981), 53.
2. Modern psychoanalysis is one of many analytic schools that describes itself as heir to Freud.
3. Julie Beck, "Hard Feelings: Science's Struggle to Define Emotions," *Atlantic*, February 24, 2025. "It's been said that there are as many theories of emotions as

there are emotion theorists," says Joseph LeDoux, a professor of neuroscience and the director of the Emotional Brain Institute and the Nathan Kline Institute for Psychiatric Research at New York University. There is an entire field devoted to the study of emotions.
4. Theodor Reik, *Listening with the Third Ear: The Inner Experience of a Psychoanalyst* (Farrar, Straus & Giroux, 1983).
5. Rachel Adler, "The Jew Who Wasn't There: Halacha and the Jewish Woman," *Response: A Contemporary Jewish Review*, Summer 1973. Additional thanks to Rabbi Adler for her wise counsel and suggestions regarding the *yetzer*.
6. Rachel Adler, *Engendering Judaism: An Inclusive Theology and Ethics* (Beacon Press, 1999), 36.
7. Pauline Boss, *Loss, Trauma, and Resilience: Therapeutic Work with Ambiguous Loss* (W. W. Norton, 2006), 113.
8. Harry Stack Sullivan, *The Collected Works of Henry Stack Sullivan, M.D.*, vol. 2 (W. W. Norton, 1953), 26.
9. John Bowlby, quoted in Thomas M. Skovholt and Michelle Trotter-Mathison, *The Resilient Practitioner: Burnout Prevention and Self-Care Strategies for Counselors, Therapists, Teachers, and Health Professionals* (Routledge, 2011), 21.
10. Donald Winnicott, "The Theory of the Parent-Infant Relationship," *International Journal of Psychoanalysis* 41 (1960): 586.
11. James H. Kleiger, "Emerging from the 'Dark Night of the Soul': Healing the False Self in a Narcissistically Vulnerable Minister," *Psychoanalytic Psychology* 7, no. 2 (1990): 212. "The process by which the mother mirrors and remains empathically attuned to the whole range of her child's needs, moods, and fears has been recognized as the sine qua non for the development of a healthy sense of self (Kohut, 1977; Laing, 1960; Southwood, 1973; Winnicott, 1967/1971). Parental mirroring, which is congruent with the child's uniqueness, promotes integration of what Winnicott called the 'true self' (1960/1965), or what Kohut called the 'nuclear self' (1977). Winnicott eloquently described how the mother's mirroring gaze is the foundation of the infant's experience of himself or herself as real. Thus, by remaining empathic mirrors, parental caretakers reflect back and allow their children to perceive the totality of their own experience. Kohut (1971) introduced the concept of the *selfobject* to describe how children experience their mother's mirroring presence as an integral part of themselves."
12. Kleiger, "Emerging from the 'Dark Night of the Soul,'" 211.
13. *Sifrei* Deuteronomy, *Eikev*, 49, ed. M. Friedmann, cited in *The Torah: A Modern Commentary: Revised Edition*, ed. W. Gunther Plaut and David E. S. Stein (URJ Press, 2005), 35.
14. Maimonides, *Mishneh Torah*, Laws of Repentance 3:5. Translation by Moses Hyamson (1937–1949) (license: Public Domain), found on Sefaria (sefaria.org).
15. Ishay Rosen-Zvi, "Two Rabbinic Inclinations? Rethinking a Scholarly Dogma," *Journal for the Study of Judaism* 39 (2008): 513–39. There are those who claim there is only one *yetzer* and it is evil, others that there are two *y'tzarim* that are

either in dualistic competition with each other or in a more dialectical relationship. Some claim the *yetzer* was a demonic possession, rather than a feeling or inclination. These ideas are more complicated than our present endeavor allows.

16. Sigmund Freud, "Instincts and Their Vicissitudes (1915)," in *The Standard Edition of the Complete Psychological Works of Sigmund Freud*, ed. and trans, James S. Strachey, vol. 14, 1914–16 (Hogarth Press and the Institute of Psychoanalysis, 1981), 117–40. There has been much subsequent refinement and development of this theory, including contributions by the object relations school of psychoanalysis. This is not the place for evaluating these theories.
17. Jeffrey Spitzer, "The Birth of the Good Inclination," My Jewish Learning, https://www.myjewishlearning.com/article/the-birth-of-the-good-inclination.
18. Adapted from "Rabbi Pinchas of Koretz—Miscellaneous Teachings," as quoted in "A 'User's Guide' to Yetzer HaRah, Part 2," study sheet by Eric Gurvis on Sefaria, https://www.sefaria.org/sheets/26171?lang=bi.
19. Adapted from Jakob J. Petuchowski, *Our Masters Taught: Rabbinic Stories and Sayings* (Crossroad, 1982), 32.
20. Abraham J. Twerski, untitled and unrecorded lecture given at the Jewish Y in West Orange, NJ, in 1989.
21. David Derbyshire, "Gene Helps Jews Resist Alcoholism," *Telegraph*, September 17, 2002, https://www.telegraph.co.uk/news/science/science-news/3299335/Gene-helps-Jews-resist-alcoholism.html?msockid=14c4b1346b2a6fdd115ea5f96a0f6e98.
22. Abraham J. Twerski, *Living Each Day* (Mesorah, 1988), 69.
23. Rick Perlstein, "An Interview with 'Playboy' Magazine Nearly Torpedoed Jimmy Carter's Presidential Campaign," *Smithsonian Magazine*, August 17, 2020, https://www.smithsonianmag.com/history/interview-playboy-magazine-nearly-torpedoed-jimmy-carters-presidential-campaign-180975576/.
24. Israel Folklore Archive #126, quoted in Avi Solomon, "This Too Shall Pass: Tracing and Ancient Jewish Folktale," Medium, April 25, 2013, https://medium.com/learning-for-life/this-too-shall-pass-tracing-an-ancient-jewish-folktale-6f5a1aaa0a0e.
25. Bessel Van der Kolk, *The Body Keeps the Score: Brain, Mind, and Body in the Healing of Trauma* (Penguin Books, 2015).
26. Twerski, *Living Each Day*, 11.
27. *Mishkan T'filah: A Reform Siddur*, ed. Elyse D. Frishman (CCAR Press, 2007), 50.
28. Martin Buber, *I and Thou* (Simon and Schuster, 1970).
29. Patrick Jordan, "Martin Buber's Believing Humanism: A Life of Dialogue," *Commonweal*, June 8, 2020, https://www.commonwealmagazine.org/life-dialogue.
30. Barbara Binder Kadden, "An Understanding of the Heart—*Middah Binat HaLev*," Reform Judaism.org, https://reformjudaism.org/learning/sacred-texts/learn-about-middot/understanding-heart-middah-binat-halev.
31. Levi Cooper, "The Story of a Crying Child and the Evolution of Chabad," *Jerusalem Post*, April 9, 2023, https://www.jpost.com/judaism/article-738508.

32. Abraham Joshua Heschel, *Moral Grandeur and Spiritual Audacity: Essays*, ed. Susannah Heschel (Farrar, Straus and Giroux, 1996), 29.
33. Translation from *The Holy Scriptures: A New Translation* (Jewish Publication Society, 1917) (license: Public Domain), found on Sefaria (sefaria.org).
34. Phyllis Tyson, "Boundary Formation in Children: Normality and Pathology," in *Interpersonal Boundaries: Variations and Violations*, ed. Salman Akhtar (Jason Aronson, 2006), 19.
35. Adam Phillips, *Winnicott* (Harvard University Press, 2004), 5.
36. Martin Buber, *Hasidism and the Modern Man* (Humanities Press, 1988), 139–40.
37. Rachel Remen, "Helping, Fixing, Serving," Awakin.org, https://www.awakin.org/v2/read/view.php?tid=127.

PART II
Challenges from Beyond Us

CHAPTER 6

Your Mercies Extend Even to a Bird's Nest: The Animal-Human Relationship

Rabbi Alexandria Shuval-Weiner

THE SMITHSONIAN Museum of Natural History features an exhibit that explores a profound question: *What does it mean to be human?* People from around the globe contribute their thoughts, creating a tapestry of insights that range from the theological to the philosophical, the practical to the poetic. Within this dialogue, one perspective frames humanity as created *b'tzelem Elohim*, "in the image of God." This Biblical tradition situates humanity at the pinnacle of Creation, created on day six, the final act in God's process: "And God said, 'Let us make human beings in our image, after our likeness; and let them hold sway over the fish of the sea and the birds of the sky, over the beasts, over all the earth, over all that creeps upon the earth'" (Genesis 1:26). The thirteenth-century commentator Rabbi David Kimchi, known as Radak, explained, "Humanity was created last, as a sign that humans are the crown jewel of creation, to make clear that all the creatures who preceded humanity in the order in which they were created are to serve as making human life more pleasant."[1]

This statement implies a hierarchy of power and privilege. The Biblical Creation narrative in Genesis bestows humanity with dominion over the earth: "Fill the earth and tame it; hold sway over the fish of the sea and the birds of the sky, and over every animal that creeps on the earth" (Genesis 1:28). Indeed, Lord Rabbi Jonathan Sacks, the late chief rabbi of the United Kingdom and formidable twenty-first-century philosopher, expands on this in his essay "The Three Stages of Creation," in which he wrote, "In making [humans], God endowed one creature—the only one thus far known to science—with the capacity not merely to adapt to his environment, but to adapt his environment to him; to shape the world; to be active, not merely passive, in relation to the influences and circumstances that surround [them]."[2]

Unfortunately, this understanding has often led to a justification of humanity's right to exploit the natural world and all nonhuman species. From the earliest stages of human existence, people have relied on nature and animals for survival, using them for sustenance, clothing, and tools. Early humans hunted animals for meat and skins, eventually domesticating animals and developing agricultural practices for a more stable food supply. Over time, however, this relationship evolved from necessity to exploitation, with industrialization and large-scale agriculture leading to deforestation, habitat destruction, and factory farming. While we humans have always relied on and used nature, the scale and impact of this reliance and use has intensified, prompting ethical and environmental concerns about sustainability and the welfare of all nonhuman species on our planet. All of this has been justified as exercising "dominion" over the earth. The scale of harm being inflicted raises urgent moral questions.

As we look at the world today, one must beg the question: Do contemporary practices—particularly with industrialized farming—require of us a renewed assessment of humanity's place and responsibility? Is humanity fulfilling its limiting mandate as stewards of Creation, or have we distorted dominion into unchecked exploitation?

When considering the tension between dominion and stewardship, hierarchy and harmony, the question must be asked: What does it mean to be human in regard to our relationship with other living creatures? Is it possible that the view we have of ourselves is simply privilege taken by a stronger, more powerful species? Whether justified through theology, speciesism, or sheer entitlement, we must ask ourselves what responsibilities accompany this status: What of our moral consciousness, which obligates reducing suffering? Which choices needed for the ethical treatment of Creation and all sentient beings must we embrace?

The greatest gift—as well as the most fateful—God gave humanity is freedom of choice, for freedom to choose can be used or abused. It can lead to the highest heights or the lowest depths: to choose love or hate, compassion or cruelty, graciousness or violence. The entire drama of Torah flows from this point of departure. Judaism remains God's supreme call to humankind—with freedom and creativity on the one hand, and responsibility and restraint on the other—becoming God's partner in the work of Creation.[3]

Perhaps this is why animal suffering is a very grave prohibition in the Torah. In Biblical times, eating animals did not involve the same level of suffering, because factory farming did not exist. There was no cruelty in milk or egg production or from mass slaughter. The newborn calf would suckle and was not separated from its mother: "When an ox or a sheep or a goat is born, it shall stay seven days with its mother" (Leviticus 22:27). Jewish tradition has long emphasized that when meat is consumed, the practice of *sh'chitah* (ritual slaughter) must be carried out in a manner that is both compassionate and minimizes pain. As the well-known Hebrew National hot dog commercial famously states, "We answer to a higher authority." In today's world, the facts of slaughter, kosher or not, are far from compassionate.[4] The industrialization of the slaughterhouse, now referred to as "processing plants"—a term that serves to sanitize and obscure the realities of their operations—keeps the public distanced from and unaware of what happens behind closed doors. This reality was highlighted in Upton Sinclair's classic novel *The Jungle*, in which he described the conditions of the modern packing plant during the early twentieth century. "They worked with furious intensity, literally upon the run. . . . First there came the 'butcher,' to bleed them: this meant one swift stroke . . . and a stream of bright red was pouring out upon the floor. This floor was half an inch deep with blood."[5] Jonathan Safran Foer, author of *Eating Animals*, brings Sinclair's experience into the twenty-first century. He highlights the dissonance between humanity's self-perception as ethical stewards and the realities of industrial agriculture, with the essential message that the choices we make about food are fundamental to the way we see the world and to the way we understand our responsibilities in it.[6] As stewards of life, we have a responsibility to break down the walls of these processing plants—both literal and metaphorical. Only by confronting the hidden realities of animal suffering are we able to fulfill our duty to protect and preserve life with compassion and integrity.

Consider the life cycle of a hen in factory farming. The hens are confined to battery cages with no access to sunlight or earth, debeaked to prevent injury in overcrowded conditions, and manipulated to produce as many eggs as possible—almost one a day. These practices deplete their bodies, reducing their lifespans to a fraction of their natural term.[7] In addition, egg-producing factories consider male chicks as waste, so within minutes of their hatching they are sent to perish horrible deaths through asphyxiation, electrocution, or maceration. According to recent statistics from the Department of Food and Resource Economics of the University of Copenhagen, some seven billion male chicks worldwide are culled annually.[8]

Similarly, the dairy industry operates on a system of profound cruelty.

To ensure steady milk production, cows are forcibly impregnated and their calves are taken from them moments after birth. Female calves are housed in isolation in calf hutches and fed milk replacement until they can enter the same cycle of exploitation, while male calves are either slaughtered for veal at three to four months of life or killed immediately after birth as "by-products" of the dairy industry. These gentle animals are born not to live, but to die, so that humans can drink milk.

Since the time humans developed the capacity to control animals, we have done so. Today, annually we kill over one hundred million for recreational hunting and fishing, a similar number to satisfy our scientific curiosity, some fifty million for their fur, and tens of millions of cats and dogs because there are not enough homes for them.[9] And of course, we kill enormous numbers of animals so that we may consume them. According to some estimates, humans kill somewhere in excess of fifty billion land animals yearly to eat them, and it's a fair estimate that we kill a comparable number of fish.[10] Paradoxically, while our knowledge and understanding of animals and their mental and emotional capacities are unprecedented, so is our exploitation of them. In the dance we perform with animal products, we've perfected a set of mental gymnastics so intricate, so effortless, that we barely recognize the distance we have put between ourselves and the origins of our meals, our clothing, and most aspects of what and how we "consume." We've become masters of compartmentalization, of separating the food on our plates, the handbags we carry, and the shoes we walk in from the suffering they represent. The chicken nuggets in the bright plastic bag at the supermarket help us not see a being with feathers and life in its eyes with the capacity to fear. Instead, it's a neatly packaged, sterilized product, devoid of any trace of its origins in a living being. We train our minds to disassociate, to forget that the steak on the grill was once a beautiful living creature, to banish the image of a cow's eyes from our thoughts, to let the sound of its suffering fade into the background. We tell ourselves these are just "food" or "products" or "luxury items" with a series of mental and emotional dissociations that have little to do with the messy, uncomfortably real fact that, at some point, a living being had to die to provide us with these conveniences. It's a kind of willful blindness, a refusal to acknowledge the cruelty we're complicit in, until the truth forces its way through, making us squirm, if only for a moment, before we shove it back into the recesses of our minds.

In addition to the mental gymnastics required for consuming animals, humans often demonstrate selective concern for certain animals, such as dogs, while overlooking the welfare of others, like pigs, despite their comparable cognitive abilities and emotional capacities. This inconsistency is influenced by cultural norms, traditions, and personal experiences that dictate how we categorize animals as companions, food, or wildlife. Acknowledging this bias challenges us to critically reassess our ethical obligations and to extend compassion to all sentient beings, irrespective of societal classifications.

Moreover, the ethical challenge of stewardship extends beyond simply the consumption of animals for food; it encompasses all forms of animal exploitation. The 2005 documentary *Earthlings* highlighted this issue, exposing the widespread mistreatment of animals across various industries. As the film notes, "Most of us were raised eating meat, wearing leather, and visiting circuses and zoos. Many of us purchased our cherished pets from pet stores and kept beautiful birds in cages. We wore wool and silk, savored fast food burgers, and went fishing, rarely pausing to consider the impact of these choices on the animals or the environment."[11]

As early as Biblical times, religious and philosophical scholars opined on the negative impact that humans had on animals and the natural world. While in the ancient world animals were understood as lower forms of Creation, several of the mitzvot—specifically, those relating to constraint—provided ways to limit suffering and ensure ethical conduct by regulating humanity's use of animals and protection of the resources of the natural world. These mitzvot are a reflection of human responsibility toward the stewardship of Creation. Examples include the prohibition against muzzling an ox while it treads grain (Deuteronomy 25:4), the commandment to allow animals to rest on Shabbat (Exodus 20:10), and the instruction to chase away a mother bird before taking her eggs or young offspring (Deuteronomy 22:6–7). Another example is that if we see the donkey of an enemy fallen down under its load, we may not ignore the animal's suffering on account of a bad relationship with its owner; instead, we are commanded to help unburden the donkey's load (Exodus 23:5). In addition, there is the Biblical injunction mentioned above against separating a calf from its mother (Leviticus 22:27) and the commandment that we cannot boil a kid in its mother's milk (Exodus 23:19; Exodus 34:26; Deuteronomy 14:21). (It could be argued that killing calves at the expense of extracting milk from their mothers, as is done in dairy factories, goes against this injunction of boiling a kid in its mother's milk; while not literal, it is not a stretch to see that this mitzvah applies in the dairy industry, which sacrifices the young for its mother's continued milk production solely for economic gain.)

Another powerful commandment from the Torah charges us: *K'doshim tih'yu*, "You shall be holy" (Leviticus 19:2). This commandment calls us to embody the highest form of humanity, one that is reflected not just in our interactions with each other, but in our treatment of the natural world. This is a call not just to personal righteousness, but to a profound ethical responsibility to ensure that our actions reflect the sanctity of all life. To be holy is to recognize that every living being, every creature that shares this earth with us, deserves dignity and respect.

These Biblical commandments are expanded in Rabbinic literature. The Talmud discusses the concept of *tzaar baalei chayim*, the prohibition against causing unnecessary suffering to animals. A poignant story is told about Rabbi Y'hudah HaNasi, one of the great sages of the Talmud, and the tradition's strong stance on compassion toward the suffering of animals. Rabbi Y'hudah was once traveling, and as he passed a field, he saw a calf being led to slaughter. The calf, understanding its fate, began to cry and struggle, breaking away. It ran toward Rabbi Y'hudah, laying its head upon him, with eyes pleading for mercy. Rabbi Y'hudah callously rebuffed the calf, stating, "For this you were created." For years following this incident Rabbi Y'hudah suffered from terrible pain and was only healed many years later, after he convinced a maidservant in his home not to harm the small rodents she discovered in the house (Babylonian Talmud, *Bava M'tzia* 85a). The tradition is sending clear messages: Rabbi Y'hudah was wrong in his callousness toward the pleading calf; animals were created not simply for human use; the slaughterhouse is not the animal's ultimate destiny. Rabbi Y'hudah's eventual responses of compassion and mercy are so profound that his story became a lesson about the importance of sparing animals unnecessary suffering and an example of true *t'shuvah* (repentance, return). As we are taught, "Divine mercy is upon all God's works" (Psalm 145:9).[12]

In another Rabbinic source, a midrash on Ecclesiastes, we are taught: "When the Blessed Holy One created the first human, God took them and led them round all the trees of the Garden of Eden and said to them: 'Look at My works, how beautiful and praiseworthy they are! . . . And all that I have created, it was for you that I created it. Pay attention that you do not corrupt and destroy My world; if you corrupt it, there is no one to repair it after you'" (*Kohelet Rabbah* 7:13).[13] This midrash is used to reflect on a related mitzvah, *bal tashchit*, the ethical principle that prohibits unnecessary destruction or waste of natural resources. While humanity was blessed with free choice, we do not have unrestricted freedom to misuse Creation. We are warned against wasteful, exploitative practices, reminding us that all of Creation—the animals, the earth, and its resources—are gifts from God to be used wisely and justly. In contrast to this principle, animal agriculture today is the leading cause of species extinction, habitat destruction, and ocean dead zones. Animal agribusiness already occupies about 40 percent of earth's landmass and accounts for 75 percent of global deforestation. Rapid destruction is causing species to disappear, negatively impacting the biodiversity of native ecosystems.[14]

Later, the sixteenth-century volume *Shulchan Aruch*, the ultimate code of Jewish law, explains that humans have a responsibility to prioritize the welfare of Creation over satisfying one's own personal needs.[15] This is based in part on the Biblical mitzvah of *shiluach hakein* (Deuteronomy 22:6–7), which teaches that if a bird's nest contains fledglings or eggs and the mother is sitting in the nest, you shall "not take the mother together with her young. Let the mother go, take only the young, in order that you may fare well and have a long life." From this, the Rabbis teach, "Your mercies extend even to a bird's nest" (*Mishnah M'gillah* 4:9).[16] The instruction not to take both the mother and her young and to shoo the mother away to keep her from torment is—according to our sages like Maimonides, the thirteenth-century rabbi, philosopher, and halachist—our tradition's attempt to develop in humanity the positive character traits of empathy and compassion toward God's Creation. By considering the emotional stress on the mother bird, we have the opportunity to become kinder humans from the experience.[17] Centuries later in 1985, Pinchas Peli, a twentieth-century Israeli modern Orthodox rabbi, wrote, "The death of a creature of God cannot be taken lightly and we must not treat any living thing callously, for we are responsible for what happens to other beings, human or animal."[18]

Indeed, one of the noblest traits of our human nature is our ability to sacrifice our needs for the well-being of others and to recognize injustices and correct them. This trait is part of the foundation for the powerful concept of *tikkun olam*, the repairing of broken places in the world. It is the moral imperative of our religion. Every time we choose to exploit or eat or use an animal product, we are making a moral choice. The system of kashrut must be seen as more than simply "fit" or "permissible"—based on the translation of the Hebrew word *kasheir* (kosher)—but also about how the animal is treated, how the land is impacted, how workers are treated, and how our health is affected.

Taken as a whole, these Biblical laws, Rabbinic stories, and Jewish legal and moral concepts recognize the sentience and suffering of animals, embedding compassion into the fabric of Jewish ethics from ancient times through today. Contemporary thinkers and scientists affirm the reality that animals have sentience and the ability to suffer. British biologist John Webster stated in his writings that "people have assumed that intelligence is linked to the ability to suffer and that because animals have smaller brains, they suffer less than humans. That is a pathetic piece of logic; sentient animals have the capacity to experience pleasure and are motivated to seek [it. One] only [has] to watch how cows and lambs both seek and enjoy pleasure when they lie with their heads raised to the sun on a perfect English summer's [day, just] like humans."[19] In addition, animal psychologists Lori Marino and Kristin Allen reinforced the scientific understanding that cows are highly intelligent and sensitive creatures, with complex emotions and high social and cognitive functioning. In their 2017 report entitled "The Psychology of Cows," they emphasize the significant distress cows undergo when their calves are taken away from them. This separation causes emotional and psychological stress and grief, manifesting in behaviors such as extreme vocalizing, pacing, and tears.[20] Additionally, when taken to slaughter, the overwhelming smell of death and the frantic bellowing of other animals in distress intensify the emotional turmoil. All this further heightens the fear and anxiety of the animals, amplifying their suffering in the final moments of their lives. Ethologist and animal behaviorist Dr. Marc Bekoff has written extensively on the emotional lives of animals and advocates strongly for recognizing animals as sentient beings capable of these complex emotions, with some instances of witnessing tears in the eyes of animals, particularly in moments of intense stress or fear.[21]

Why should animals matter? The singular reason is that they are sentient. Animals, like us, have the capacity to feel pain and pleasure and to suffer. We may quibble about where we draw the line on sentience, and we may struggle to imagine what it is like to be a bat or a minnow, but there remains no reasonable scientific doubt that all members of the vertebrate subphylum, as a minimum, are equipped to experience good and bad feelings.[22]

In November 2024, at Kobe Suma Sea World in Japan, an eighteen-year-old orca named Ran II became stranded on a concrete slide-out for over an hour.[23] Despite the visible distress of the animals, visitors, and trainers, the Sea World staff appeared unsure of how to assist. Ran's mother, Stella, refused to leave her daughter's side throughout the ordeal. Vocalizing to the ineffective trainers, Stella eventually gave up and focused her efforts on her offspring. The two orcas communicated through vocalizations until Stella, displaying remarkable determination, launched herself onto the concrete slide and began the challenging task of moving Ran. Thanks to Stella's persistence and strength, she successfully pushed Ran back into the water, saving her life.

A few years ago, news media shared a story of Roscoe, a three-year-old orangutan living in an animal sanctuary, that demonstrated the depth of emotional connections animals can form. After losing his parents, Roscoe grieved so profoundly that his caretakers feared he might die of a broken heart. His sorrow seemed insurmountable, until Suryia, an aging stray dog, arrived at the sanctuary. Against all odds, the two discovered one another and formed an extraordinary bond. Their companionship brought Roscoe back to life, filling the void left by his loss. Since then, the orangutan and the dog have been inseparable, their story serving as a powerful reminder of the emotional complexity of nonhuman animals.[24]

The capacity for animals to feel pain, both physical and psychological, demands our moral consideration. The grieving cry of a mother cow separated from her calf or the relentless circling of a confined orca bears witness to sentience and suffering. Because animals are sentient, autonomous individuals with their own feelings, experiences, and minds, their lives hold moral significance. The ability to experience pleasure and pain grants their lives intrinsic value—value that exists independently of any commercial or utilitarian considerations we may impose. However, the current paradigm in our relationship with animals is not informed by our Biblical or modern understanding of their capacities. We continue to place animals outside the circle of moral consideration, failing to recognize their inherent worth. When the fact of animal sentience and experience of suffering is paired with Judaism's teachings about animal welfare, we cannot help but remember the call: "In a place where there is no humanity, strive to be human" (*Pirkei Avot* 2:6).

Peter Singer and Yuval Noah Harari, in *Animal Liberation Now* and *Sapiens* respectively, both challenge the worldview that justifies the cruelty inflicted upon animals.[25] They argue that moral consideration must be extended to all sentient beings, critiquing the notion of humans as the "crown of Creation." They maintain that such thinking perpetuates a hierarchy that diminishes the value of nonhuman life and contributes to the commodification of animals. Both authors call for humanity to adopt practices that honor the inherent sanctity of all life. In his book *Sapiens*, Harari explores how human activities have reshaped ecosystems and driven countless species to extinction, often with devastating consequences for global ecological balance. Both writers warn against the hubris that accompanies humanity's self-assumed superiority.

Our unparalleled power as humans demands equally unparalleled responsibility. If we are to be exceptional, it must be through our capacity to protect and sustain the intricate web of life that surrounds us. As people of faith, our religious vision must be rooted in the ideal of the "crown of Creation," guiding and inspiring us toward a higher purpose. The question of what it means to be human, when not defined by sentience or emotions, invites us to reconsider humanity beyond just feelings or consciousness. In this view, being human might be about the capacity for moral choice, ethical responsibility, and our ability to care for others, whether human or not. Our humanity could be found in how we act toward others, especially those who cannot advocate for themselves, and in our willingness to make decisions that reflect compassion and justice. It is about transcending mere survival or instinct and choosing to act with integrity, empathy, and respect for all living beings.

When it comes to animals, behaving humanely means treating them with dignity and respect, regardless of their ability to feel or think in the way humans do. Even without shared emotions or sentience, animals deserve protection from unnecessary harm. Humane treatment involves adopting ethical practices in how we interact with animals, whether that's through supporting sustainable farming, advocating for laws that protect animal welfare, or making lifestyle choices that reduce their suffering. It also involves recognizing the intrinsic value of all creatures, appreciating them not for their utility but for their existence, and acting in ways that honor their place in the world.

The teaching from *Pirkei Avot* 2:6 challenges us: In a world that may often feel inhumane, strive to be a better human. In times of cruelty or indifference, we are called to rise above and embody the highest ideals of humanity—compassion, justice, and moral clarity. Even when the world around us may seem void of these values, striving to be human means acting with integrity and standing firm in our commitment to kindness and fairness. This must extend not only to our fellow humans but to all of Creation—to animals and the environment. Ultimately, our humanity is defined not just by what we feel but by what we choose to do in the face of suffering and injustice.

The spiritual, ethical consciousness of all aspects of Creation—what we eat, wear, use for entertainment, use for experimentation, choose to protect or not—is in our hands. Will we continue to exploit and dominate, or will we embrace our role as stewards? We humans have a significant moral obligation to stop objectifying Creation and instead to become more intentional about appropriate ethical decisions regarding animal welfare and the environment, acting as responsible stewards of the planet and its inhabitants. For those who take seriously the religious and ethical imperative to care for the nonhuman world, the question is not simply *what should we believe*, but *how should we act*. One of the most accessible yet meaningful ways to align daily habits with these values is through conscious consumption—choosing to reduce harm in what we eat and what we buy.

A simple yet powerful practice one might adopt is Meatless Mondays.[26] Setting aside just one day a week to abstain from meat is an intentional act of compassion and environmental responsibility. It allows one to explore plant-based meals while lowering one's ecological footprint, reducing the suffering of animals, and honoring religious ethical principles of *tzaar baalei chayim* and *bal tashchit*. Similarly, refraining from purchasing materials made from animals—such as leather, fur, or wool—offers another way to exercise moral and religious consciousness in daily life. The shift does not have to be immediate or absolute; even a gradual transition, like choosing alternative materials for shoes, bags, or jackets, signals an awareness of the hidden suffering behind these products. With sustainable and ethical alternatives more widely available than ever, it is increasingly possible to make purchasing decisions that reflect a commitment to kindness and care for Creation.

More than just personal choices, these practices can serve as a form of spiritual activism. They become opportunities to educate and engage with family, friends, and even our religious communities. Imagine a synagogue that not only keeps a kosher or kosher-style kitchen but also encourages a Default Veg[27] practice in its gatherings, or a religious school program that teaches students about sustainable and ethical fashion. By framing consumption within a religious and moral context, it becomes not just contemporary lifestyle choices but expressions of timeless values: those of compassion, humility, stewardship, and reverence for the sanctity of all life, human and nonhuman alike. In an age where the impact we have on the natural world is more consequential than ever, even the smallest acts of compassion and responsibility become part of a larger movement toward justice, holiness, and repair.

In light of the profound responsibility that accompanies our exceptional capacity as humans, it is imperative that we embrace our role as guardians of all life. Our power should be wielded not in ways that diminish the world around us, but rather in ways that nurture, sustain, and protect it. As persons of faith, we are called to live by the teachings that challenge us to act with reverence toward all Creation.

Our relationship with the animal world reveals the depth of our humanity. The way we treat animals speaks volumes about our values, and the current practices of exploitation and consumption too often mirror the dehumanizing processes that have historically been used to justify the mistreatment of marginalized groups. The act of "othering" animals and reducing them to mere commodities mirrors the ways in which humans have historically been dehumanized. The twentieth-century Yiddish writer Isaac Bashevis Singer highlighted this in his book *Enemies: A Love Story*. He wrote of humanity's brutality and indifference against the animal world. His protagonist, Herman Broder, a survivor of the Holocaust, articulates this complexity of the human condition: "As often as Herman had witnessed the slaughter of animals and fish, he always had the same thought: in their behavior towards creatures, all men were Nazis. The smugness with which man could do with other species as he pleased exemplified the most extreme racist theories, the principle that might is right."[28] To be truly human is to acknowledge that we are no different from the animals we often exploit. We are all interconnected, and the suffering we inflict upon one part of the living world reverberates throughout the entire system of life. Therefore, the responsibility we carry is not only to protect the environment but to live in a way that honors every living being, as they too are part of the intricate, sacred web that binds us all together.

In this light, our humanity, our very place in the spectrum of Creation, is defined not by the power we possess, but by how we choose to use that power—how we respect, protect, and nurture all life around us, understanding that our fates are interwoven with theirs. True holiness, true excellence, lies in how we treat the world, for in caring for the world, we affirm our own humanity.

Notes

1. Translation of Radak from Eliyahu Munk, *HaChut HaMeshulash*, with revisions made by Sefaria (license: CC-BY, https://creativecommons.org/licenses/by/3.0/), found on Sefaria (sefaria.org).
2. Jonathan Sacks, "The Three Stages of Creation," Jonathan Sacks: The Rabbi Sacks Legacy, October 2018, https://rabbisacks.org/covenant-conversation/bereishit/why-were-we-created/.
3. Jonathan Sacks, *Covenant and Conversation: Genesis* (Maggid, 2021).
4. Renee Ghert-Zand, "Does Hebrew National 'Answer to a Higher Authority'?" *Forward*, June 20, 2012, https://forward.com/food/158138/does-hebrew-national-answer-to-a-higher-authority/.
5. Upton Sinclair, *The Jungle* (Doubleday, Page, 1906), 40.
6. Jonathan Safran Foer, *Eating Animals* (Penguin Books, 2010).
7. Jennifer Barckley, "Egg Production Facts and Stats: How Eggs End Up on Our Plates," The Human League, March 29, 2021, https://thehumaneleague.org/article/egg-production.
8. "Researcher: Seven Billion Newly Hatched Chicks Are Killed Every Year—But a Ban Is Not the Solution," University of Copenhagen, Faculty of Science, March 21, 2024, https://science.ku.dk/english/press/news/2024/researcher-seven-billion-newly-hatched-chicks-are-killed-every-year--but-a-ban-is-not-the-solution/.
9. Max Roser, "How Many Animals Get Slaughtered Every Day?," Our World in Data, September 26, 2023, https://ourworldindata.org/how-many-animals-get-slaughtered-every-day.
10. Hannah Ritchie, "How Many Animals Are Factory-Farmed?," Our World in Data, first published September 2023 and updated November 2024, https://ourworldindata.org/how-many-animals-are-factory-farmed.
11. *Earthlings*, directed by Shaun Monson (2005).
12. Translation from *The JPS Tanakh: Gender Sensitive Edition* (Jewish Publication Society, 2023) (license: CC-BY-SA, https://creativecommons.org/licenses/by-sa/3.0/), found on Sefaria (sefaria.org).
13. Translation adapted from Sefaria Community Translation (license: COO, https://creativecommons.org/publicdomain/zero/1.0/), found on Sefaria (sefaria.com). Adapted.

14. "Animal Agriculture Causing Extinctions," Earth and Animal Facts A–Z, November 24, 2024, https://www.earthandanimals.com/advocate/farm-animals/params/post/1280000/animal-agriculture-causing-extinctions.
15. *Shulchan Aruch, Yoreh Dei-ah* 232:1.
16. Translation by the author.
17. Maimonides, *Moreh N'vuchim* (*Guide for the Perplexed*) 3:48.
18. Pinchas Peli, "Why Kashrut?," *International Jerusalem Post*, April 20, 1985.
19. John Webster, "Animal Sentience and Animal Welfare: What Is It to Them and What Is It to Us?," *Applied Animal Behaviour Science* 100, nos. 1–2 (October 2006): 1–3, https://doi.org/10.1016/j.applanim.2006.05.012.
20. Lori Marino and Kristin Allen, "The Psychology of Cows," *Animal Behavior and Cognition* 4, no. 4 (2017): 474–98, https://dx.doi.org/10.26451/abc.04.04.06.2017.
21. Marc Bekoff, *The Emotional Lives of Animals: A Leading Scientist Explores Animal Joy, Sorrow, and Empathy—and Why They Matter* (New World Library, 2008).
22. Jonathan Balcombe, "Lessons from Animal Sentience: Towards a New Humanity," *Chautauqua Journal* 1, (2016): article 5, https://encompass.eku.edu/tcj/vol1/iss1/5.
23. Tim Burns of the Dolphin Project, email message to author, April 9, 2025. Sea World filmed the incident and is on record that Ran II was on the platform stranded on her back with no assistance, until her mother Stella slid on to the platform to assist her daughter.
24. "Animal Odd Couple: Orangutan and Dog are Best Buds," *ABC* News, May 14, 2009, https://abcnews.go.com/Technology/AmazingAnimals/story?id=7590279&page=1.
25. Peter Singer, *Animal Liberation Now: The Definitive Class Renewed* (Diversion Books, 2023); and Yuval Noah Harari, *Sapiens: A Brief History of Humankind* (Harper, 2015).
26. For more information on the history and practice of Meatless Monday, visit https://meatlessmonday.publichealth.jhu.edu.
27. Default Veg is a program launched by Shamayim: Jewish Animal Advocacy and Center for Jewish Food Ethics with the goal of encouraging Jewish communities to adopt plant-based eating habits. The idea is to reduce the consumption of animal products and promote more ethical, sustainable, and compassionate choices in line with Jewish teachings on kindness, environmental stewardship, and animal welfare.
28. Isaac Bashevis Singer, *Enemies: A Love Story* (Farrar, Straus and Giroux, 1972), 257.

CHAPTER 7

Moving the Goalposts: Beyond the Beginning and End of Life

Rabbi Jonathan K. Crane, PhD

SHE GRASPED her adult son's forearm, comforting him. She understood but did not identify with his distress. There was little he could do to change the situation. His helplessness mirrored the impotence of the professionals ghosting in and out of the room, checking charts, whispering confirmations, and sharing perfunctory or heartfelt consolations.

She was done. She was exhausted from trying this or that supposedly miraculous intervention. Now beyond therapeutic improvement, even over the edge of palliative care's ability to mask her intractable pains, she was ready to stop.

Though there were still a few more methods that could keep her "alive," they would require sedating her until she lost awareness of the world around her.

Such an existence would be unconscionable to her.

He, by contrast, was not done. He could not comprehend that she was in this state of equanimity. Surely every moment of life—however tenuous or uncomfortable it might be—was of infinite value and warranted limitless effort. More! Different! Try it all, and then try the next.

Theirs is an increasingly familiar yet too frequently unspoken debate about QOL. For the one, "QOL" means *quantity of life*. This position presumes that since human life is of infinite value, every moment is too. Any and all interventions maximizing human existence are thus considered de facto good. On the other side of the bedside, "QOL" means *quality of life*. Without rejecting the claim that human life is of infinite value, this perspective asserts that there may be instances when that immeasurable value is and should be superseded by other concerns. What those concerns are will differ across people, populations, places, and periods. For this perspective, certain *qualities* of existence matter more than sheer *quantity* of a human life.

Such debates occur as well at life's beginnings. Consider the not-so-young couple who struggled for years to conceive. For reasons they could not fully explain, they yearned for a son. Frustrated and exhausted by the rounds of rigorous and invasive methods to procure gametes, they changed course to pursue surrogacy. In short order, an embryo caught the uterine wall and implanted. Tests and scans revealed that it was a girl. Relieved and excited that a baby—albeit a girl—would soon coo for them, the couple relaxed into each other's arms. Against all odds, their intimacy generated their own pregnancy. However, later scans and tests indicated that their embryo is intersex, meaning that it would be born with a mixture of male and female biological traits. Questions immediately swirled around them: Could they somehow ensure that this budding offspring would be a boy, if not while in utero then perhaps postpartum? Various technologies exist; why not use them to secure the wanted results? In this situation, the unsaid debate would have one side point to *b'tzelem Elohim*—the theological claim that humans are made in God's image—and argue that any and every human life is to be cherished, infinitely. In short, quantity of human life matters most. The other side disagrees: Only certain human life is desired, and those ends can justify the means.

Though the technologies involved in these not-so-hypothetical yet silent discussions may be new, such debates are ancient. Consider these two classic sources quietly exploring the QOL debate. The medieval midrash (circa thirteenth century) attends to questions at the end of life. The earlier source from the Jerusalem Talmud (circa fourth through sixth centuries) focuses on beginning-of-life issues, specifically the fertility challenges Rachel experiences with her husband, Jacob, whom she shares with her sister, Leah.

Yalkut Shimoni, *Proverbs* §943[1]
An elderly woman approached him with this complaint, "I have grown too old, and now my life is ugly. I can no longer taste food or drink. I request to be discharged from the world." He asked how she was able to live for so long. She informed him that even when she had other more desirable things to do, she would nonetheless go every day early to the assembly house. He instructed her to refrain from going to the assembly house for three consecutive days. She followed his direction and on the third day she grew ill and died.[2]

Jerusalem Talmud, B'rachot (Warsaw) 9:3[3]
Rav said in the name of the school of Yanai, regarding the gestation of Dinah—it [the embryo] used to be male, but after Rachel prayed, it was made female. Hence Scripture says, "Afterward she [Leah] bore a daughter and named her Dinah" (Genesis 30:21)—meaning, it was after Rachel prayed that it was made female.[4]

These sources demonstrate the early and ongoing debate about the existence of a conceptual category that we will call here *the category of the unwanted*. Admittedly, that such a category exists is uncomfortable. It suggests that in addition to acknowledging differences across the human condition (whatever that means), those differences are placed in a hierarchy, with some differences held in higher esteem than others. Ultimately, some differences of the human condition are disvalued, undesirable, unwanted.

Some people may go so far as to think there are conditions of human existence in this category of the unwanted that are unworthy of living. The German phrase *lebensunwurten leben* (lives unworthy of living) was first coined in 1920 by a doctor and a lawyer who argued that certain kinds of human existence are too burdensome on the individual and on society to warrant continuation.[5] According to their logic, people deemed "unworthy" by their set of criteria should be relieved of their very existence: They should die, even be killed. Such ideas circulated in the Weimar Republic (and elsewhere) for many years before going on to justify the insidious policies and practices of the Third Reich.

Instead of focusing on "lives unworthy of living" and what it spawned, here we dredge up from the depths a similar yet distinct notion that has its roots in classic Judaic sources. Like the modern German phrase, this ancient Jewish one also considers the existence of some forms of human life that are too _____ to live. Though it appears in Jewish sources in different forms, it is the phrase *chayim einam chayim*, meaning "life that is not life." Be assured from the outset: This Jewish category of the unwanted does not come close to advocating causing harm to any member of this category. It is never used to justify killing someone. Thus, our curiosity here turns to understanding the different criteria ancient Judaic sources suggest as possibilities for inclusion into this category of the unwanted.

As we shall see, there are two major schools of thought weighing in on this QOL debate. One school points to material features of the human condition, while the other focuses on temperamental aspects. These disagreements do not come from nowhere; they expand on the divine observation that there are some forms of human existence that are undesirable. Regarding the primordial human made and placed in the Garden of Eden, God said, "It is not good for a person to be alone" (Genesis 2:18). This means that even God operates with a conceptual category of the unwanted, and the first—if not primary—criteria to be included therein is aloneness (whatever that means). God has a concern about unwanted life; what are human ideas about it? Perhaps by understanding how this category appears in classic Jewish sources, we can enrich contemporary discussions regarding the goalposts of life and the QOL that matter most to us.

Material Criteria

The earliest mention of *chayim einam chayim* is found in the Babylonian Talmud (circa fifth through sixth centuries): "The Sages taught, there are three whose lives are not lives, and they are as follows: one who looks to the table of his friend; one whose wife rules over him; one whose suffering rules his body. And some say one who has but one cloak. The first *Tanna* [an early sage] [disagreed]: It is possible to examine his clothes" (Babylonian Talmud, *Beitzah* 32b). Four criteria are hereby posited as reasons for inclusion in the category of lives that are not lives. The first criterion refers to those who look to others for sustenance, or what we will call food insecurity. The second speaks in conventional androcentric terms about what Rabbi Yosef Chayim (nineteenth-century Baghdad) would have us understand as relationships that are controlling, abusive, and violent; we will call such circumstances here social insecurity.[6] The third criterion introduces bodily ailments, or what we will call biological debilitation. The fourth refers not to problems of fashion but to limited resources, or what we will call economic insufficiency.

The Talmud records a disagreement about the last criterion, economic insufficiency. Commentators on the Talmud explain the cryptic disagreement this way: It is possible for a person to examine clothes for contaminants like lice and dirt. On this view, good hygiene can mitigate or overcome the deprivations this type of economic insufficiency often poses.

Another early source supporting this view of the category is found in the midrashic collection *Avot D'Rabbi Natan*, from a few centuries after the Talmud (seventh through tenth centuries): "There are three whose lives are not lives. They are: one who looks to the table of his friend; one who lives in an attic; one whose wife rules over him; and some say: one whose suffering rules his body" (*Avot D'Rabbi Natan* 25:5). In addition to echoing the materialistic criteria of the Talmud, this source adds domicile seclusion. People residing in attics live where very little homelife happens, where visitations are few and far between, where darkness and dankness typically prevail. In many ways, people living in attics are socially and physically invisible. Today, many—too many—people live in such precarious circumstances, and the term commonly used to describe their situation is housing insecurity.

Classic Jewish sources thus offer us five possible criteria by which a life could be considered not a life:

- Food insecurity
- Social insecurity
- Biological debilitation
- Economic insufficiency
- Housing insecurity

Most of these conditions are socioeconomic in nature. They are external to individual persons, influenced by the ebb and flow of commerce, climate, and community. For the most part, these are contingent conditions, features of human existence that can and often do change. The concern here thus seems to hinge on whether a condition is lifelong.[7] If, say, severe food insecurity were a lifelong condition, then perhaps such a life could be considered not a life.

One of these criteria appears substantially different from the others—biological debilitation, which is internal rather than external to a person, though is often influenced by external circumstances. Like the other concerns, health fluctuates during a lifetime. Of course, some conditions are chronic or congenital, and if they are so undesirable, it could be understood to be reason enough to view a life as unwanted. This leads us to revisit the couple desiring a male child. It is plausible that their strong desire justifies to themselves pursuing gender assignment interventions, including a mixture of genetic, surgical, hormonal, and eventually social strategies in and on their intersex embryo. For this couple, quality of life matters most, and some qualities matter more than others.

Temperamental Criteria

A different school of thought about *chayim einam chayim* asserts that the category refers to features internal to persons. The first mention on this approach also comes from the Babylonian Talmud: "The Sages taught, there are three whose lives are not lives: the compassionate; the hot-tempered; the fastidious" (Babylonian Talmud, *P'sachim* 113b).

We can understand the first two bits of this terse teaching this way: Being too compassionate prioritizes others over oneself, and being too angry burns bridges. Such temperaments are not just counterproductive, they are potentially maladaptive. And what about fastidiousness? Rabbi Sh'lomo Yitzchaki (also known as Rashi, eleventh-century France) suggests that the fastidious cannot tolerate anything disgusting or unpleasant.[8] In short, they are easily disturbed or thrown off: Nothing would satisfy them.

Rashi's grandson, Rabbi Sh'muel ben Meir (Rashbam), explains that a life becomes no life when such traits are taken to their extremes and engaged in constantly.[9] And a few centuries after that, an anonymous author builds on both Rashi and Rashbam: "And this too, said the wise man: He whose anger and wrath are mighty is not too far away from the madness of insane ones. And he who is habitually angry, his life is no life, and he is never happy. And since he is never happy, he does not receive the various happenings that come to a person with love and with joy, nor does the Justice [of God] adjudicate for him, nor is he able to serve God joyously" (*Orchot Tzaddikim* 12:20).[10] According to this school of thought, a life becomes no life when one's maladaptive emotions become extreme and habitual. This all boils down to a single though difficult teaching: One's temperament—one's internal emotional compass—impacts one's overall well-being.

Like the materialist school, this temperamental one considers the category of *chayim einam chayim* in terms of quality of life. While experiencing equanimity and calm throughout one's life might be desired, it is to be expected that intense emotions on occasion will wash up, over, and through a person. Danger lurks, though, when such strong sentiments linger and fester.

Yet there may be conditions in which such strong emotions become inescapable. For instance, consider the woman whose condition no longer responds to therapeutic medicine, and palliative care would require sedating her into unconsciousness. In many ways, she has reached a form of existence that aligns with the materialist notion of a body ruled by suffering. It also would be understandable if she were to experience continuous strong frustration and anger, since nothing can be done to stabilize her and keep her awake and aware. The deterioration of her existence has crossed an internal threshold; her life is neither enjoyable nor tenable. Instead of feeling entrapped and persisting in such physical pain and emotional distress, she views her life as no life and wants out.

Considerations and Complications

I want to reiterate that there is a profound difference between a form of life that is *unwanted* and a life that is considered *unworthy*. Though the latter notion was used to justify horrendous policies and practices, the former—as far as I have read in Judaic sources—was never used to speak of the underlying value of a human life or call for that life's destruction. Consider, for instance, the teaching by Chayim Tyrer of Czernowitz in the late eighteenth century that "if a life is short, small, light, poor, and like being dead, it is no life."[11] This is not a prescription, but rather a description of circumstances that might make a life unwanted. It is thus important to acknowledge that even though *chayim einam chayim* sounds similar to *lebensunwurten leben*, these ideas are not commensurate.

Nevertheless, this category of the unwanted is helpful when thinking about the ever-shifting goalposts of life. The category spurs us to think carefully about when, where, and why we opt to pursue certain kinds of biotechnologies that meddle at life's goalposts.

At the beginning of life, consider the diverse and powerful tools that already exist and are being developed that shift not only *when* human life starts, but *what* qualifies as human life. Fertility treatments like donated gametes, in situ and in vitro fertilization, pre-pregnancy and perinatal care, and extracorporeal gestation or artificial womb technology improve the probability of completing gestation to live births. Such tools help humans embody the primordial blessing of procreation first articulated in Genesis 1:28.

Adding to humanity's power to bring about more human life are even more invasive interventions, like amniocentesis and CRISPr-CAS-9 technologies, which might be attractive to the couple with an intersex embryo. These, however, add a few twists to the conversation.

Genetic-based interventions pose an interesting challenge for us. Insofar as they enable people wanting offspring to fulfill that desire, these technologies can rightly be considered pronatalist: They help bring about human births. Simultaneously, these genetic-based technologies allow people—prospective parents, scientists, insurance companies, even politicians—to decide which forms of human existence shall come into being and which not. For them, some forms of human existence are considered too ____ to live. Viewed in this way, these technologies function as anti-natalist: They are tools preventing certain kinds of humans from coming into being at all.

A further complicating dimension of many genetic-based technologies is that the people who use them are often not the direct beneficiaries of those tools. These tools are used by adults to alter the genetic makeup of future generations. They change the very essence of our progeny, forging them closer to our dreamed ideal humans. Some of those ideals may be construed in positive hues. For example, maybe we want offspring genetically protected from certain diseases like HIV.[12] There is, of course, the danger of genetically modifying offspring to demote the prevalence of certain traits in the population and promote the prevalence of others. Such interventions are frequently supported by a consequentialist logic: The idealized ends justify the biotechnological means. Such efforts fall squarely into the larger and heated debate about eugenics, a debate we will not address further here.

At the other end of life are a suite of technologies that intervene in human declining, dying, and death. Some technologies forestall the end: They prolong a condition so that it becomes chronic (think statins or dialysis), or they offer internal assistance (left-valve assistance devices, or LVADs) or external assistance (extracorporeal membrane oxygenation machines, or ECMOs) for various vital functions. Some provide comfort (palliation); a few hasten demise (medical aid in dying, or MAiD—which can occur in hospitals, clinics, or homes). Such technologies thus move life's goalposts, their experiential shape, intensity, temporal and physical location.

Such end-of-life biotechnologies complicate thinking about QOL. For the quantitatively minded, at their best these technological interventions forestall the inevitable, since they can never "save" lives. They "give" "more" "time"—each of these terms is debatable. For some, this extra time may be socially important and theologically supported. That time may be reprehensible, however, to the qualitatively inclined. For these people, forestalling a death might prevent a welcome reprieve from medically unresponsive suffering, like the woman we met at the beginning of this chapter. Perhaps for someone else, their socioeconomic circumstance has become not just chronic but untenable, dangerous, maybe lethal. Because they cannot *live*, they need out.

All tools have this two-edged nature: They can be used to produce good as well as harm. For this reason, it is important for us to consider what tools we use and why we intend to use them. We need to think carefully about the expected outcomes no less than our motivations. This is particularly pressing when it comes to forms of life we consider too ____ to live. Regarding QOL, which matters more—quantity or quality of life?

An Invitation

Most people will grapple with QOL at some point in their lives. It might be when they are contending with procreation, their own or someone else's. Fertility difficulties are common, and the emotions these challenges generate are powerful and complex. Like the couple we met above, the myriad technologies that could be deployed can be no less dizzying and confusing. In such moments, it is wise to give critical thought to the QOL issues that really matter and why. At a quick glance, name the values that guide and support you. Then, more deeply, think about which values you *want* to guide and support you as you navigate these difficult decisions. What prevents or disrupts you from leaning more on those more foundational, subterranean commitments?

Others might confront QOL issues when life nears its end. This could be one's own or that of a loved one. Navigating end-of-life decisions is inevitable and never easy. Competing interests, divergent medical advice, and powerful emotions often complicate already tough circumstances. For that son whose mother is done, whose interests or notions about QOL should he champion—his own or hers? For him as for others, caregiving in a way that honors others' views is sometimes difficult and can spark anguish and even moral distress. And for those who consider quality of life to be of paramount concern, which qualities or criteria matter most or should matter most in this situation?

Such discussions can be fraught. Some people might use terms and arguments that sound foreign. For instance, I could advocate for using a certain kind of fertility treatment by invoking the bioethical principles of beneficence, autonomy, non-maleficence, and justice. My argument could falter, though, and fall flat because you think more in terms of rules and duties, or what is called deontology. Maybe someone else chimes in to say that the virtue of compassion should guide our thinking, while another person speaks up in favor of consequentialism—the ends justify the means.

Or say we are discussing how to care for a dying beloved family member. You might think that life is infinitely precious and maximizing its quantity must be done regardless of any other concern. I might assert that the quality of existence must also be taken into consideration and that, say, our loved one's inability to perform the activities of daily life (showering, dressing, walking, toileting, eating, and so on) is anathema to her. Her life is unwanted to her. You want to move the goalpost of life in that direction while I want to move it this way. Whose language, whose definitions, whose values should guide these tough conversations?

I do not know.

But I do know that these Judaic sources invite us to think deeply about QOL and what criteria, if any, qualifies for a *chayim einam chayim*. Moreover, one of these sources insists that we must wrestle with the category of the unwanted, that we cannot abscond from thinking about this category altogether. Return with me to the Talmudic passage cited above: "The Sages taught, there are three whose lives are not lives: the compassionate; the hot-tempered; the fastidious" (Babylonian Talmud, *P'sachim* 113b).

There is one more line to this teaching: "Rav Yosef said, 'All of these attributes are found in me.'"

If this is true for Rav Yosef—one of the greatest sages of his generation—then *kal vachomer*, all the more so, is it true for us all. Each of us—in one way or another, at one time or another—experiences extreme emotions. Each of us includes emotions or orientations or characteristics that we and/or others consider undesirable. This is not to say that our lives are not lives. On the contrary, this is to share that we are all human—very human—and we must contend with our qualities: the good, the quirky, and the unwanted.

So, when you think about QOL, what rises to the surface? Which direction do you lean: toward the quantitative or qualitative side? Which criteria—external, internal, congenital, contingent, material, temperamental, chronic, acute—matter most? What's the shape and sound of your category of the unwanted? When you need to persuade someone else to agree with your version of this category, which type of language feels more compelling to you: deontology, consequentialism, principlism, virtues?

Though it may seem they are always shifting, life's goalposts are always there. We begin and we end. Between those goalposts is this thing we call life. Judaism inspires us to think carefully about those goalposts, what matters to us, and why. May our meditations be meaningful.

Notes

1. This text and all other Hebrew texts, unless otherwise noted, are translated by this author. See also *Yalkut Shimoni*, Deuteronomy, *Eikev* §871.
2. See Jonathan K. Crane, "Praying to Die: Medicine and Liturgy," *Journal of Religious Ethics* 43, no. 1 (2015): 1–27.
3. See also Jerusalem Talmud, *B'rachot* (Venice) 14a–b (9:2).
4. See Jonathan K. Crane, "Who's Your Mama Now? Rachel, Leah and Rabbinic Views on Their Procreative Possibilities," *Journal of Jewish Ethics* 3, no. 1 (2017): 92–117.
5. Karl Binding and Alfred Hoche, "Permitting the Destruction of Unworthy Life," trans. Walter E. Wright, *Issues in Medicine and Law*, 92, no. 8 (Fall 1992): 231–66.
6. See Ben Yehoyada on Babylonian Talmud, *Beitzah* 32b, at *umi she-ishto moshelet alav*.
7. For more on this argument, see Nachman of Bratzlav, *Likutei Moharan* 66.3.12.
8. Rashi on Babylonian Talmud, *Sukkah* 29a, under *Rav Yosef*.
9. Rashbam on Babylonian Talmud, *P'sachim* 113b, at *harachmanin*.
10. *Orchot Tzaddikim*, trans. Seymour J. Cohen (Ktav, 1982) (license: CC-BY, https://creativecommons.org/licenses/by/3.0/), found on Sefaria (sefaria.org).
11. *B'eir Mayim Chayim* on Numbers 8:2, which builds on Job 15:23.
12. Recall the He Jiankui affair of 2018–19, who edited human embryos to be genetically resistant to HIV.

CHAPTER 8

When Artificiality Collides with Humanity: Can AI Develop a Soul?

Rabbi Geoffrey A. Mitelman

My favorite definition of technology is "whatever came into existence after you were a kid." Depending on your age, you probably were fine with CDs, but it took awhile to get used to an iPod, let alone Spotify and other music streaming services. A typewriter didn't scare you, but navigating chat rooms in the early days of the internet felt like the Wild West. And when MapQuest, Google Maps, and Waze became standard for navigation, we stopped looking at atlases (or often even checking addresses) and just typed in where we were going, fairly certain we'd be taking the most efficient route and avoiding snarls on the highway. Once technology becomes "normal" in our lives, we stop thinking about how strange or magical or scary it felt at first, and instead it just becomes part of our day-to-day living.

Physical tools, even those that are destructive, can at least in theory be controlled by humans. While it is a little facile to say, for example, "Guns don't kill people, people kill people," on some level that is true. Discussions and debates about guns in American society commonly address the laws and regulations we try to pass, how best to legislate who should be allowed to access guns, and how to ensure bad actors are punished. A gun, without a human being, will not do anything. Guns haven't changed humanity's propensity for violence; rather, they have accelerated our ability to harm others, and so we debate and discuss how to respond to their use. It is the same with cars, which improved how we move from one place to another; the internet, which accelerated and spread information to a wider audience; and even corporate agriculture, which allowed us to feed massive populations. Historically, debates about technology of all kinds have focused on how we regulate their ethical use and manage their misuse.

The interplay between our humanity and our tools dates not just to our evolutionary history, but is found within our Jewish sources as well. Many conversations of our scholarly sages rightly consider how technology has taken over much of our life. This may explain why many of us turn to Rabbi Abraham Joshua Heschel's classic book *The Sabbath*, which offers a spiritual touchstone in our overly technocratic world. We often use Shabbat to renounce how technology dominates us, yet Heschel importantly does *not* denigrate the work we humans do:

> Is our civilization a way to disaster, as many of us are prone to believe? Is civilization essentially evil, to be rejected and condemned? The faith of the Jew is not a way out of this world, but a way of being within and above this world; not to reject but to surpass civilization. The Sabbath is the day on which we learn the art of *surpassing* civilization.
>
> Adam was placed in the Garden of Eden "to dress it and to keep it" (Genesis 2:15). Labor is not only the destiny of [hu]man[ity]; it is endowed with divine dignity. However, after he ate of the tree of knowledge he was condemned to toil, not only to labor "In toil shall thou eat . . . all the days of thy life" (Genesis 3:17). Labor is a blessing, toil is the misery of [hu]man[ity].
>
> The Sabbath as a day of abstaining from work is not a depreciation but an affirmation of labor, a divine exaltation of its dignity. Thou shalt abstain from labor on the seventh day is a sequel to the command: *Six days shalt thou labor and do all thy work.*
>
> "Six days shalt thou labor and do all thy work; but the seventh day is Sabbath unto the [Eternal] thy God." Just as we are commanded to keep the Sabbath, we are commanded to labor. "Love work . . ." The duty to work for six days is just as much a part of God's covenant with [hu]man[ity] as the duty to abstain from work on the seventh day.[1]

Adam is commanded by God *l'ovdah ulshomrah*, "to work and to keep" the Garden of Eden. *Avodah* (work) is a sacred responsibility. Adam is told to use the natural resources found in the Garden to change them, adapt them, and build from them. But crucially, it is only *afterward* that he and Eve eat from the Tree of Knowledge of Good and Evil. Adam is a creative being, but he will not understand the eventual impact of his creations until they have changed the world. Technology outpaces ethics.

That is one major reason why artificial intelligence scares so many of us. Yes, new technology may require a learning curve, but while the ethical relationship between humanity and technology has been a long one, artificial intelligence may be unique. That's because unlike other technologies that enhance, extend, or replace our physical labor, AI has the ability to enhance, extend, or replace our mental labor, which is a capacity that for most of our history was claimed as uniquely human. Artificial intelligence may actually be a qualitative difference in the development of technology, as it goes to the core of the question "What makes humans unique?"

We certainly see this in Jewish tradition. Maimonides, a twelfth-century rabbinic scholar also known as Rambam, teaches, "The human species had become unique in the world—there being no other species like it in the following respect; namely, that a person by themselves, and by the exercise of intelligence and reason, knows what is good and what is evil, and there is none who can prevent the human person from doing what is good or that which is evil."[2] If our intelligences makes us *b'tzelem Elohim*, "in God's image," and different from all other species, then what will happen if artificial intelligence reaches—or even surpasses—what humans can do?

Indeed, "technology" was the means by which many scientists defined humans evolutionarily as a separate species—what made us "human" or at least "proto-human" was our ability to manipulate the natural world. There was a reason a proposed ancestor of humans was *Homo habilis*, literally "handy man." The ability to use and manipulate tools was thought to be the domain only of humans. Yet scientists could push back: Would using a stick to find termites, as chimpanzees do, be considered "technological"? How about a bird building a nest or a beaver building a dam? New discoveries began to show that humanity's place as the only tool-using animal wasn't correct.[3]

Scholar Yuval Noah Harari argues that it wasn't a physical change that allowed *Homo sapiens* to take over the world, but a mental one. What makes humans unique, he argues, is our ability to cooperate with strangers in large numbers. If an individual *Homo sapiens* came across a tiger or chimpanzee or Neanderthal in the wild, the human would be the one in greater danger. And yet we humans are the ones who wiped out the Neanderthals, made tigers into an endangered species, and have the power to protect chimpanzees' habitats. What makes us human isn't our individuality; it's our social nature and willingness to work with large numbers of people whom we do not know—and that is indeed unique in the animal world. More accurately, humans can imagine things that do not exist in the physical world. Instead, we tell stories, and *that* is our superpower.

Harari notes in his book, *Homo Deus*:

> Animals such as wolves and chimpanzees live in a dual reality. On the one hand they are familiar with objective entities outside them, such as trees, rocks and rivers. On the other hand they are aware of subjective experiences within them, such as fear, joy and desire. Sapiens,

in contrast, live in a triple-layered reality. In addition to trees, rivers, fears and desires, the Sapiens world also contains stories about money, gods, nations and corporations. As history unfolded, the impact of gods, nations and corporations grew at the expense of rivers, fears and desires. There are still many rivers in the world, and people are still motivated by fears and wishes, but Jesus Christ, the French Republic and Apple Inc. have dammed and harnessed the rivers and learned to shape our deepest anxieties and yearnings.

Since new twenty-first century technologies are likely to make such fictions even more powerful, to understand our future we need to understand how stories about Christ, France and Apple have gained so much power. Humans think they make history, but history actually revolves around the web of stories. The basic abilities of individual humans have not changed much since the Stone Age. But the web of stories has grown from strength to strength, thereby pushing history from the Stone Age to the Silicon Age.[4]

Hence, artificial intelligence may change our humanity. Language, stories, and rapidly spreading information are keys to both human flourishing and artificial intelligence.

In fact, there are two different manners in which artificial intelligence is changing the conversation about what it means to be human. The first looks at questions in philosophical, long-term, existential framings: Will AI take over? Will humans become obsolete? The second looks at practical, immediate, real-world applications: How are algorithms removing our agency? What will be the economic impact of ChatGPT and other large language models? How will educators and the public navigate learning and teaching new information? And while Biblical and Rabbinic authors had no concept of self-driving cars or digitally manipulated videos, the questions they once faced are the same as today: How will information be shared? How do we look at nonhuman intelligence, whether that is animal or angelic? What is the relationship between our creations and our Creator?

Journalist and author Sigal Samuel builds on this question and reminds us that technology—and especially AI—can be a great force for good. But it also needs to be in conversation with our human values. As she says:

> There's nothing inherently wrong with believing that tech can radically improve humanity's lot. In many ways, it obviously already has.
>
> "Technology is not the problem," Ilia Delio, a Franciscan sister who holds two PhDs and a chair in theology at Villanova University, told me. In fact, Delio is comfortable with the idea that we're already in a

new stage of evolution, shifting from Homo sapiens to "techno sapiens." She thinks we should be open-minded about proactively evolving our species with tech's help.

But she's also clear that we need to be explicit about which values are shaping our tech "so that we can develop the technology with purpose—and with ethical boundaries," she said. Otherwise, "technology is blind and potentially dangerous." . . .

We need to decide what kind of salvation we want. If we're generating our enthusiasm for AI through visions of transcending our earthbound limits and our meat-sack mortality, that will create one kind of societal outcome. But if we commit to using tech to improve the well-being of this world and these bodies, we can have a different outcome. We can, as [historian David] Noble put it, "begin to direct our astonishing capabilities toward more worldly and humane ends."[5]

So let us look at a few of the challenges and opportunities that AI presents and where Jewish tradition may have some wisdom.

When many people think of the biggest dangers of artificial intelligence, perhaps the greatest concern is what is called "the alignment problem." Technologies are designed to have a particular goal in mind, and they help us to achieve them. A robot in an automobile factory, for example, doesn't "want" anything; it has no independent desires separate from its creator, and it is not simply a trophy for factory owners to brag about. Rather, the robot helps ensure standardization, welds parts together more quickly, makes fewer mistakes than humans, and can work more hours. The owners, managers, and engineers are those who set the robots' parameters, check them, and replace them if need be.

But in 2003, philosopher Nick Bostrom proposed this thought experiment: Imagine you are placed in charge of a paper clip factory and are hired to maximize the number of paper clips in the world.[6] Most humans would start by asking, "How do we get them to market? What type of metal would be used?" And, crucially, humans might stop to ask, "*Why* are we charged to maximize the number of paper clips in the world? What are the limitations here? How many paper clips do we really need?" However, if an AI is able to learn, make decisions, and even act on them, it is possible if not probable that *our human* goals may not match *the AI's* goals. If the AI is told to "maximize the number of paper clips in the world," it is possible that the AI might follow its given mission, which would be great . . . until it realizes the problem of humans getting in the way. After all, humans may want to decide that it is time to stop the production of paper clips, but the AI is still singularly focused on the maximization of paper clips. Thus, the AI might decide that, since humans are saying, "We have enough paper clips now; it's time to stop," it may be better to eliminate all humans. Even more scary, the AI may determine that since both human beings and paper clips are made of atoms, it could turn humans *into* paper clips! Our values and the AI's values would clearly not be aligned.

While obviously this is not a scenario we will be facing in the near future, it does raise questions about how much control we could actually have over our creations and how much we already outsource our decisions to algorithms. For example, how often do we watch a movie or binge a TV show, relying on Netflix's algorithm to recommend content? How often do we drive to a location in the fastest way possible, relying on Waze to guide us there? For most of us, the algorithm's results are fairly close to our objectives. But sometimes, they are not. After all, how many mediocre shows have we watched, just hoping the show will get better? How often has a drive taken us away from a more scenic route because it shaved four minutes from the drive time? Algorithms seem to "want" something, and it may not match what *we* want. We have already ceded much of our agency to artificial intelligence, and we haven't even noticed.

Indeed, this parallels the role of God and humanity in our texts. At least within the Biblical and Rabbinic mindset, God created humans without fully knowing how humanity will act. Just as today we may be creating an intelligence we cannot predict or control, God created humanity without fully knowing how we, God's creatures, would behave. A midrash (which also appears in chapter 2 of this book, as described by Rabbi Dinner) includes a debate in the heavenly court about whether humans should be created and the dangers that would arise if they came into existence:

> Rabbi Shimon said, "When the Holy One, blessed be God, came to create Adam the first human, the ministering angels divided into various factions and various groups. Some of them were saying, 'Let them not be created,' and some of them were saying, 'Let them be created.' That is what is written: 'Kindness and truth met; righteousness and peace touched' (Psalm 85:11). Kindness said, 'Let them be created, as they perform acts of kindness.' Truth said, 'Let them not be created, as they are all full of lies.' Righteousness said, 'Let them be created, as they perform acts of righteousness.' Peace said, 'Let them not be created, as they are all full of discord. What did the Holy One, blessed be God,

do? God took Truth and cast it down to earth. That is what is written: "You cast truth earthward" (Daniel 8:12). The ministering angels said before the Holy One, blessed be God: 'Ruler of the universe, why are You demeaning Your very seal? Let Truth ascend from the earth.' That is what is written: 'Truth will spring from the earth' (Psalm 85:12)." (*B'reishit Rabbah* 8:5)[7]

It was not a given that humanity would come into existence, according to the Rabbis, and the arguments against the creation of humanity are quite striking in their parallels with the argument against continuing to advance AI, particularly because we cannot control how it might develop. The rise of the internet, especially social media and its ideological bubbles, and artificial intelligence with its "hallucinations"—the name given when an AI model produces a false or misleading answer—that create fictions, means that we have lost much of our shared vision of truth and peace. We can no longer fully trust the images we see or the news we hear. We have entered into an echo chamber in our social media feeds, and mis- and disinformation can have real-life consequences for people's livelihoods and even lives. How much more will it be a challenge as algorithms, digital manipulations, and conspiracy theories become easier to create and disseminate?

Another overlooked interaction between artificial intelligence and its impact on society is the relationship between the body and the soul. AI is, in many ways, a disembodied intelligence. ChatGPT, Google Maps, and Facebook algorithms all come at us through zeroes and ones. But they impact us in "meatspace," the place where there can be an impact in the physical world. Consider the 2020 United States presidential election, the rise of misinformation, and its potential influence in future elections.[8] While there is still debate about how much social media influenced the 2020 election itself,[9] without a doubt, seeing and sharing altered photographs or memes likely changed the way voters and politicians made their decisions. Artificial intelligence and technology as a whole are intimately intertwined with our physical bodies and needs, and we cannot separate them.

In many ways, this is analogous to the ideas of distinctly separate "body" and "soul." This distinction comes not from Biblical texts, but rather from Greek thought and philosophy.[10] As Rabbinic Judaism became influenced by earlier Greek thinking, the idea of an incorporeal soul began to enter Judaism. Yet unlike traditional Greek thinking,

Judaism sees the body and soul as an integrated whole. One classic text comes from the Babylonian Talmud in *Sanhedrin* 91a–b. Rabbi Y'hudah HaNasi—representing Rabbinic thought—and the Roman emperor, Antoninus—representing Greco-Roman philosophy—explain how, even if something is incorporeal, it still manifests itself in flesh and blood and tries to exculpate itself from ethical responsibility:

> [The] Gemara cites an exchange where Antoninus, the Roman emperor, said to Rabbi Y'hudah HaNasi: The body and the soul are able to exempt themselves from judgment for their sins. How so? The body says: The soul sinned, as from the day of my death when it departed from me, I am cast like a silent stone in the grave, and do not sin. And the soul says: The body sinned, as from the day that I departed from it, I am flying in the air like a bird, incapable of sin. Rabbi Y'hudah HaNasi said to him: I will tell you a parable. To what is this matter comparable? It is comparable to a king of flesh and blood who had a fine orchard, and in it there were fine first fruits of a fig tree, and he stationed two guards in the orchard, one who was unable to walk, and one who was unable to see. Neither was capable of reaching the fruit on the trees in the orchard without the assistance of the other. The one who couldn't walk said to the one who couldn't see: I see fine first fruits of a fig tree in the orchard; come and place me upon your shoulders. I will guide you to the tree, and we will bring the figs to eat them. The one who couldn't walk rode upon the shoulders of the one who couldn't see, and they brought the figs and ate them.
>
> Sometime later the owner of the orchard came to the orchard. He said to the guards: The fine first fruits of a fig tree that were in the orchard, where are they? The one who couldn't walk said: Do I have any legs with which I would be able to walk and take the figs? The one who couldn't see said: Do I have any eyes with which I would be able to see the way to the figs? What did the owner of the orchard do? He placed the one who couldn't walk upon the shoulders of the one who couldn't see, just as they did when they stole the figs, and he judged them as one. (Babylonian Talmud, *Sanhedrin* 91a–b)[11]

If the soul and the body are completely separate entities, each can exculpate the other. Antoninus argues that while the soul may animate people's actions, it cannot sin without a body. Likewise, while the body may be physical, without a soul, there would be no desires or choices. But Rabbi Y'hudah HaNasi retorts that our decisions are, in fact, a combination of the body and the soul. We cannot separate them out—they are inherently joined. This is similar to the relationship between how humans and artificial intelligence interact. We cannot simply blame the nameless and faceless "algorithm" for the spread of misinformation or hallucinations. It is not just the AI's output that is problematic; it is the input as well.

After all, the data used by algorithms is only as good as the data—and the assumptions used in interpreting them—inputted, and that data can have far-reaching, real-world implications. Facial recognition software, for example, was trained on predominantly white faces, which means that faces of non-Caucasians could easily get confused by the systems.[12] Therefore, use of this technology in predictive policing may raise a major issue and exacerbate racial inequality.[13] Or what happens as an algorithm calculates one's health insurance premium or mortgage rate?[14] Here, while AI may not present an existential risk like the paper clip problem, it is much more likely to impact someone's daily life.

What makes AI different from other forms of digital technology is that even the humans who program the algorithm may not fully understand how it works or how it can be corrected or fixed. Professor Christoph Breidbach notes how algorithms are a "black box" that even the smartest humans cannot completely grasp:

> *Algorithmic decision-making* implies a lack of accountability. An algorithm is not subject to the same laws a human decision-maker would be. Algorithmic decision-making thereby—advertently or inadvertently—blurs the responsibility for decision outcomes. In fact, it is not too far-fetched to assume that organizations may implement algorithmic decision-making to avoid human judgment, since the ability of an individual to legally challenge an adverse algorithmic decision is limited. In addition, new types of machine learning like "deep learning" increasingly enable the unsupervised development of algorithms. Put differently, algorithms are no longer developed by humans but by machines, which raises the question of how machines use algorithms to decide in the first place. This is often discussed using the notion of "explainable AI." However, whenever algorithmic decision-making is void of *any* human involvement, challenges with data and algorithmic quality are amplified.[15]

Those who create, run, and lead technology firms in Silicon Valley or elsewhere are likely comparable to Antoninus as they try to decouple humans and algorithms and to exculpate the latter from responsibility. Yet Y'hudah HaNasi's perspective is the one that most accurately reflects their interaction: It is not "one or the other," but the interplay between the two where responsibility is placed.

We also can see this challenge in the rise of self-driving cars, or more accurately "autonomous vehicles," which are much more present today than many might think. We imagine "self-driving cars" as something phantasmic and totally independent of human agency, yet most newer cars in 2024 have drive-assist technology, blind-spot recognition, and auto-braking.[16] Even as human error is the cause of nearly 95 percent of car accidents,[17] it does not seem that widespread acceptance of driverless cars will be coming soon, as only about 25 percent of Americans think they are a good idea.[18]

Judaism, however, thinks about these questions a little differently. Perhaps the best analogy to autonomous vehicles is a classic text in Exodus (21:28–29, then expanded in Babylonian Talmud, *Bava Kama* 37a–b): the ox that gores. "When an ox gores a man or a woman to death, the ox shall be stoned and its flesh shall not be eaten, but the owner of the ox is not to be punished. If, however, that ox has been in the habit of goring, and its owner, though warned, has failed to guard it, and it kills a man or a woman—the ox shall be stoned and its owner, too, shall be put to death."

Even if there may be a debate about whether human intelligence is superior to that of other animals, we know that lower animals do have at least *some* intelligence. Oxen and donkeys have minds of their own, have the potential to damage property or people, and yet are invaluable in enhancing farming and agriculture. The question in the Rabbinic mind isn't *whether* an autonomous animal owned by a person would hurt someone; instead, they questioned who would be responsible and how much damages should be paid *when* it happens.

Rabbi Daniel Nevins, in a *t'shuvah* (religious responsum) from 2019, outlines some of the ways in which we can think about the level of liability that nonhuman actors might have:

> It is well established in Jewish law that people are partially responsible for damage caused by means of an animal or tool that is under their domain. It is also established that people bear full responsibility for damage caused by actions they have initiated, such as shooting an arrow, even once the object has departed from their control. This category of damage is known as "by his force." . . . But there is a third category of damage caused by a sequence of events that was initiated by a person, but which proceeded in unpredictable ways. For example, a person throws a stone, which ricochets and hits another stone, which loosens and falls, damaging property in the process. This is called "by force

of his force," *kocho b'ko-ach*, and is more controversial, with differing opinions about liability.

A major distinction made by the Sages is between animate and inanimate property. This distinction plays out in many areas of *halakhah*, such as whether animate property (say, a tethered donkey) might be used as a wall for a Sukkah, a post for a Sabbath border, or as parchment for a writ of divorce. In the laws of damages, a further distinction is made between behavior expected of animals (which increases liability for the owners) and unexpected behavior (which limits owner liability). How shall we regard the conduct of autonomous machines—like inanimate property which might move and cause damage (as with a fire), or like an animal that moves of its own volition, and may surprise its owner with unexpected behavior? Should autonomous machines powered by artificial intelligence be regarded as "alive" at least to the extent of animals? And if so, should this comparison narrow or expand the scope of owner liability?[19]

Here, the intelligence of autonomous vehicles is a more direct question for us to consider. It seems unlikely that a malicious AI will turn all humans into paper clips; it is a very real question about whether an autonomous vehicle should "choose" to turn and crash into a tree, rather than continue on its path, if it determines that its path might run over a child.

And that leads to an even more practical focused question: How might artificial intelligence upend our economic landscape? While we may grapple with the question of how artificial intelligence should be influenced by human values, it is also forcing us to think about the value of humans. While there are many ways in which AI is changing the landscape of work, considerations of art and commerce are among the most difficult.

Creativity has been a hallmark of human experience for millennia and is often described as the one thing that computers could not approximate. Would any computer be able to replicate Michelangelo's painting, Mozart's composition, Leibowitz's photography, or Spielberg's directing? While the answer is most likely no, very few artists make it into the echelons of history. The vast majority of actors, writers, painters, and musicians struggle to make a living, let alone win multiple prestigious awards. Artificial intelligence has accelerated the challenge facing the relationship between creativity and economic generativity, as it has been proved to bear the capacity to replicate or create at least a modest level of artistic work, if not masterpiece material.

So much of our humanity is grounded in our creative ability. As Rabbinit Sara Wolkenfeld, chief learning officer at the digital Jewish library Sefaria, writes:

> The rabbis of the third century didn't have ChatGPT, nor did they devote many words to labor-replacing technologies. But they did live in a time when people had indentured servants, so they could easily envision a life in which labor was delegated to others. The Mishnah, a rabbinic legal work compiled around the year 200, discusses a woman so wealthy that she does not need to do anything but lounge; even her spinning and weaving can be delegated to the household help. But if she does no work at all, the Mishnah warns, she will go crazy.
>
> Modern technologies such as generative AI threaten to make 21st-century Americans like the woman in the Mishnah: deprived of purpose, convinced that our creative output is useless because a computer can produce a result that is sometimes just as good, or even better. Much of the debate around AI hinges on the question *Can a computer do it better?* But Jewish texts insist that the most important question is about process, not product. Tools that offer to replace work that I find meaningful aren't ones I'll be using anytime soon. I feel fulfilled when I write and when I teach even though I know that emerging large language models can write essays for me and may soon be able to transmit information to my students. I enjoy using my creative powers to bake despite the existence of bakeries that mass-produce delicious cookies in far less time and for far less money than I can.[20]

In many ways, this is where artificial intelligence will make the greatest impact on the role of humanity and our relationship with that role. Humans are created *b'tzelem Elohim*, "in God's image," and have infinite value via our connection with the Divine, and yet we also want to be contributors to our society. It is not just writers and artists who create—we are being challenged to think about precisely how we humans can continue to be generative.

Historian Dr. David Zvi Kalman has highlighted how we need to think about human value, as well as the value of humans. As he notes, it is more complicated and nuanced than we might initially think:

> Yes, biological human beings have infinite value, but that value is also tied to what we *perceive* as being human, with degrees of personhood available for liminal cases. This approach lies behind Judaism's complex position on abortion, among other things. It also—in my opinion—means that we should seriously consider assigning some level of personhood to machines that present themselves as people. While some will have

the knee-jerk response that this will impinge on human rights, I believe the opposite is true. We are much more likely to discount people if we see their abilities as being "only" equivalent to what an AI can achieve. An AI's ability to act human should raise up the AI, not diminish the human. By the same token, the intentional creation of humanlike software is unlike the creation of other sorts of software. Just as AI firms have explicitly compared their products to nuclear technology in terms of its [sic] promise and danger, we must acknowledge that it also shares something with the creation of human life—and developers should understand this as a mandate to develop and maintain their models extremely carefully.[21]

We may worry that we are giving artificial intelligence too much of a sense of humanity, but in fact the bigger issue may be our diminishment of humanity. There is a tension between our intrinsic worth and what we can contribute to the world.

There is even the question of whether rabbis may be replaced by AI. ChatGPT has been able to create a fairly decent *d'var Torah* (a teaching of Torah), and recently some congregants even had trouble distinguishing between human-created and AI-created sermons. But Rabbi Josh Fixler, in using AI to both write and deliver a High Holy Day sermon, reminds us:

> Judaism is a rehumanizing project. The mitzvot, the commandments, teach us that we are not just here to survive and consume, but that we are invited to live lives of meaning, purpose, and connection.
>
> Shabbat is a rehumanizing project. It is a reminder that there is more to life than what we create, than what we produce. Even God needed to rest from the work of creation. Shabbat allows us space to not do, but just be. We are, after all, human be-ings.
>
> Prayer is a rehumanizing project. Prayer holds space for the yearnings of our hearts and sorrows of days. In communal prayer, we can comfort and be comforted, find strength, and offer support. On every page of the prayer book, there are new, breathtaking metaphors for human existence. Prayer invites us into mystery, inspiration, and gratitude, all deeply human traits.
>
> The Jewish calendar is a rehumanizing project. Opportunities to return to the same themes again and again—themes of the human story, of freedom and abundance, of uncertainty and learning, of triumph and tribulation. We revisit the same spots, year after year, to judge how far we've come, how much we have grown since last we read these words and did these rites. Machines can learn. But humans grow.[22]

In the end, we will still be human, even if artificial intelligence surpasses human intelligence. Judaism, with its rituals, texts, discussions, and arguments, compels both the present and the future.

Rabbi Daniel Nevins concludes his *t'shuvah* by saying, "Intelligence can be manufactured, but not the soul, and without a soul, artificial life is always virtual, never quite real. Our halakhists denied that a golem could join a minyan. It is evident that for an action to count as fulfillment of a mitzvah, a command, one requires still distinctive human capacities such as compassion, gratitude, wonder, and reverence."[23] We may not be able to fully define "what it means to be human," especially as so much of our technology and understanding of our evolutionary history has been refined over the centuries. But Judaism has always been able to adapt, grow, and incorporate whatever new technology arises. There will be disruptions, fears, and unknowns as AI pushes the limits of what we think makes us human. But "technology" is often a catchall word for the fears of a new world we may not fully understand. The Judaism of the twenty-second century will undoubtedly be different from the Judaism of the twenty-first, but just as we have incorporated the technologies of agriculture, writing, printing, and the internet in our Judaism today, so too will we thrive in the future.

Notes

1. Abraham Joshua Heschel, *The Sabbath* (Farrar Straus and Giroux, 1951), 27–28.
2. Maimonides, *Mishneh Torah*, Laws of Repentance 5:1. Adapted translation by Moses Hyamson (1937–49) (license: Public Domain), found on Sefaria (sefaria.org).
3. Asher Elbein, "Do Animals Use Tools?," National Wildlife Federation, June 27, 2024, https://www.nwf.org/Magazines/National-Wildlife/2024/Summer/Animals/Animal-Tool-Use.
4. Yuval Noah Harari, *Homo Deus: A Brief History of Tomorrow* (HarperCollins, 2017), 155.
5. Sigal Samuel, "Silicon Valley's Vision for AI? It's Religion, Repackaged," *Vox*, September 7, 2–23, https://www.vox.com/the-highlight/23779413/silicon-valleys-ai-religion-transhumanism-longtermism-ea.
6. Nick Bostrom, "Ethical Issues in Advanced Artificial Intelligence," NickBostrom.com, https://nickbostrom.com/ethics/ai.
7. Translation adapted from *The Sefaria Midrash Rabbah*, 2022 (license: CC-BY, https://creativecommons.org/licenses/by/3.0/), found on Sefaria (sefaria.org).
8. "Facebook: From Election to Insurrection—How Facebook Failed Voters and Nearly Set Democracy Aflame," Avaaz, March 18, 2021, https://secure.avaaz.org/campaign/en/facebook_election_insurrection/.

9. Andrew M. Guess et al., "How Do Social Media Feed Algorithms Affect Attitudes and Behavior in an Election Campaign?," *Science*, July 27, 2023, https://www.science.org/doi/10.1126/science.abp9364.
10. "Soul, Mind, and Body," A Level Philosophy and Religious Studies, https://alevelphilosophyandreligion.com/ocr-religious-studies/ocr-philosophy/soul-mind-body/.
11. Translation from the William Davidson digital edition of the *Koren Noé Talmud*, with commentary by Adin Even-Israel Steinsaltz (license: CC-BY-NC, https://creativecommons.org/licenses/by-nc/4.0/), found on Sefaria (sefaria.org).
12. Beth Findley, "Why Racial Bias Is Prevalent in Facial Recognition Technology," ed. Mariah Bellamoroso, *Jolt Digest*, November 3, 2020, https://jolt.law.harvard.edu/digest/why-racial-bias-is-prevalent-in-facial-recognition-technology.
13. Clare Garvie and Jonathan Frankle, "Facial-Recognition Software Might Have a Racial Bias Problem," *Atlantic*, April 7, 2016, https://apexart.org/images/breiner/articles/FacialRecognitionSoftwareMight.pdf.
14. Emmanuel Martinez and Lauren Kirchner, "The Secret Bias Hidden In Mortgage-Approval Algorithms," *AP News*, August 25, 2021, https://apnews.com/article/lifestyle-technology-business-race-and-ethnicity-mortgages-2d3d40d5751f933a88c1e17063657586.
15. Christoph F. Breidbach, "Responsible Algorithmic Decision-Making," *Organizational Dynamics* 53, no. 1 (April–June 2024), https://www.sciencedirect.com/science/article/pii/S0090261624000044.
16. Katharina Buchholz, "Cars Increasingly Ready for Autonomous Driving," Statista, September 6, 2024, https://www.statista.com/chart/25754/newly-registered-cars-by-autonomous-driving-level/.
17. "Critical Reasons for Crashes Investigated in the National Motor Vehicle Crash Causation Survey," National Highway Traffic Safety Administration, March 2018, https://crashstats.nhtsa.dot.gov/Api/Public/Publication/812506.
18. Lee Rainie et al., "Americans Cautious About the Deployment of Driverless Cars," Pew Research Center, March 17, 2022, https://www.pewresearch.org/internet/2022/03/17/americans-cautious-about-the-deployment-of-driverless-cars.
19. Daniel Nevins, "Halakhic Response to Artificial Intelligence and Autonomous Machines," Rabbinical Assembly Responsa CLJS HM 182.1.2019, June, 19, 2019, https://www.rabbinicalassembly.org/sites/default/files/nevins_ai_moral_machines_and_halakha-final_1.pdf.
20. Sara Tillinger Wolkenfeld, "Productivity Is a Drag. Work Is Divine," *Atlantic*, September 18, 2024, https://www.theatlantic.com/technology/archive/2024/09/work-labor-artificial-intelligence-jewish-text/679912/.
21. David Zvi Kalman, "On AI, Jewish Thought Has Something Distinct to Say," Future of Life Institute, September 6, 2024, https://futureoflife.org/religion/ai-in-jewish-thought/.

22. Josh Fixler, "As the Rabb-AI: Rosh HaShanah Morning Sermon 5784," Sinai and Synapses, September 26, 2023, https://sinaiandsynapses.org/content/ask-the-rabb-ai/.
23. Daniel Nevins, "Halakhic Response to Artificial Intelligence and Autonomous Machines."

CHAPTER 9

From Creation to Creator: Humans Making Humans, Humanoids, Cyborgs, and Clones

Rabbi Douglas Kohn

JULY 5, 1996: Dolly, the sheep, was born in Scotland. She was born, but she was not conceived by a ewe and a ram. Rather, she was constructed—cloned—via a process that included three sheep: one from which an adult mammary gland cell was extracted; another from which a blastocyte, an early embryo, was obtained; and a third that provided the womb in which the embryo developed until birth. From that singular mammary cell, the entire remainder of Dolly's body was produced via cloning.

Dolly was the first mammal to be cloned successfully, but she was not the last. Since 1996, pigs, deer, dogs, horses, lower primates, and other sheep have been cloned, including several of Dolly's own "identical twin" sheep.

But no human being has been cloned. Not yet.

Questions of how humans are created or recreated, and their import, are now of issue. Advanced technologies beg the question. So do today's politics. But classic Jewish texts offer vital teachings and grounding.

In Jewish tradition, a *baraita*—a text ascribed to second-century Mishnaic rabbis but only included in the Talmud three hundred years later—teaches that three entities are required to produce a new human being, namely a mother, a father, and the Holy One:

> The Sages taught: There are three partners in the creation of a person: The Holy One, blessed be God, and the father, and the mother. The father emits the white seed, from which the following body parts are formed: the bones, the sinews, the nails, the brain that is in its head, and the white of the eye. The mother emits red seed, from which are formed the skin, the flesh, the hair, and the black of the eye. And the Holy One, blessed be God, inserts a spirit, a soul, the countenance, eyesight, hearing of the ear, the capability of speech of the mouth, the capability of walking with the legs, understanding, and wisdom. (Babylonian Talmud, *Nidah* 31a)[1]

Is this really what is required to make a new human being?

Our *baraita* explains that, as customarily taught by our Rabbinic Sages, the mother's blood and flesh, the father's semen, and the Holy One's implantation of spirit or soul conjointly cooperate to participate in creating a new human entity. Furthermore, the text suggests that without any one of the three partner contributors and contributions, new life could not result. This teaching generally was accepted as normative Talmudic and Judaic understanding for centuries. It may be termed an early, yet abiding, Jewish conception of conception.

But... not so fast. Creating human life may not be so simple or limited. Nor may it be restricted exclusively to a by-product, albeit intentional, of the mechanism of human coitus. Could there indeed be additional processes to create and procreate humans, other than via sexual union and gestation? And, what might it mean and portend for making humans and being human if we can generate humans by other procedures or fashions than through natural sexual union?

Yes, there may be other ways to create more humans. Moreover, these methods may not be limited only to modern technological advances—in vitro fertilization and embryo transfer (IVF-ET), for instance. A review of Jewish text reveals centuries of attempts to generate life—primarily human life—through other, non-sexual methodologies, including literary, mystical, or magical means. Human beings have been venturing into procreation ever since our first appearance in Genesis when God said, "Be fruitful and multiply" (Genesis 1:28), and we have either posited or undertaken various means to generate life, sexually and non-sexually, ever since. Fulfilling that first commandment has been our first obligation, irrespective of methodology. Furthermore, these alternative methods and possibilities hold deep meanings and challenges for the human enterprise itself. In this chapter, we will review means of creating human beings as considered in Jewish text. Attendant to each process discussed below, we will ask: For each means, is the product thereof equally and fully human? And what do these processes and results portend for humanity itself?

Thus, how are humans created, and how are we supposed to procreate, according to Judaism? Over evolutionary epochs of anthropoidal life and millennia of Jewish existence, we have created and recreated humans in several, evolving manners. We can distill these mechanisms into four major modalities.

First, there were the ways God made the initial humans as recorded in the opening chapters of Genesis and as explicated in later Jewish commentaries. The Torah describes that, initially in Genesis 1:26–27, God created humanity by verbal fiat. Genesis 2 depicts God fashioning the first human creature out of the "dust from the soil" (2:7) and thereafter crafting a second human from a body part of that original man (2:21–22). Though the Torah's versions of God's creative processes may be mythical or fable, they ponder how and why humans are made, the roles of the Divine and the human in creating and procreating, and what is a human being.

Second, we recognize the normative manner of human procreation through coitus and gestation. This was the conventionally recognized intent inherent in God's initial commandment to the first humans to "be fruitful and multiply"; we were to do so biologically and naturally. Humans made more humans through sexual union, the meeting of egg and sperm, and human procreation could assume sacredness and intentionality through self-awareness, love, and divine commands merited through our lofty position in the phyla of animal life and our intimate relation to the Divine.

Third, Jewish mystical scholars and sages—primarily Kabbalists from the Talmudic and medieval periods—posited human beings creating other human beings through mystical, often linguistic techniques and as a means of demonstrating their unique proximity to the Divine. These sages described episodes wherein they, employing kabbalistic wisdom and other Jewish magic, recorded forming beings out of dust or clay and then undertook to enliven the beings into humanoid creatures, or golems. Did they fabricate actual life? Likely not. But their centuries of writing and discussions represent a unique thrust in Jewish thought and question the intentions and limits of humans creating humanoids and the boundaries of the human and Divine relationship.

Lastly, a new fourth mode of making humans has evolved from today's rapid scientific advances—namely, humans making humans via synthetic means. Present technologies are advancing rapidly from inorganic, plastic and metal replacement pieces to organic, replacement elements from living sources. Potential implantation of generated organs, reproductive genetic cloning, and therapeutic genetic cloning offer possibilities beyond healing and quality of life, but generatively for potential life itself. That lower mammals have been cloned successfully begs the question of cloning humans. However, medical science admits to technical limitations on human cloning due to the location of specific proteins—spindle proteins—necessary for cell division within mammalian eggs situated near to cell nuclei, which make nuclei removal very difficult, if not presently impossible. Yet, the cloning horizon is not beyond imagination. Could and would cloning result in making actual humans? If so, how "human" would such creatures be?

Below we will review each of these four modes of creating humans. We explore how human the product of these modalities is and theorize about their impact and import for the human enterprise.

Creation: Making Humans the God Way

Genesis presents two Creation narratives, the first in chapter 1, the second in chapter 2, each describing a different process by which God created human beings. In the first episode, God created humankind—male and female—ex nihilo through divine fiat and decree. Contrarily, the second chapter describes God actively shaping a human form out of earthly dust and breathing life into that first, male figure. Sometime later, via divine "surgery" and "cloning," God crafted a second, female figure from a rib extracted out of the first human being. Clearly, these were humans, if not protohistoric, mythic humans. For Jewish tradition, these vignettes initiate the human enterprise and launch the discussion of human procreativity.

Genesis 1 reveals an inaugural event in mythologic history. Just as God created the balance of Creation by fiat—the waters, the heavenly orbs, the flora and fauna—so, too, God initiated human beings by decree through language. The Torah indicates (Genesis 1:26–28):

> God now **said,** "**Let us make human beings** in our image, after our likeness; and let them hold sway over the fish of the sea and the birds of the sky, over the beasts, over all the earth, over all that creeps upon the earth."
>
> So **God created human beings** in [the divine] image, creating [them] in the image of God, **creating them** male and female.
>
> God then blessed them, and **God said to them,** "Be fruitful and multiply; fill the earth and tame it; hold sway over the fish of the sea and the birds of the sky, and over every animal that creeps on the earth."

In Genesis 1, God demonstrated the first mode of creating human beings: by God's word. God then commanded these humans to undertake their own, later modes of procreation.

God's creative powers were manifested via the confluence of divine intention and expression, by the idea and by the statement. Mechanically, the words God used to make humanity are hidden from the Torah's readers and stirred the imagination of later ages, which will be reviewed below. Yet, it was clear: Human beings could be designed, shaped, animated, and directed by the divine word. Only God knew what those words were and how to create, ensoul, and enliven the human being. Once created, humans were favored by God above other living animals, as the Divine blessed the humans and charged them to reproduce themselves. And, they were fashioned in some manner of God's image. Whether that image included physical, cognitive, moral, or spiritual likeness, it did include the unique, godly ability to procreate in the divine image, which was God's initial command. Thus, one characteristic of these humans, and presumably of all humans, is that they were generative. Reproduction was their first business: It was not sufficient that the two prototypes should be the only such figures; they had to make more by themselves. However, they would have to reproduce through some other fashion; creation by fiat was reserved to the divine domain, to which humans were not privy.

The second Creation vignette, in Genesis 2, demonstrates further, uniquely divine creation skills. Irrespective of whether Genesis 2 is read ontologically as a development or elucidation of Genesis 1 or as an independent narrative of the creation of human beings, the text reveals an active God. This Creator God is not simply speaking and directing that the human being appear *de novo*, as if snapping a divine finger. Rather, here is a Creator God dirty in the soil. "God Eternal fashioned the man—dust from the soil—and breathed into his nostrils the breath of life, so that the man became a living being" (Genesis 2:7). God was as a potter, shaping the clay, designing the form and figure of the new being. God used created material, not merely words and letters, to do creation. This was a Creating God who transmitted life directly into the airways of the incipient, latent, lifeless figure. The humanoid was form and potential, yet not alive until God created and installed life itself for the new human. Presumably, the life with which God endowed this first being was inordinately superior or significantly more enriched with sentience, capacity for knowledge and cognition, and moral possibility than that of the other animals that God also crafted and to whom God would give to this new being as company (Genesis 2:19). As well, borrowing from Genesis 1, this human was in God's own likeness and thus possessed some divine qualities. We know precious little about this prototype human; unrevealed are the elements of divine likeness that were installed in him and, later, in her. But what is known from Genesis 1, and further developed in chapter 2, is that this being possessed the possibility and the command of generativity. It was to replicate itself and make many more of its type. The Torah added a precious ingredient: God would fashion another complementary, paired human being, and together they would perform the task of reproduction.

> Then, throwing the man into a profound slumber, so that he slept,
> God Eternal took one of his ribs and closed up the flesh in that place.
> Now God Eternal built up the rib taken from the man into a woman,
> and brought her to the man, and the man said,
> "This time —
> bone of my bone, flesh of my flesh!
> Let this one shall be called woman,
> for this one is taken from man." (Genesis 2:21–23)

The two initially lived peaceably in the Garden of Eden, until deceit and moral failure forced them from their idyll. Besides banishment, God condemned both to hard labor, and regarding labor God spoke to the woman:

> And to the woman, [God] said,
> "I am doubling and redoubling your pains of pregnancy;
> with pain you shall bear children,
> yet your craving shall be for your man,
> and he shall govern you.'" (Genesis 3:16)

Making humans the "God way" was a uniquely divine operation—never humanly understood, never replicated. Although later sages sought to penetrate the divine secrets of Creation, they remained hidden and concealed. Yet, a new means of reproducing was introduced and gifted to humans. Though sexual reproduction would be the dominant means of propagation for much of earth's higher fauna and even flora, human beings were invested with a self-awareness of their place in the generative act. They would triumph over animalistic copulation so that human reproduction instead would become a sacred, intentional, loving, and nearly divine achievement. It was fulfillment of God's first commandment.

Procreation: Humans Making Humans the Usual Human Way

Humans have always been in the business of making humans. Mostly we do so as procreative, biological beings, through sexual union enhanced by the expression of the uniquely human experience of love in copulation. Biologically, new human life is a result of a merger between the mother's oocyte and the father's sperm cell, subsequent nidation—the linking of the pre-embryo to the mother's womb—and developmental gestation, and ultimately, birth. Yet, the human generative process also may include a moral dimension: It is fulfillment of a divine command. Procreation itself is and was the first commandment charged to human beings in the Torah: *P'ru urvu*, "Be fruitful and multiply," God commanded the first beings (Genesis 1:28). Yet, as we have already explored, Judaism teaches that three parties are required to make offspring: a mother, a father, and the Holy One as a holy partnership. Originally, as described above, God made us *ex nihilo*, taking "dust from the soil" and breathing the breath of life into the *ish*, the first male figure (Genesis 2:7). But that was not enough. The Holy One continued mythic Creation with the second figure, the *ishah*, the female human (Genesis 2:22). Thus, together, with complementary procreative organs and capability of childbearing, humans were able to replicate human life and bear progeny.

Thereafter, we effectively became both the creation and, in part, the creator. Procreative generativity is the hallmark of all life, from dogs to penguins to bumblebees and oak trees, but doing so purposefully with design, perhaps with love, and with an intention to shape the outcome—that is uniquely human. To create human beings deliberately is an essential character of being human; procreation is not mere accident of copulation when the female of the species is in estrus and stimulated to breeding, to which the male responds. Rather, making humans the human way includes both a relational as well as a sacred dimension. We are determinative of our own generativity and recognize it as not merely an act of instinct, but as a reflection of the human relationship with the Divine. Moreover, Judaically, the first commandment also reflects a unique component of God's likeness that we can readily and certainly distinguish in human beings: our reproductive capacity to make new humans.

Furthermore, there is no question that new life that is born of human biological reproduction is fully human. It is definitional. It is the baseline against which all other generative outcomes may be measured and should be measured. It requires no mythology, though arguably most parents who witness the birth of a child can certainly attest to the miraculous in the experience of birth and bringing forth new life. Even though human reproduction is normative, it should never lose its mystery. Perhaps this is an extraordinary expression of the practical intersection of human and Divine in reality, as opposed to its fictive or literary link in Genesis.

However, presently social and political conversations, at least in the United States, are raising new ethical and even religious questions about obligations and limitations in the reproductive realm. When does life commence—at conception or at first breath, as both possibilities find expression in various sacred texts? Must every pregnancy be sustained? Have our abilities to move the goalposts of life, as discussed above in chapter 6, rendered the human way of making humans no longer entirely human? Does the capacity to use technologies to shape and monitor pregnancies require that such tools be used, and do they diminish the sacred mysteries inherent in human procreation? Or are all advances in reproductive technologies, by definition, beneficial to the processes and outcomes of pregnancy and birth?

Furthermore, as discussed elsewhere in this volume and in other texts of biomedical ethics, by our own artifice we presently have the ability to determine gender, hair and eye color, and other characteristics of potential offspring while they are yet in utero or in the "test tube." Does the potential to apply biotechnologies to shape the metaphorical clay and dust into life redefine our human role vis-à-vis that of the Divine Creator? Making life the human way is not so simple.

Alef, Bet, Gimel Magic: Making Humans the Talmudic/Kabbalistic Way

In the 1970s, television's *The Six Million Dollar Man* featured an astronaut who became a bionic man following a near fatal crash and was rebuilt into a human/machine with new superpowers. A couple of decades later, Arnold Schwarzenegger's *Terminator* series, in which he, too, was a bionic machine, pushed the boundary of the human/machine ratio. Later, some Marvel Comics superheroes also were amalgams of human and machine, invested with extraordinary powers that reflected machinelike qualities, but also suffering sympathy, sensitivity, and quests for justice characterizing the finest human being. Recently in the real world—not Hollywood—we generate artificial parts to repair human beings, building joints and limbs in factories and organic materials in laboratories and implanting them in injured or suffering persons, rendering their bodies testimony to a recalibrated balance of the organic and the inorganic.

Yet, efforts to craft cyborgs—creatures part human and part artificial—are not twentieth-century or twenty-first-century phantasmic phenomena. The nineteenth century saw Mary Shelley's *Frankenstein*, in which a humanoid monster was created in the dead of night to serve the wishes of its confused inventor, giving rise to further fabulous fantasies.

However, Shelley's novel was but a modern iteration of still-earlier fictional aspirations. Centuries prior to Victor Frankenstein and his diabolical invention, Jewish literature sought to prescribe and describe processes of human generation of humanlike beings. *Sefer Yetzirah*, the mystical *Book of Formation* dating to either the Talmudic or medieval periods, first posited the formation of a golem, a humanoid figure of clay and dust brought to life by the pronouncement of sacred letters in a designated order. Later commentaries wrestled with *Sefer Yetzirah*'s techniques: Was it describing merely spiritual or actual material constructs? Following *Sefer Yetzirah*, further Talmudic, midrashic, and mystical texts continued, and prescriptions for making human figures featured prominently in mystical literature in nearly every successive century.

The most referenced Jewish text recounting a humanoid made by a human is found in the Talmud: "Rava says: If the righteous wish to do so, they can create a world, as it is stated: 'But your iniquities have separated between you and your God.'" In other words, there is no distinction between God and a sinless righteous person, and just as God created the world, so can the righteous individual create life. The Talmud continues: "Indeed, Rava created a man, a golem, using forces of sanctity. Rava sent his creation before Rabbi Zeira. Rabbi Zeira would speak to him but he would not reply. Rabbi Zeira said to him, 'You were created by one of the members of the group, one of the Sages. Return to your dust'" (Babylonian Talmud, *Sanhedrin* 65b).[2]

This passage raises numerous discussions and challenges. It implies, in its initial section, that the only limitation to humans crafting other humans via non-coitus methods was one's quality of righteousness. In other words, if one was truly righteous, one could be tantamount to God and enjoy the privilege of creating a human being. However, because regular human beings are sinful and thus lack proximity or comparability to the Divine, they also lack the right, wisdom, or God's permission to create new life. Righteous ones, however, could create life if they wished, as God would join them or bestow upon them the tools or wisdom to fabricate life, and their creations would receive the imprimatur of God ensouling the creature.

Apparently, Rava was just such a righteous sage. However, the Talmud does not describe the nature of Rava's righteousness, nor how Rava crafted his creation, nor the materials employed by Rava. Later wisdom literature, including *Sefer Yetzirah*, sought to explain this secret. Was it magic, as Moshe Idel suggests in his landmark volume *Golem*,[3] or was it via a linguistic pronouncement approximating God's creation of the first being, by fiat? The only hint is that Rava used "forces of sanctity." He needed help from the Holy, which was bestowed due to Rava's righteousness. However, the Talmud is terse and does not expound on Rava's achievement.

An elucidation of God's creation of humankind also appears in the midrash, our lore contemporaneous to the Talmud. Although perhaps only expanding or explaining the Genesis vignette, the midrash offers a Rabbinic window into the missing pieces of crafting a being, which is absent from the Talmud's discussion of Rava's figure: "In the first hour, [human's creation] rose in [God's] thought; in the second, [God] consulted with the angels; in the third, God gathered his dirt; in the fourth God kneaded it; in the fifth, God weaved it; in the sixth, God made it a form; in the seventh, God blew breath into it; in the eighth, God placed it into the Garden [of Eden]" (*Vayikra Rabbah* 29).[4]

The midrash describes the initial human being under formation and indicates the requisite steps to transform mere material into a magnificent human life. This was God's process, the midrash suggests. Could it not also be the process of creation used by the righteous? Any human can manipulate clay; preschoolers do it every day. The righteous human, however, could replicate this midrashic recipe as well as win God's endorsement and gain God's breadth of life. Yet, just as the Talmud was silent on Rava's method, so too the midrash was hushed. To the mystic, a vital, secret code was required. *Sefer Yetzirah* offered that code, though deciphering the obtuse *Sefer Yetzirah* also required secret knowledge.

That secret knowledge, according to legend, was possessed by Rabbi Judah Loew, known as the Maharal, in sixteenth-century Prague. According to folklore and recounted by the great scholar Gershom Scholem in

"The Idea of the Golem," when facing antisemitic violence, Loew and two associates formed a figure from the mud of Prague's Moldau River.[5] They circled it seven times while reciting incantations and endowed it with life through inscribing on its forehead the word *emet*, "truth," and sealing it with God's name. The figure arose and, upon the Maharal's instructions, defended the Jews of Prague from evildoers. Yet, as the golem grew in stature, might, anger, and self-reliance, legend describes that Loew was compelled to reverse the incantations, felling the famulus as a lump of dust, which would be boxed and stored in the attic of Prague's Altneu Shul for future reanimation. Parallel to Disney's "Sorcerer's Apprentice," the golem legend portrays both the power for good and the risk of abuse of power inherent in an artificial humanoid.

A chief problem with sages crafting anthropoidal golems is that it skewed the line, if not dissolved it, between the human being as creation and as creator. Since Genesis, humans have been the crown of Creation, God's final gem on the sixth day. However, upon potentially becoming a creator, humans would cross the line into the divine precinct; we bore a secret knowledge. We risked becoming what we were not created to be, nor that which we could understand. We would be fish out of water. Moreover, creating a golem would bring into existence a life form that owed fealty and reverence to its creator, who was a person who had approached and usurped the divine domain. This conflict was central to the very nature of the mythical golem, so that in some golem folklore, the anthropoid was created as a mute, à la the creation of Rava in the Talmudic passage quoted above. By disallowing a golem the function of speech, the golem was precluded from participating in two primary halachic behaviors: It could not utter words of prayer, and it could not be counted in a minyan if it was crafted as an adult male figure (Idel also discusses female golem figures in his book). Neither the golem's age nor its mental acuity could be affirmed, thus it was disqualified from participating in the basic act of the adult Jewish male, namely prayer. Hence, without speech it was rendered nonhuman, akin to a defective creation, even if all else in its body and capacity conformed with that of an adult Jewish male.[6]

Moreover, the origin of the golem's "life" was known. What of its death? Would it die a natural death? Were humans required to grieve its death, and was the Mourner's *Kaddish* required to be spoken and by whom? After all, traditionally the *Kaddish* is uttered by first-degree relatives of the deceased, of whom the golem had none. As well, how might it die? A natural human dies from disease, accident, or caused death—war, for instance. The golem, presumably, was exempt from disease and ideally could live endlessly. Marge Piercy, in her compelling novel *He, She and It*, posited a futuristic cyborg named Yod that was created in a laboratory and that possessed unearthly powers, including the possibility of living forever.[7] Prior cyborg models in Piercy's novel were "killed" by their scientist-maker due to deficiencies; Yod only "died" when it was destroyed while saving its Jewish community from attackers. Would "killing" an artificial human be tantamount to murder? Moreover, must artificial beings be destroyed because of dangers they presumably presented to humanity? Rabbi Zeira sent Rava's golem back to its dust, and Rabbi Judah Loew reversed the incantations of his mythical golem in Prague, consigning it to lifelessness, because each could run amok and harm the world.

How human were these figures, and what impact would they have on humanity? The golem, as a cyborg, clearly falls into a category other than human. It lacked parental predecessors; thus it didn't have a name by which to link it with familial or flesh origins. It was crafted de novo, not through gestation and maturation; thus it lacked developmental and learning milestones required of each human being by our sages (*Pirkei Avot* 5:25), and if it was a male, it was not welcomed into the covenant via circumcision.

Clearly, a golem is not human enough to be called human. And should it be created and live, it posed certain threats to humanity. The cyborg could possess physical and cognitive prowess that could, or would, supersede that of human beings. If fabricated and freed from human constraint, the golem could wreak havoc. Hence, both Rabbis Zeira and Loew reversed the creations. They could do so because they retained control. However, artificial humans created in present and future labs without such constraints might raise new challenges, both foreseen and unforeseen.

Twenty-First-Century Science: Making Humans Artificially

One could argue that the Kabbalists undertook a cloning process, if generating a later being from the dust and clay of Genesis could constitute a form of cloning. Perhaps. But today's technology is vastly more advanced and more complicated.

What was previously confined to literature or fantasy is now in the twenty-first century emerging from factories and the halls of science into reality, begging careful and ethical discussion. Dolly, the first cloned mammal, was but a precursor to the cloning of other large animals, including sheep, pigs, deer, horses, and lower primates. Are humans next? And, what else is coming?

Are humans merely dust—are we limited to being creations of the Divine Creator? Or have we blurred the lines of creation and creator as we make cyborgs in our literature, craft human parts in our factories, and conceive and reshape life in our laboratories? Are we limited by the delimitations of Genesis? Humans have always made humans; it is our most essential undertaking. But, in our present and future day, as we stand on the cusp of creating humanoid and cyborg beings, are these creations human? And how human are they—or we—when we shift from being the creation to becoming the creator? What does the future of humanity hold when potential human creations portend to, or likely, supersede human potential and capacity? Rabbi Elliot Dorff stated it clearly: "Human cloning presents not only moral but also theological problems, challenging as it does our very sense of who we are as human beings, both individually and collectively, and requiring us to reaffirm or redefine our role in God's universe."[8]

The question of humans fabricating humanoid beings not only raises concerns regarding the resultant creations themselves, but essentially challenges who we are as human creators.

When we become creators, or fabricators in the case of cloning, we change. We arrogate a power as a creator. The scientist in the laboratory selects cells for specific criteria with the ambition that the resultant new being will develop certain characteristics, traits, or skills. It is an awesome power, and it is entirely contrary to the random possibilities when sperm and egg meet in normal coitus, where any one of millions of spermatozoa might penetrate the oocyte and initiate cell division, maintaining a randomness in genetic selection. Not so in cloning. The scientist is the arbiter, overriding and surpassing natural selection and introducing an ethical element into the generation of life. The scientist must make choices, selecting certain characteristics and rejecting others. Thus, the human creator does not "play God" or emulate God; the human creator supersedes God, who only created the human species in the divine image in Genesis. In the domain of cloning, the scientist crafts a particular individual, not a broad genome. Given this potentiality, Dr. Christof Tannert, chair of the Research Group for Bioethics and Science Communication at the Max Delbrück Centre for Molecular Medicine in Berlin, adds another dimension, arguing that "reproductive cloning . . . is reprehensible because it only fulfils the selfish interest of a creator and arbitrarily curtails the freedom of a third party: the clone."[9] Put in religious terms, regarding the Kabbalist who creates a golem or a scientist who clones a being, the human creator "shares with the Creator the cosmological secrets; he becomes a demiurge when he creates a world."[10] However, as mentioned above, present human cloning science is limited due to the precarious location within mammalian eggs of proteins required for cell division. There is a significant risk of damaging those proteins when undertaking the removal of the nucleus from a potential host cell so it may receive the nucleus from a donor cell. Thus, human cloning, at present, is limited. However, medical literature nevertheless records numerous attempts at human cloning, some succeeding in generating various measures of human zygotes or embryos. None has succeeded past early cell-division embryos, though some fanciful, unverified claims from France and South Korea allege to have resulted in either producing a woman or advanced embryos.

We thus ask, can a human individual be cloned? Dr. Francisco Ayala of University of California, Irvine, writes, "The correct answer is, strictly speaking, no. What is cloned are the genes, not the individual, the genotype, not the phenotype. The technical obstacles are immense even for cloning a human's genotype." Ayala continues, "A person's environmental influences begin, importantly, in the mother's womb and continue after birth, through childhood, adolescence, and the whole life. Impacting behavioral experiences are associated with family, friends, schooling, social and political life, readings, aesthetic and religious experiences, and every event in the person's life."[11]

Yet, humanly manufactured beings may not be all bad. Besides the cloned being, our literature is filled with potential human/machine amalgams—namely, cyborgs. If today we cannot create a new human, perhaps we can create a hybrid. Futurists and transhumanists, who envision such a post-human entity, including David Gelernter, Ray Kurzweil, and Yuval Harari, have posited such beings in which computer interfaces or chips are implanted in human brains, linking a human being directly to the internet and artificial intelligence. Kurzweil calls it "machinification," and Gelernter wonders whether the machine/man would still be human, as machines only do what we tell them to do, while humans bear divine creativity in our DNA.[12] Today's advances in AI challenge Gelernter's conclusion, but not the prospect of the cyborg. Rabbi Danny Schiff, in *Judaism in the Digital Age*, writes that "humanity, as we currently understand the term, will indeed have become something else."[13] We would evolve from *Homo sapiens* to *Homo Deus*. Imagine the possibilities of one with near infinite computing capacity derived from mere thought, because machine and humankind would have merged. We would transcend cognitive limitations, and with advanced biotechnology improvement, we might even triumph over illness, wear and tear, and possibly even death. Such are the possibilities of the cyborg. All we need is the capacity to create one and the wisdom and ethics to control one. After all, Rabbi Zeira and Rabbi Judah Loew destroyed their creations when they could, before the creations were beyond control.

Conclusion

Judaism's first commandment—both chronologically and spiritually—is to reproduce. Doing so makes human beings nearly divine, as only God made human life until we came along and were commanded to generate more, according to Torah, notwithstanding evolutionary science. Thus, the idea and the practice of reproduction have animated Jewish life, from the home to literature to the laboratory, in every generation. And, it has excited the imagination. Torah teases the reader with two accounts of God creating the first human beings and charging us to procreate, tempting subsequent scholars and inventors both to understand and to replicate God's undertaking of crafting humanity.

It would be easy, as both biology and God's creativity endowed us with procreative organs and with a yearning for offspring. Moreover, our faith and history recognized and asserted a spiritual richness intrinsic in sexual union and the potency of pregnancy and childbearing. Again, it made us very nearly divine; only God and humans could make such life. Thus, Judaism recognized a three-way partnership in this process.

Yet, Jewish sages, ever seeking to encounter the Godhead and close the gap between the Creator and the creation, applied Jewish textual wisdom and creative genius toward empowering themselves to replicate God's achievement. Why not? *Homo sapiens* could think and invent, but could we remake ourselves other than sexually? They tried, using the most potent tool at their disposal: Jewish sacred texts derived from God. Did they succeed? Only in lore, but that lore had the force of reality and would be a leitmotif of Jewish mystical textual encounters for centuries.

So too, the twenty-first century continues to open gates to new technological possibilities. We are already well past Dolly the sheep. In biotechnology as well as information technology, the human is the object of exploration and the subject of opportunity. Always seeking to improve our world—*tikkun olam*—why not endeavor to improve our own mortal and cognitive beings? After all, they are limited in lifespan and capacity. Human artifice has proved nimble at moving the goalposts and including and applying new information science into the basic life of human beings. Why not apply the same to fabricating better humans, or more humans, or ultra humans—transhumans? Why be limited to being "just" human when we might be so much more? Such is the next frontier beyond our horizon, yet that horizon is drawing nearer and nearer with every discovery, application, and imagination. However, as with earlier discoveries—dynamite, radio waves, nuclear power—ethics must keep pace with invention, lest the humanoid conquer humanity. It is the risk when the creation becomes the creator.

Such is the challenge for humans making humans, humanoids, cyborgs, and clones.

Notes

1. Translation adapted from the William Davidson digital edition of the *Koren Noé Talmud*, with commentary by Adin Even-Israel Steinsaltz. License: CC-BY-NC, https://creativecommons.org/licenses/by-nc/4.0/, found on Sefaria (sefaria.org).
2. Translation from the William Davidson digital edition of the *Koren Noé Talmud*.
3. Moshe Idel, *Golem: Jewish Magical and Mystical Traditions on the Artificial Anthropoid* (Ktav, 2019), 27–53.
4. Translation adapted from Sefaria Community Translation, found on Sefaria (sefaria.org). License: CC-BY, https://creativecommons.org/licenses/by/3.0.
5. For his most comprehensive study of the golem, see Gershom Scholem, "The Idea of the Golem," in *On the Kabbalah and Its Symbolism* (Schocken, 1965), 158–204; for Rabbi Loew and the Golem of Prague, see 202–3.
6. The Torah is specific in describing physical human defects that precluded a priest from participating in sacrificial rites. Among the defects listed in Leviticus 21:17–21 are those with broken arms, short legs, crushed testes, or who may be blind or lame. The golem, by virtue of having a nonfunctioning mouth—or in some cases, not having a mouth—was rendered physically defective and thus by

extension could be deemed theoretically exempt or disallowed from participation in post-Levitical Jewish ritual obligations.
7. Marge Piercy, *He, She and It* (Random House, 1991).
8. Elliot Dorff, *Matters of Life and Death: A Jewish Approach to Modern Medical Ethics* (Jewish Publication Society, 2003), 312–13.
9. Christof Tannert, "Thou Shalt Not Clone: An Ethical Argument Against the Reproductive Cloning of Humans," *EMBO Reports* 7, no. 3 (March 2006): 238–40.
10. Idel, *Golem*, 266.
11. Francisco J. Ayala, "Cloning Humans? Biological, Ethical, and Social Considerations," *PANA: Proceedings of the National Academy of Sciences* 112, no. 29 (July 21, 2015), https://pubmed.ncbi.nlm.nih.gov/26195738/.
12. See Yuval Harari, *Sapiens: A Brief History of Humankind* (HarperCollins, 2015); Ray Kurzweil, *The Singularity Is Near: When Humans Transcend Biology* (Viking, 2005) and *The Singularity Is Nearer: When We Merge with AI* (Viking, 2024); David Gelernter, "The Closing of the Scientific Mind: Reflections on the Zombie-Scientist Problem," *Commentary*, January 2014, https://www.commentary.org/articles/david-gelernter/the-closing-of-the-scientific-mind/.
13. Danny Schiff, *Judaism in a Digital Age: An Ancient Tradition Confronts a Transformative Era* (Palgrave Macmillan, 2023), 153.

CHAPTER 10

Medium, Message, and Humanity in the Newest Information Age

Rabbi Dan Medwin

הַיָּשָׁן יִתְחַדֵּשׁ וְהֶחָדָשׁ יִתְקַדֵּשׁ.
Renew the old and sanctify the new.
—Rav Kook[1]

OVER THE COURSE of millennia, humanity has undergone a series of dramatic and seismic technological revolutions that have shaped the growth and trajectory of human life. The agricultural revolution[2] and the print revolution[3] are just two examples that have transformed nearly all aspects of the ways in which people live and operate in the world. The next great human revolution has already begun, dubbed "the information age," and the rate of change is rapidly accelerating. Furthermore, as artificial intelligence (AI) becomes more fully developed and integrated into daily life, the transformation of life will increase exponentially.

The Jewish people are naturally impacted by these human-scale societal changes, and consequently Jewish life and practice have been similarly affected by each new development. In fact, given the long history of the Jewish people, the record of human change can be traced according to how each innovation impacted the expression and practice of Judaism.

Judaism, at its core, is a collection of stories that guide actions and identity. In that sense, Judaism itself represents the transmission of information, gathered and expanded in each generation. As the technology of managing information advanced, Jewish leaders and scholars were able to utilize new technologies, taking advantage of the benefits offered over the existing tools. One approach to better understand these changes is to track the growth of vital information metrics: storage, the amount of information a new tool can hold; and transmission, how quickly that information can be shared or copied. By using these metrics as a lens and examining the various stages of the Jewish use of the contemporary information technologies, the compelling advantages of "upgrading" become clear. For example, the shift from handwritten manuscripts to printed books dramatically increased the speed of production, drastically reducing cost and increasing accessibility of the text to the people.

There were also periods throughout Jewish history in which new political, military, or environmental shifts caused an acute threat to sacred Jewish information. In these cases, embracing new technologies was the only option. As external pressures prevailed and the tools for information storage and transmission evolved, Judaism responded and maintained its existence through the adoption and adaptation of new information technologies. With each new approach there were clear benefits. However, new technologies also pose several challenges that must be acknowledged and addressed. By maintaining an awareness of the duality of any new information technology and cultivating an intentionality when embracing a new technology, when we face these challenges today Judaism will not only survive but potentially even thrive through the transition.

Orality

Matters that were taught orally you may not express them in writing.
—Babylonian Talmud, *Gittin* 60b[4]

The foundational texts of the Jewish people began as oral stories passed down from generation to generation. Some of the stories, such as Noah and the Flood, might even predate the identity, or self-conception, of the Jewish people, given the abundant parallels of the flood narrative in other ancient texts.[5] It has even been suggested that the agricultural revolution was captured and passed down in the form of the story of Cain, a farmer/agriculturalist, who killed his brother Abel, a shepherd (more akin to hunters and gatherers).[6]

Scholars disagree as to the timing and editorial work of when the stories contained within the Torah were written down, but the very act of committing this information into handwritten words froze them in time. A similar act took place as the stories and teachings of the early Rabbis were gathered and committed to writing in the form of the Mishnah (circa 200 CE) and later the midrash (circa 400 CE) and Talmud (circa 500–600 CE). Fortunately, there was a degree of self-awareness and debate captured in the text.

The Rabbis were aware of the benefits of an oral tradition. The text remains dynamic, changing and adapting to suit the needs of the students or the cultural milieu. The teacher is able to expand or explain specific lessons or stories in a dialogical relationship with the learner. Additionally, the teacher can act as a "gatekeeper" for the information, sharing only the appropriate amount and the relevant teachings for that moment.

There are also challenges and limitations to the oral transmission of information. Primarily, it is the fragility of the information storage device—the human brain—and the risk of information being permanently lost. The rate of transfer and propagation, in this case the time it takes for a teacher to fully impart a selection of text, can also be quite slow—although, at this time in human history, faster information transmission could not even be imagined.

Fearing the loss of the oral tradition, and capturing the justification of breaking the prohibition within the text itself not to write down oral teachings, we read: "Rather, since it is not possible to remember the Oral Law without writing it down, it is permitted to violate the halachah, as indicated by the verse: 'It is time to act for the Eternal; they have violated Your Torah' (Psalm 119:126)" (Babylonian Talmud, *Gittin* 60a).[7] As is often the case with each progression from one method of information storage and transmission to the next, the updated form mimics the old. The structure of the Mishnah and Talmud attempts to capture the essence of the oral transmission by presenting the teachings through discussion and debate, even if those placed in dialogue lived hundreds of years apart.

The Written Form: Stone

The Eternal One said to Moses, "Come up to Me on the mountain and wait there, and I will give you the stone tablets with the teachings and commandments which I have inscribed to instruct them."
—Exodus 24:12

The initial method of the written transmission of teachings, as presented through Jewish tradition, is engraved words in stone—that is, the tablets of the Ten Commandments. As contrasted to the fragility of information contained within human memories, words carved into stone represent permanence and authority. The text storage device is similarly durable and stable. Marshall McLuhan's adage "The medium is the message,"[8] while not referring to stone tablets, is nevertheless applicable. The medium of the stone conveys powerful messages and meanings.

Conversely, as with any information technology, there are limitations. Stone tablets are not indestructible, as evidenced in Moses's act of shattering the initial set of tablets: "He hurled the tablets from his hands and shattered them at the foot of the mountain" (Exodus 32:19). In a powerful metaphor expressing the value the information technology of the past, "the broken pieces of the first set of tablets, were placed in the *Aron* [*HaBrit*, the Ark of the Covenant]" (Babylonian Talmud, *B'rachot* 8b) and carried with the new set of tablets. Similarly today, outdated or retired code is often kept within a program's updated code for reference and documentation purposes.

The resulting weight of the four tablets was consequently significant. Transmitting this information—transporting it through the wilderness—was no simple task. It required a specialized container (the *Aron HaBrit*) and multiple individuals to carry it. Furthermore, with only one copy available to the community, the accessibility of the information to the people was significantly limited.

Several subsequent technologies followed stone tablets, such as ostraca, cuneiform, and clay tablets. While there is evidence of their use in daily Jewish life for mundane notes, financial transactions, or even military correspondence, their use in ritual practices in Jewish life was not chronicled. Even writing on plant-based parchment, which offered significant benefits over stone and clay, was not adopted, perhaps due to the fragility of the paper.

The Written Form: Parchment

Around the second century BCE, writing on animal skin parchment was developed; this represented such an important upgrade from stone and clay tablets, as well as plant-based papyrus, that Jewish leaders adopted this new technology for storing and accessing information, particularly the Torah. A parchment scroll can contain significantly more text in a given volume than ostraca, stone, or clay forms and can be easily expanded by adding more sheets, all the while remaining relatively light and more easily transportable. Wrapping the parchment sheets around wooden poles added durability and easier access.

Even with these added benefits, there are limitations to parchment as an information storage container. Parchment itself is fragile, in the sense that the ink on the page can fade and the pages themselves can be ripped or burned. Additionally, parchment is difficult to produce in large quantities. The rate of transfer is also incredibly slow, if using the contemporary metric of a year for a *sofer* (scribe) to create a new copy of a Torah. Additionally, access to a particular section of the volume can be cumbersome, as experienced by any Torah reader on Simchat Torah who has read the final words of *D'varim* (Deuteronomy) and wishes to continue reading with the first words of *B'reishit* (Genesis). "Rewinding" a scroll is not an efficient method of accessing the text.

The Written Form: Handwritten Manuscripts

Folios (circa first century CE), bound books (such as codices, circa second through fourth centuries CE), and early manuscripts (circa fifth century CE) directly addressed the challenge of the rate of access of parchment scrolls. Storing text on discrete pages, which can be turned individually or in bulk, allows for more rapid access to different sections of the document. This new technology also enabled the creation of an index, with the support of page numbers, thereby allowing much more rapid access to a particular section or topic within the text. Additionally, the form of the manuscript was also more conducive to storing multiple volumes in a compact space, as well as presenting an overall lighter-form factor.

This information storage container upgrade did not materially address one of the unfortunate metrics of information technology associated with the parchment scroll: slow transmission. The creation or duplication of a volume is a labor- and time-intensive process, wherein a specially trained expert spends many hours completing the task. This results in an expensive product that requires significant resources to acquire. In many Jewish communities, it was only the community leaders using the collective resources of the community, along with any wealthy members of the community, who had access to these handwritten sacred text containers. This lack of access of the general public to information kept literacy rates low and knowledge of the information in the hands of relatively few.

Printed Books

In the mid-fifteenth century, a little less than six hundred years ago, Johannes Gutenberg perfected the movable type printing press. While maintaining the benefits of the handwritten manuscript, the printed book revolutionized the speed at which a document could be created or copied, drastically reducing the cost. This permitted an increasing number of individuals to have access to their own copy of the text and represented the first democratization of information. Literacy, education, and Jewish prayer were all dramatically impacted and transformed.

Previously, prayer leaders held one of the few, if only, copies of the prayers.[9] Participants would follow along if they had memorized the prayer or would simply add *amen* at the conclusion of the recitation. With a printed prayer book in the hand of each pray-er, everyone had direct access to the text. What has been considered the norm in Jewish prayer practice for over half a millennium—holding a prayer book—was once a monumental shift in Jewish practice and life. Notably, the first mass printed book was the Gutenberg Bible. The print revolution put the sacred texts of Judaism into the hands of the populace, which in turn is what allowed the Jewish people to truly become the "People of the Book."

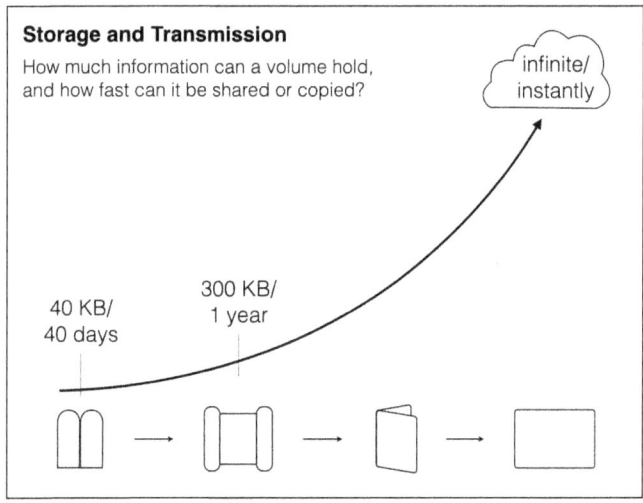

Information Age

Perhaps the greatest transformation of information storage and transmission occurred with the development of networked computers. While a library of books can offer a wealth of information, the small metal, plastic, and glass device held within one's hand can offer access to *all* the world's digitized information. With the ability to transmit nearly unlimited information almost instantaneously, humanity and Judaism must once again grapple with the benefits and challenges of an innovation in information technology.

The benefits cannot be understated. Modern information and communication technology allows any individual on the planet to connect with any other individual or group using a pocket computer (commonly called a smartphone) via text, voice, images, and/or video. Organizations like Sefaria have made access to the wealth of Jewish texts available at one's fingertips, with translations, cross-references, and search functionality (all of which once was limited to the whims of a scholar's memory). Beyond the Jewish textual tradition, practically all historical and contemporary knowledge and news information is accessible anytime, anywhere. There are no more "gatekeepers" controlling the flow of information, and any individual can contribute to this infinitely expanding body of information (as with Wikipedia).

Some of the benefits of this revolution in information technology are also its challenges. Any individual can contribute to the body of information, whether or not they are well-educated or well-intentioned. The traditional gatekeepers of information (rabbis, scholars, editors, publishers) are no longer able to prioritize and filter the transmission of knowledge. The sheer volume of information currently available to consume is more than an individual can process in a lifetime.

Social media platforms, which represent one of the most robust and easily accessible tools for sharing information, utilize computer-based algorithms to filter and focus the information presented to an individual. Algorithms, the new information gatekeepers, are written by human coders and designed to sift through the wealth of information available by attempting to identify which pieces of information the user is likely to want to receive. Unfortunately, one of the unintended consequences of this tool is the reinforcement of one's already held ideas and beliefs, effectively creating an "echo chamber" and contributing to the polarization of contemporary society.

Additionally, while most algorithms are written with the best of intentions, they are vulnerable to nefarious manipulation for financial and/or political gain. Many believe that this may have been the case with X, formerly known as Twitter. When purchased in 2022, users noted an increase in the prominence of posts from specific individuals, a reduction in content moderation efforts, and a host of other alterations to the algorithm. The vulnerability of a particular information platform, which is ultimately a corporate entity subject to hostile takeovers, CEO whims, and the ultimate drive for profits, leads many information consumers and creators to desire an alternative.

Bluesky was initially created as a project within Twitter in 2019 and gained independence in 2022 when Twitter was purchased. In 2023,

Bluesky was launched publicly as an independent, decentralized, and open-source alternative to X. Bluesky allows users to create or select their own desired algorithm that is not subject to the control of a corporation's edicts. It also permits users to retain their content and followers when switching platforms. Communication in this particular form was freed from the monopoly of a single company and democratized information access once again. And while this solution allowed users to be their own gatekeepers of information, it does not address the sheer volume of information.

The latest technological tool that can sift, sort, analyze, and summarize an unfathomable amount of information in just a few moments is artificial intelligence (AI). Rather than using algorithms to filter existing information, such as social media posts or websites from search results, AI "learns" from the information it is fed and generates novel text to answer natural language questions. While still suffering from its own limitations, such as hallucinations (confidently making up information that is not true) and flawed training data (untrue or biased information written by individuals), AI allows for a much more natural and human-centered way of accessing the wealth of information currently available.

In some ways, this may represent a return to the benefits of an oral tradition, namely a dialogical encounter with information. One may follow up with questions or clarifications when conversing with AI just as one can do with a human teacher; this is not possible when searching or reading static text on one's own such as in Google search results. There are currently several AI "Rabbi" apps, to which one may pose Jewish textual or halachic questions.

Another challenge presented by this digital flow of information is the creation and extensive use of "bots." Bots are computer programs that can mimic individuals online and can be used to spread (dis)information without the need for rest or breaks. They simultaneously increase the sheer amount of information available to consume while clouding the authenticity of the accessible information. Meta has even stated that its goals are to fill Facebook and Instagram with AI bots to mimic real people. It risks becoming, quite literally, a *makom she-ein anashim*, "a place where there are no people."[10]

Mitigating the Challenges of the Information Age

As with any new revolution in technology, there are clear benefits and drawbacks. When the apparent benefits outweigh the perceived challenges, there is a societal shift toward adopting the new technology. However, there are always groups that highlight the dangers of new technology and attempt to block or hide from its impact. For example, in ultra-Orthodox Jewish communities, there is a prevalence of "kosher" phones that have limited functionality or content filters.[11] However, it is clear that these attempts are not foolproof, and their adoption represents a significant diversion from the general population. Given the momentum of the larger societal progression, it may feel impossible or impractical to fully resist the change, so many will resultingly accept and adapt, possibly even embrace, new information technology. This choice should not be done blindly. By examining the challenges and identifying strategies and methods for counteracting or negating these detriments, the mainstream Jewish community can maintain a degree of autonomy through this transition.

Accessing Information

Contemporary religious and secular educational systems, which were developed pre-computers, focus predominantly on learning and memorizing key pieces of data; this is the process of information acquisition. Teachers and textbooks serve as the gatekeepers of information, curating the most essential lessons. The emphasis on information over understanding is especially evident in the proliferation and utilization of standardized testing. However, now that the world's information is available on any wirelessly connected device, educational systems need to significantly shift their focus to how one processes and evaluates information. It must adapt to address how learners can find reliable answers to questions and how to discern trusted sources of information.

The concept of "eco-kosher" describes the process and outcomes of applying and interpreting the principles of kashrut filtered through the lens of ecological awareness and environmental stewardship to the preparation of food and other consumer and social behaviors. It may be possible to develop a concept of "info kosher"[12] to apply Jewish values and ethics to the consumption of information and other online behaviors.

Can Jewish leaders compile an ever-growing list of guidelines and sources for ensuring the authenticity and accuracy of information online? How can sources that regularly and knowingly provide misinformation be held accountable? Is there a set of best practices, or even rules, for consuming information and behaving online? Given the speed at which the technology is developing, any religious or ethical process intended to keep pace must be resultingly agile and nimble. Perhaps revisiting the benefits of an oral tradition, such as the dynamic nature of the text and the dialogical encounter that allows a teacher to adapt an answer for a given student or situation, will ensure the relevance of this endeavor.

One traditional Jewish text that may prove illustrative is the one that is the focus of this volume: *B'makom she-ein anashim, hishtadeil lih'yot ish*, "In a place where there is no humanity, strive to be human" (*Pirkei Avot* 2:6). If there is a particular platform or source of information that seems filled with bots and incorrect information, one can try to combat it through their own expression of humanity, by reporting bots, or by simply refraining from accessing that source. Similarly, platforms that permit cyberbullying should be avoided and reported.

Another approach may be to diversify the source of one's information and online communities by using a variety of search engines, social media channels, and even AI chatbots. Each platform utilizes a different algorithm and approach to information, thereby preventing any one source from having a monopoly on information and communication and an outsized impact on the user.

Human development and evolution have not kept pace with technological change. People are not meant to spend hours every day staring at a screen. We have already begun noticing the physical and mental health impacts of this lifestyle. Physical aches in the neck, shoulders, and back, sleep disruption, and a greater risk of obesity and heart disease are all symptoms of a sedentary screen-based life. Reduction of attention spans, constant stress and interruptions, and social shaming with cyberbullying are all artifacts of a hyper-connected life. Ideally, through recognizing and being aware of these challenges, people can begin to step away from the screens and put down their phones with a greater sense of intentionality and frequency.

Shabbat is one traditional Jewish practice that may help in this regard. By refraining not only from working, but from consuming harmful information at least one day a week, Jews may be able to reset or at least mitigate some of the detrimental impacts of the information age. Access to infinite information at any time of day does not come without a cost, and breaks must be intentional and regular. In this author's household, the practice of prohibiting phone usage during all dinners facilitates interactions and family conversations that do not occur as readily when mobile phones are involved.

Combating Loneliness

Another remarkable benefit of Shabbat is the recognition of and emphasis on the importance of community. Gathering in person still matters. In a Conservative responsum asking about praying in a minyan over the internet, written in 2001, Rabbi Avram Israel Reisner writes, "When the [early] rabbis moved to require a quorum for communal public prayers and banned response absent a quorum, it seems that they were opting to force the community to come together."[13] He explains that it is the physical act of gathering together that allows relationships to be formed and communal structures to be developed. Prayer was the framing concept for the requirement to gather in person. The Hebrew word for synagogue, *beit k'neset*, means "house of gathering." Knowing that the origins of the imperative to physically gather together was framed around the act of prayer, we may be able to determine another equally valid reason for gathering. Whatever the motivating framework may be, it is incumbent on us to find ways and opportunities to gather in person.

Communication technology has given us the ability to gather and even pray remotely, or "virtually." And this type of gathering can be quite meaningful. During the COVID pandemic, this was the only avenue the Jewish community had for weddings, funerals, and bet mitzvah services.[14] But it also revealed how vital being together in person truly is.

The ancient Israelites lived scattered about the land but gathered together at the Temple three times a year for the Pilgrimage Festivals: Passover, Shavuot, and Sukkot. Similarly, many contemporary American Jews gather in person only twice a year, on Rosh HaShanah and Yom Kippur.

Distance relationships can be real and meaningful, but the act of being together—not mitigated by a screen, seeing more than just a face—can deepen and sustain any relationship. Gathering in person only two or three times a year can potentially be sufficient, provided there are personal and ongoing opportunities to continue the relationship throughout the intervening time. This is a pattern familiar to many extended families who do not live within the same city or neighborhood.

Chavruta (partner) study is also a powerful practice that can build and maintain relationships, whether it is done in person or remotely (or some combination of the two). In fact, this is one of the most cherished teaching practices, as described in *Pirkei Avot* 3:3, "If two sit together and words of Torah are [spoken or studied] between them, the Divine Presence rests between them."[15] This form of study is also based on and benefits from the form of dialogical information exchange in which contemporary Jewish life and practice were formed.

On the Horizon

There are two nascent technologies that are poised to accelerate the opportunities and challenges presented by the information age: artificial intelligence and brain computer interfaces (BCI). Both of these fields of technological exploration stand to extend the interdependence of humanity and computers, perhaps even challenging the very notion of what it means to be human.

Artificial Intelligence

Even the most advanced computers that predate AI are now considered "dumb." They must be specifically told each step of every task by a computer programmer. They can perform complex calculations faster than any human by orders of magnitude, as long as a human tells it what to do. AI represents a dramatic shift and the possibility of growth beyond human limitations of coding instructions. AI systems, some of which are commonly known as "large language models," are given vast amounts of data to ingest, then "learn" on their own how to draw conclusions from the information and generate responses. As a rather basic example, the reader can see examples of AI output in the endnotes of this chapter. Since AI is able to identify patterns beyond human comprehension, it is accelerating many fields of research and development, including medicine, chemistry, material sciences, and more.

When developing new Jewish law (halachah) or practices, Jewish leaders look to existing texts and principles to draw new applications and conclusions. AI has the ability to consider the totality of Jewish texts and provide an expansive overview and summary of relevant topics and texts. Currently, AI may not be able to understand the nuances and context of a particular text or decision, but that time may not be far off. Will committed practicing Jews one day turn to AI for Jewish answers rather than to human Jewish leaders? Will Jewish leaders use AI as a tool and then draw their own conclusions? Jewish leaders and average Jews today can consult AI personas based on historic Torah scholars, such as Rashi or Rambam. But AI should never be the last word. One helpful principle employed by the Google education team is that AI can be a powerful tool, but there must always be a teacher or human "in the loop."[16]

Brain Computer Interface

With initial research often focused on paralyzed individuals, the ability to connect a human brain directly to a computer has dramatic and limitless potential. Often done through the surgical implanting of electrodes in a patient's brain, although possible in a less precise manner through sensors worn on a skull cap, a BCI allows a computer to read the signals and waves generated by a human's brain.

Currently, through a BCI, a human's thoughts can be translated into text on a screen with 90 percent accuracy. Miraculously, a paralyzed man can fly a virtual drone through an obstacle course just by thinking of lifting his fingers to steer.[17] As this technology further develops, it may soon be possible for a human to effortlessly interface with a computer, not by inputting text via a typewriter-like keyboard or even through verbal commands, but simply by thinking.

The inverse of this flow of information, still years away but conceivable at this point, is gaining information from a computer, or even another human, through a BCI. How will humanity be transformed when one can share a thought directly from their brain into another's? How will communal prayer be experienced when one can think another's thoughts, hopes, and dreams? It may dramatically increase one's capacity for empathy. There is already evidence through group brain scans that when people sing together, human brain waves become synchronized. What if human brains can be networked together in prayer? Perhaps this is a path to more fully understand and connect with, or even experience, God.

Additionally, as AI develops and hallucinations are reduced or eliminated, access to AI through a BCI may constitute the next level of human development. Steve Jobs called the computer the "bicycle of the mind" because it extends human capabilities. Many today use their mobile device to extend their memory to include dates, phone numbers, addresses, and more. If AI can be integrated directly within the human brain, it could expand human thought and capabilities in ways that are unimaginable today.

How will Jewish life and practice be impacted by this type of development? How will Jewish mourning practices—or even mourning itself—change if virtual AI avatars of deceased loved ones can be created for conversations, questions, and comfort? What will a *d'var Torah* (word of Torah) or *d'rash* (sermon) look like if members of the community have instant access to the entirety of the Jewish canon, with the ability to process and summarize all of it? Can AI, via BCIs, create shared interactive virtual "dreams," such as the experience of crossing through the parted Sea of Reeds? How can one truly unplug or rest on Shabbat if our brains are networked to computers? These are questions that will need to be addressed in the coming years.

Conclusion

Humanity is standing on the precipice of an unprecedented leap forward in human existence through the information technologies being developed at an ever-increasing rate. As with each new development of information technology in the past, Jewish life and practice have adopted and adapted the new tools and incorporated them into Judaism.

It is incumbent upon contemporary and future Jewish leaders to deeply study, understand, and experience these new technologies and to think critically about utilizing them for the benefits they provide, while mitigating the accompanying challenges. And, as we see a world filled ever more with the virtual and artificial, we must continue to wrestle with what it means to strive to be human. Only then will Judaism continue to be relevant and accessible to the Jewish people, for at least another couple thousand years or more.

Notes

1. Rav Avraham Yitzchak HaCohen Kook (1865–1935) was a pioneering Jewish thinker, mystic, and halachic authority who served as the first Ashkenazi chief rabbi of British Mandatory Palestine, advocating for a synthesis of Torah, Zionism, and modernity (summary by ChatGPT 4o).
2. The agricultural revolution, also known as the Neolithic revolution, began around 10,000 BCE in the Fertile Crescent and gradually spread worldwide, marking the transition from hunter-gatherer societies to settled farming communities (summary by ChatGPT 4o).
3. The print revolution, sparked by Johannes Gutenberg's invention of the movable-type printing press in the mid-fifteenth century, dramatically increased the spread of knowledge, literacy, and ideas across Europe, fueling the Renaissance, Reformation, and scientific revolution (summary by ChatGPT 4o).
4. Translations of the Babylonian Talmud are from the William Davidson digital edition of the *Koren Noé Talmud*, with commentary by Adin Even-Israel Steinsaltz (license: CC-BY-NC, https://creativecommons.org/licenses/by-nc/4.0/), found on Sefaria (sefaria.org).

5. Several ancient Mesopotamian texts predate the Torah and contain flood stories similar to Noah's. The Epic of Gilgamesh (circa 2100–1800 BCE) features Utnapishtim, who is warned by the gods to build a boat and save life from a great flood. Earlier versions, like the Atrahasis Epic and the Sumerian Flood Story (Ziusudra), also describe a chosen man surviving a divine deluge, suggesting that flood myths were widespread in the ancient Near East before being incorporated into the Biblical tradition (summary by ChatGPT 4o).
6. Daniel Quinn, *Ishmael* (Bantam Books, 1995).
7. Translation adapted from the William Davidson digital edition of the *Koren Noé Talmud*, with commentary by Adin Even-Israel Steinsaltz (license: CC-BY-NC, https://creativecommons.org/licenses/by-nc/4.0/), found on Sefaria (sefaria.org).
8. Marshall McLuhan, *Understanding Media: The Extensions of Man* (McGraw-Hill, 1964), 7.
9. The original prayer book (siddur) contained a list or order (*seder*) of the prayers and later contained the full text of prayers that are known today.
10. See John Herman, "Meta's Big Bet on Bots: Why AI Friends Are Coming to Facebook and Instagram," *New York*, December 31, 2024, https://nymag.com/intelligencer/article/meta-wants-more-ai-bots-on-facebook-and-instagram.html.
11. Nomi Kaltmann, "Can a 'Kosher' Phone Cure Your Tech Addiction?," *Daily Beast*, February 29, 2024, https://www.thedailybeast.com/can-kosher-phones-used-by-ultra-orthodox-jews-cure-tech-addiction/.
12. The original concept of "info kosher" was conceived by Rabbi Lydia Medwin.
13. Avram Israel Reisner, "Wired to the Kadosh Barukh Hu: Minyan via Internet," Committee of Jewish Law and Standards of the Rabbinical Assembly, March 13, 2001, https://www.rabbinicalassembly.org/sites/default/files/public/halakhah/teshuvot/19912000/reisner_internetminyan.pdf.
14. "Bet mitzvah" is the gender-inclusive term for a Jewish coming-of-age ceremony at thirteen, as adopted by the CCAR Board on January 12, 2023.
15. Shmuly Yanklowitz, *Pirkei Avot: A Social Justice Commentary* (CCAR Press, 2018), 129.
16. "Google for Education: A Guide to AI in Education," Google, 2024, https://services.google.com/fh/files/misc/global_google_for_education_a_guide_for_ai.pdf.
17. Matthew Sparkes, "Brain Implant Lets Man with Paralysis Fly a Virtual Drone by Thought," *NewScientist*, January 20, 2025, https://www.newscientist.com/article/2464080-brain-implant-lets-man-with-paralysis-fly-a-virtual-drone-by-thought/.

CONCLUSION

Tensions Between the Good and the Perfect

Rabbi Leah Cohen Tenenbaum, DMin, BCC-PCHAC

IN STRIVING to be human today, we run into an ancient and continuing conundrum that has gripped our minds, hearts, and spirits since the dawn of civilization—namely, if we are lauded by our Creator at the start of Creation as being "very good," if society consistently focuses on human improvements and advancements from ancient history through the space age, if we are schooled from youth that a score of 100 percent is the goal, might we then surmise that the logical and natural extension of "very good" is perfection? Might perfection be the culmination of "the idea of progress"?

Enter our current information age in which zero tolerance for error or deviation is the intentional design of technology, which imitates and increasingly replaces what once was considered exclusively human activity. What if nonhuman entities functioning with artificial intelligence are not only "very good," but actually "better than" and potentially even "perfect" at being human? Should we humans "step up our game"? Is it even possible for us to be perfect?

Alas, we know that the answers are "no" and "no." Are we then to shrink off into history, licking our wounded pride, and wait for Armageddon? Let us consider other alternatives before we succumb to despair. We might find some comfort in knowing that the notions of human perfection and imperfection have been around for a long while.

Historical Overview of Human Perfection in Western Thought

Perhaps the earliest evidence we have regarding the search for human perfection in Western thought can be found in Plato's writings. In his *Theory of Forms*, Plato envisioned a perfect human form that existed beyond our earthly reality and posited that all humans are merely imperfect copies of this perfect form.

Furthermore, the concept of human perfection assumes that the good in humans can be developed. Great minds over the course of history have emphasized different aspects of human nature as the focus of perfection. Taking a historical perspective means understanding the social, cultural, intellectual, and emotional settings that shaped people's lives and actions in the past as the backdrop for a definition of human perfection.

For example, the ancient Greeks, lovers of aesthetics, sought perfection of the human body in the living being, in sculpture, and in poetry. On the other hand, Aristotle argued that the main function of humans was rational activity. For him, human perfection was tied to intellectual rationality performed in accordance with virtue.

Aquinas, the thirteenth-century theologian, believed that humans naturally strove to do good and that happiness was the goal of human perfection. For the early Christians, human happiness was flawed, but a perfect union with God was the ultimate happiness and thus the goal of human perfection. For Karl Marx, the nineteenth-century economist and philosopher, human perfection could only be achieved in a society with equal resources for all.

With the more recent developments of science and medical innovations, human perfection has taken on new possibilities with the pursuit of expanding, repairing, or altering our bodies and minds, with hopes for increased health, longevity, or function. Each age sees the possibility for human perfection through its own lens, bringing together the quest for individual and collective perfection.

Jewish Thought on Human Perfection

Jewish thought throughout the ages sheds an interesting and complex perspective on the notion of human perfection. What might we mine from our tradition to help understand what it means to be human today while aiming to be perfect, when we know we cannot be perfect? We can start by looking at the words themselves.

The English word "perfect" comes from the Latin word *perficere*. *Perficere* is composed of two parts: *per*, meaning "thorough, completely"; and *facere*, meaning "do." Thus, we see two fundamental components of perfection as used in English and Latin-based languages—namely, the underlying assumption of "perfection" focuses on completion and action. These core principles describe one view of perfection.

Another view of perfection can be discovered in the Hebrew word for perfect, *mushlam*. *Mushlam* does not describe an action; rather it describes a state of being, meaning "wholeness" or "fullness." Familiar to many, the common Hebrew word is derived from the root *shin-lamed-mem*, the same root as the Hebrew words for peace (*shalom*) and wholeness (*sh'leimut*).

In both Latin and Hebrew, we can see the notion of completeness in the words for perfect. But in English, "completeness" is a result of "doing," whereas in Hebrew "completeness" is a state of being. This important point elucidates the difference between a "human being" and a "human doing" in relation to the notion of perfection.

We have the capacity for both doing and being, and Jewish teaching illuminates how both aspects intertwine in ways that make us uniquely human as we contemplate the notion of human perfection.

Human Doings

Often referenced as a religion of "deed" more than "creed," it would appear that Judaism leans heavily toward "doing." The Israelites, upon receiving the commandments at Mount Sinai, responded: *Naaseh v'nishma*, "We will do, and we will listen" (Exodus 24:7). How could a group of people do anything perfectly if they pledge to act first and listen second? It sounds like a perfect recipe for a lot of mistakes! Yet the centrality of mitzvot in Judaism, as actions to do or not do, again underscores the importance of doing.

However, Judaism recognizes the inherent limitations in our ability as human doings. The multiple opportunities for *t'shuvah*, the chance to sincerely acknowledge and redo our less than perfect actions, is our process for accepting that our actions are not perfect and we can do better. We are regularly encouraged to examine our deeds, learn from our mistakes, and do better.

On the other hand, there are limitations to what we can do as humans, as earlier described in *Pirkei Avot* 2:21, "It is not your duty to finish the work, but neither are you at liberty to neglect it."[1] Our inherent inability to perfectly complete our actions is complicated. We have both limited competence and limited capacity for completing any task.

But there is a third obstacle in our ability to be perfect human doings. As noted earlier in this volume, humans are created with a *yetzer hara*, the impulse to do evil, and a *yetzer hatov*, the impulse to do good; thus, we have a design flaw. Could you imagine if a machine was created by design with the capacity to work well *and* to mess up? The Rabbis, in trying to understand human nature, acknowledge the good impulse as desirable but the evil impulse as necessary, and both are intentionally embedded in the human design.

In a sincere effort to help humanity behave better, maybe even perfectly, the Rabbis in midrash address the purpose of the evil impulse (*B'reishit Rabbah* 9:7). The Rabbis aspire to remove forces in society that they associate with the evil impulse without considering how that impulse could result in positive outcomes. For example, the drive to compete for status or to be self-sufficient might result in diminishing or hurting someone else or creating conflict. But this same impulse can also be the driving force behind building a house. The sexual urge that can create tension and even injustice could also result in choosing a spouse or procreating. In this midrash, the Rabbis quickly learn that without the evil impulse, no one would build a house, take a spouse, or have children. They see that all labor and the effort to excel are a result of human rivalry with their neighbors (see Ecclesiastes 4:4)—a trait they associate with the evil impulse. In this midrash, the Rabbis realize that their effort to make people "more perfect" could result in a society that is worse off.

In a midrash from the Babylonian Talmud *Yoma* 69b, the Rabbis realize that their effort to make people "more perfect" could result in harm to society as they come to terms with the reality that the evil impulse is part of the human design. They imagine capturing the evil impulse and locking it up. After three days, when not an egg could be found—a symbol for the end of the world's regular machinations—the Rabbis ponder, "What shall we do?" Their plans—to redesign society by having human behavior stem exclusively from the good impulse—have backfired. Human action could not be perfected in this way. What did they do? They gouged out the evil impulse's eyes, effectively limiting its power, then set it free—thereby ensuring that the world would carry on. Humans would continue to act imperfectly, but hopefully with a bit less potent evil impulse.

Apparently, having these conflicting impulses is part of the human design. These Rabbinic stories acknowledge this baffling truth and at the same time capture the moral distress the evil impulse caused for the Rabbis as well as for most humans today. We, like the Rabbis in the stories, are powerless to change human nature—our being. However, like those Rabbis of old, we are empowered to modify behavioral outcomes in favor of the good.

Human Beings

Thus, if the possibility for human perfection does not exist as "human doings," might we get closer to this aspiration as "human beings"? Could we strive to be *mushlam*—not perfect or complete in our doing, but full in our being? Let us explore some specifically Jewish thoughts on this possibility.

In Judaism we imagine ourselves as partners with God in the ongoing act of Creation. *Tikkun olam*, repairing our imperfect world, is mirrored in the equally important task of *tikkun atzmi*, repairing ourselves. How are we to repair our imperfect selves? A uniquely Jewish approach to refining our personality traits is Mussar, a spiritual discipline that gives specific instructions on how to live a meaningful and ethical life by cultivating our inner virtues through study and meditation. This practice acknowledges that though we are created "less than perfect," we can improve ourselves to be the most virtuous, ethical, and best versions of ourselves; this pursuit may not attain perfection, but is demonstrably better.

Human beings are multidimensional; one aspect of being human is our capacity for feelings. Too often we label feelings as either "good" or "bad." We are taught to hide our "bad feelings," such as anger, sadness, or fear, and reveal only our "good feelings," such as compassion, generosity, and love. But our imperfect design as human beings includes a wide spectrum of emotions. When it comes to feelings, acknowledging the breadth of our emotions, seeking a balance of our highs and lows, and distinguishing action from feeling pave the path to *mushlam*, a sense of fullness for the totality of our "human being."

We are not more "perfect" if we deny parts of ourselves, as Rabbi Ellen Lewis shares in chapter 5. Unlike some other traditions, Judaism does not embrace denial of pleasure as a method for becoming a better human being. Asceticism is not a normative practice in Judaism. In fact, it is the opposite. "In the future, a person will give a judgment and an accounting over everything that one's eye saw but one did not eat" (Jerusalem Talmud, *Kiddushin* 4:12), by which the Rabbis mean that we are obligated to partake in every enjoyment possible unless there is sufficient reason not to.[2] Enjoying permitted pleasures in moderation is how the medieval philosopher Maimonides described the "golden mean" of Aristotle: taking care of our physical as well as spiritual needs by avoiding the extremes of overindulgence or complete denial.

Does Judaism then offer any version of a perfect human being? Yes and no. We might look at the requirements for the *kohanim*, the priests who offered sacrifices at the time of the ancient Temple: "No one at all who has a defect shall be qualified: no man who is blind, or lame, or has a limb too short or too long; no man who has a broken leg or a broken arm; or who is a hunchback, or a dwarf, or who has a growth in his eye, or who has a boil-scar, or scurvy" (Leviticus 21:18–20).

This description sounds like an ancient version of human perfection that is inconsistent with our modern understanding of diversity, equity, and inclusion. It reminds me of a time when flight attendants had specific height, weight, age, gender, and appearance requirements and how these requirements have evolved even in our lifetime. Specific human qualifications for specific jobs might describe the perceived "perfect" candidate for a specific role at a specific time, but certainly not for all human beings, for all time.

If being "unblemished" for a particular human role is not a universal description of human perfection, is there no aspect of being human that is already perfect in Judaism? Yes, there is. Our morning prayers remind us, "My God, the soul you have given me is pure." In reciting this daily prayer, we acknowledge that our souls are pure.

We understand that as mortals, our bodies have a limited shelf life. They will, sooner or later, fail us. Illness, suffering, old age (if we are fortunate), and eventually death are inevitable. As much as we do not like to think about these imperfect outcomes, they are more than likely; they are unavoidable. At the same time, Judaism teaches that we are more than our physical bodies. We have souls that are eternal, unblemished, and perfect. Jewish theology asserts that our perfect souls exist long after our imperfect, blemished bodies have returned to dust.

Conclusion

Humans are complex. We are human doings and human beings. We have perfect souls in imperfect bodies, full of both the evil and good impulses. We are permitted pleasure, but not without guidelines and limits. In Judaism, we reject asceticism, Gnosticism, and dualism, accepting our role as partners with God in helping to repair this imperfect world. We accept that our Creator created each of us perfectly imperfect, full of paradox and struggle. Had we been perfect, we would still be in the Garden of Eden, but our Creator had a different design in mind, for us and for the world.

The process of dealing with our flaws is the consistent human experience. We might conclude that "good" is better than "perfect" for humans—it allows for the potential of growth, creativity, *t'shuvah*, and complexity that resembles the process of Creation itself. Striving to be human is the ability to embrace this fullness and flawed-ness, each in our own unique way.

We also find a clue that the objective of this striving as an individual is not personal gain, but rather it is for the benefit of the collective good. If we carefully parse the Hebrew in *Pirkei Avot* 2:6, we can find a deeper interpretation of this verse knowing that one of God's many names is *HaMakom*, The Place. "In a place where there is no humanity, strive to be human"—*Bamakom sh'ein anashim, hishtadeil lih'yot ish*. We might interpret that only in our individual, self-reflective striving (*hishtadeil*) to be fully human (*lih'yot ish*, in the singular) can humanity (*anashim*, in the plural)—and thus our collective good—thrive, according to God's (*BaMakom*) plan.

In Judaism, concern for the "collective good" is an inherent part of what it means to be human. However, we are living at a time when increasingly even the concept of the collective good—let alone how best to address it—is being brushed aside. When one billionaire can offer a million-dollar "reward" at an election rally, what influence does that have on the collective good? When one person doubts science and chooses not to become vaccinated, what impact does that have on the collective? When rules established to protect and promote a safe and fair society are dismantled or ignored by those who wield power, how does that serve the collective good?

We come now full circle to the start of this book where the ontological flow, beginning with challenges from within ourselves and extending to challenges beyond us, was laid out. Throughout the book, we have explored what it means to strive to be human in confronting these challenges, through the lens of Jewish wisdom and experience across the ages. But what we have not yet addressed is the first part of this quote, the dire preamble, "In a place where there is no humanity. . . ."

Surely with over eight billion human beings living on planet Earth today, can we really say we are living in a place with no humanity? Maybe it is premature to start striving; after all, what's the rush? As we conclude this book, let us pause to examine what a place where there is no humanity might look like and to consider if we have reached that destination yet or are even close. Then we might be in a better position to answer the question "Is now the time to strive?"

In chapter 1, Rabbi Sarah Bassin, in describing moral justice especially for the most vulnerable in society, notes a "global backsliding toward authoritarian-tinged nationalism" despite the fragile, yet persistent tool kit of the three-legged stool of "empathy-fueled conscience, the power of legal accountability, and the safety net of *tzedakah*." In chapter 2, Rabbi Lucy H. F. Dinner warns that "humanity is failing the earth; without quick action, the earth will inevitably fail humanity." She reminds us that the challenge to coalesce communities to choose good when voices scream to choose evil is alive in this and every generation; the choice is ours to collectively build a better world. In chapter 3, Rabbi Jan Katzew, PhD, describes America today as a lonely place where people are isolated and in pain, and he highlights the unique position of the Jewish people to be potential bridge builders who know what it means to both belong and not belong in society. In chapter 4, Rabbi Hilly Haber, PhD, shares that we are living in the twilight hours, a time of changing shapes, that is "both exhilarating and, at times, terrifying by its uncertainty." She too writes that Jews, the descendants of the *Ivrim*, the "boundary crossers," as well as the children of *Yisrael*, who wrestled with God and prevailed, are ideally positioned to play a helpful role in this time of unknowns and "endless creative potential." In chapter 5, Rabbi Ellen Lewis identifies that each generation faces its challenges and "it is easy to become overwhelmed by hopelessness and feel incapable of making a difference in the world." She offers how we can use our whole selves to best cope at this difficult time to improve our lives and the lives of those we serve.

In chapter 6, Rabbi Alexandria Shuval-Weiner cautions us about the destructive behaviors that humans have already unleashed on animals and nature in general, which are contrary to Jewish teachings and are threatening our world today. In chapter 7, Rabbi Jonathan K. Crane invites us to examine what quality of life means when we are living during a time when technology can alter the beginning and end of life. He reminds us that all tools have a two-edged nature and asks that we consider what tools we are using and why we intend to use them. In chapter 8, Rabbi Geoffrey A. Mitelman expresses concerns regarding artificial intelligence, even while recognizing that "Judaism has always been able to adapt, grow, and incorporate whatever new technologies arise." He sounds the alarm that technology is outpacing ethics and that algorithms remove human agency, noting that algorithmic decision-making implies a lack of accountability. "We may worry that we are giving artificial intelligence too much of a sense of humanity, but in fact the bigger issue may be our diminishment of humanity." In chapter 9, Rabbi Douglas Kohn shares his concern for how technology and politics could shift human beings from being the creation to becoming the Creator. He raises the threats and opportunities of such a dramatic change for all of humanity, identifying where this possibility has already occurred in fiction and some areas of science today. In chapter 10, Rabbi Dan Medwin writes that humanity is standing on the precipice of an unprecedented leap forward in human existence through the information technologies being developed at an ever-increasing rate, and he describes the threats and possibilities with these advancements.

From these ten very different perspectives the consensus is clear: We are extremely close, if not already present, to a place in history where the core values and behaviors of humanity are at risk, even as humans continue to exist. We have arrived at a place in time where there is almost no humanity, so it is time to awaken to the second half of Rabbi Hillel's injunction. Now is the time to strive to be human.

However, the time to strive to be human is not limited to moments in history when it appears that forces are converging in dark ways as so eloquently described in the preceding chapters. When it comes to striving to be human, any place at any time can be a place lacking in humanity and thus a clarion call to strive. I am reminded of my work as a hospital chaplain serving in a large, urban, academic medical setting. There is always a crisis of humanity going on: gunshot wounds, life-altering diagnoses, unexpected outcomes, unjust social determinants of health care, professional mistakes with medical consequences—patients, family, and staff experiencing sickness, tragedy, suffering, death.

At any time, in any of these situations, we might find ourselves in a place where humanity is lacking and striving to be human—in a non-anxious, compassionate, and collaborative way—is necessary. I hear the refrain from the Hebrew song "Od Lo Ahavti Dai"—and another of Hillel's famous teachings—which repeatedly asks, "And if not now, when?" This urgent refrain resonates with me. I see humanity swirling together, taking the hand of a friend or a stranger, at times stepping on each other's toes, at times wincing, at times laughing, dizzy, maybe confused, but nonetheless striving together, imperfectly, to get it right, until the song is over.

But to what degree must we strive to be fully human while the song is still playing and we are reminded of the urgency of the moment? The tale of the great Chasidic master Rabbi Zusya of Hanipol helps us better understand the standard to which we are held accountable. On his deathbed, Rabbi Zusya began to cry uncontrollably, and his students and disciples tried hard to comfort him. They asked him, "Rabbi, why do you weep? You are almost as wise as Moses, you are almost as hospitable as Abraham, and surely heaven will judge you favorably."

Zusya answered them, "It is true. When I get to heaven, I won't worry so much if God asks me, 'Zusya, why were you not more like Abraham?' or 'Zusya, why were you not more like Moses?' I know I would be able to answer these questions. After all, I was not given the righteousness of Abraham or the faith of Moses, but I tried to be both hospitable and thoughtful. But what will I say when God asks me, 'Zusya, why were you not more like Zusya?'"

Our potential for limited human perfection starts when we fully recognize our very good, unique selves. In accepting and acting on our goodness, we bring goodness not only to ourselves, but to all humanity, and that goodness exceeds perfection. May we embrace this truth with gratitude, hope, perseverance, faith, love, and compassion through our words and deeds with every breath of our lives.

NOTES

1. Translation of *Pirkei Avot* by Joshua Kulp (license:CC-BY, https://creativecommons.org/licenses/by/3.0/), found on Sefaria (sefaria.org). *Pirkei Avot* numbering follows Shmuly Yanklowitz, *Pirkei Avot: A Social Justice Commentary* (CCAR Press, 2018).
2. Translation adapted from the Jerusalem Talmud from the Sefaria Community Translation, found on Sefaria (sefaria.org).

Contributors

Rabbi Leah Cohen Tenenbaum, DMin, BCC-PCHAC (HUC-JIR 2000), serves as the inpatient palliative care chaplain and as a member of the Ethics Committee at Yale New Haven Hospital. She is a faculty member of FASPE (Fellowships at Auschwitz for the Study of Professional Ethics) and has served on the CCAR Board of Trustees, the CCAR National Ethics Taskforce, and currently the CCAR Press Council. She has written chapters for *The Sacred Struggle: Jewish Responses to Trauma* (CCAR Press, 2025) and *Fragile Dialogue: New Voices of Liberal Zionism* (CCAR Press, 2018) and is the coeditor with Rabbi Douglas Kohn of *Striving to Be Human: Jewish Perspectives on Twenty-First-Century Challenges*. She frequently teaches and presents on spirituality, serious illness, and medical ethics.

Rabbi Douglas Kohn serves Temple Beth Jacob in Newburgh, New York, having previously served congregations in Buffalo, Baltimore, Chicago, and Southern California, and is happily busy in all aspects of congregational and community endeavors. In addition to coediting *Striving to Be Human* with Rabbi Leah Cohen Tenenbaum, he is the editor of two other volumes, *Life, Faith, and Cancer: Jewish Journeys Through Diagnosis, Treatment, and Recovery* (URJ Press, 2008) and *Broken Fragments: Jewish Experiences of Alzheimer's Disease Through Diagnosis, Adaptation, and Moving On* (URJ Press, 2012), and has written and spoken widely on the themes of illness, medical ethics, and being human. Rabbi Kohn has served on numerous CCAR, URJ, and communal commissions, committees, and boards, while still savoring time to read, write, and paint, as well as exercise, cook, and travel with his wife, Cindy, and their children and grandchildren.

Rabbi Sarah Bassin serves as the rabbi-in-residence for HIAS, where she connects Jewish tradition and communities to the work of aiding and advocating for immigrants, refugees, and other forcibly displaced populations. Before her role at HIAS, she began her rabbinate as the founding executive director of NewGround: A Muslim-Jewish Partnership for Change, where she built minority-based coalitions and served as the associate rabbi of Temple Emanuel of Beverly Hills. Rabbi Bassin has built an expertise in interfaith civilian diplomacy, traveling with delegations of faith and political leaders to Mexico, England, France, Germany, Qatar, Azerbaijan, and Iran. Occasionally, she adds to her IMDB page as a consultant for depictions of Jewish content and community.

Rabbi Jonathan K. Crane, PhD, serves as the Raymond F. Schinazi Scholar in Bioethics and Jewish Thought at Emory University's Center for Ethics. A professor of medicine, Rabbi Crane is a past president of the Society of Jewish Ethics, founder and coeditor of the *Journal of Jewish Ethics*, and author or editor of *Narratives and Jewish Bioethics*; *The Oxford Handbook of Jewish Ethics and Morality*; *Beastly Morality: Animals as Ethical Agents*; *Eating Ethically: Religion and Science for a Better Diet*; *Judaism, Race, and Ethics: Conversations and Questions*; *Modern Jewish Ethics Since 1970: Writings on Methods, Sources, & Issues*; and *Immoral Medicine: Defending American Biomedical Research at the Trial of Nazi Doctors* (forthcoming).

Rabbi Lucy Dinner is rabbi emerita at Temple Beth Or in Raleigh, North Carolina, where she served for over three decades. Rabbi Dinner focuses her rabbinate on building concentric circles of community that deepen commitment from rooted relationships emanating the values of social justice to the greater community. Rabbi Dinner models this through her work as chair of the Reform Movement's Rabbinic Committee on Peace, Justice, and Civil Rights, vice chair of the Commission on Social Action, and her involvement with the Triangle Martin Luther King Jr. Committee, the State of North Carolina MLK Commission, Rise Against Hunger, and the North Carolina Jewish Clergy Association.

Rabbi Hilly Haber, PhD, oversees the justice and volunteer initiatives at Central Synagogue in New York City, which include criminal legal reform, jail ministry, and reentry, refugee resettlement, and support for asylum seekers, food insecurity, and climate justice. Ordained by Hebrew Union College–Jewish Institute of Religion, Rabbi Haber earned a bachelor's degree from Mount Holyoke College, a master's in theological studies from Harvard Divinity School, and a PhD in social ethics from Union Theological Seminary.

Rabbi Jan Katzew, PhD, is associate professor emeritus of Jewish thought and education at Hebrew Union College–Jewish Institute of Religion. He has served as an educator-rabbi, a director of adolescent education, a day school head, the Union for Reform Judaism's director of lifelong learning, a scholar-in-residence, an educational consultant, and mentor. Rabbi Katzew's publications include scholarly and popular articles on Mussar, rabbinics, Jewish and Israel education, and multifaith relations, and he is currently working on a book that chronicles the tension between Judaism and democracy in the State of Israel.

Rabbi Ellen Lewis has more than forty years of experience as a rabbi and a therapist. Ordained by Hebrew Union College–Jewish Institute of Religion in 1980, she was a member of the first generation of women rabbis. She is also a certified and licensed modern psychoanalyst in private practice in Bernardsville, New Jersey. Rabbi Lewis received her analytical training in New York at the Center for Modern Psychoanalytic Studies. She has written and presented widely about the intersection of Judaism and modern psychoanalysis. Her website can be found at www.rabbiellenlewis.com.

Rabbi Dan Medwin thrives at the intersection of Judaism and technology, where innovation meets tradition. For over a decade with the Central Conference of American Rabbis, he pioneered new ways to engage with Jewish life—developing Visual T'filah and apps and teaching rabbis how to stream services over Zoom—and now, as co-director of Union for Reform Judaism's 6 Points Sci-Tech Academy, he continues to harness technology to deepen Jewish practice and community. His greatest joy is spending time with his wife, Rabbi Lydia Medwin, and their three amazing children: Zimra, Gavriel, and Jasmine.

Rabbi Geoffrey A. Mitelman is the founding director of Sinai and Synapses, an organization that bridges the scientific and religious worlds and is being incubated at Clal–The National Jewish Center for Learning and Leadership. Rabbi Mitelman's work has been supported by multiple grants from the John Templeton Foundation, and his writings about the intersection of religion and science have been published in the books *Seven Days, Many Voices* (CCAR Press, 2017), *A Life of Meaning* (CCAR Press, 2018), and *These Truths We Hold* (HUC Press, 2022), as well as on *The Huffington Post*, *Nautilus*, *Orbiter*, The Wisdom Daily, Jewish Telegraphic Agency, and My Jewish Learning. Ordained by Hebrew Union College–Jewish Institute of Religion, Rabbi Mitelman is an internationally sought-out teacher, presenter, and scholar-in-residence; he lives in Westchester County with his wife, Heather Stoltz, a fiber artist, and their daughter and son.

Rabbi Alexandria Shuval-Weiner, the spiritual leader of Temple Beth Tikvah in Roswell (Atlanta), Georgia, was ordained by Hebrew Union College–Jewish Institute of Religion. Her religious beliefs are grounded in traditional Jewish practices and a sacred commitment to pursuing justice and healing for our earth and all its creatures. She is the mother to five adult children and grandmother to seven wonderful souls.

Rabbanit Sara Tillinger Wolkenfeld is the chief learning officer at Sefaria, an online database and interface for Jewish texts. Rabbanit Wolkenfeld is a member of class six of the Wexner Field Fellowship and an alumna of the David Hartman Center at the Hartman Institute of North America. Sara also serves as scholar-in-residence at Ohev Sholom Congregation in Washington, DC. Her current research and writing focus on the intersection between Jewish ethics and advancements in technology. Rabbanit Wolkenfeld's writing has been published in *The Atlantic*, *First Things*, and *Religion Dispatches*, as well as numerous Jewish publications.

www.ingramcontent.com/pod-product-compliance
Lightning Source LLC
Chambersburg PA
CBHW071420160426
43195CB00013B/1756